THE VALLEY AND THE HILLS

For my father
Jack Rawls
who all his life loved
the valley and the hills

THE VALLEY AND THE HILLS

An Illustrated History of
BIRMINGHAM
&
JEFFERSON COUNTY

Leah Rawls Atkins

Sponsored by
Birmingham-Jefferson Historical Society

Windsor Publications, Inc.
Woodland Hills, California

Preceding page: *Taken from Shades Mountain in the early 1920s, this view looking north across Shades Valley to Red Mountain shows Edgewood Lake and the intersection of old Columbiana Road and Lakeshore Drive.*

Published 1981
Printed in the United States of America

First Edition

Library of Congress Cataloging in Publication Data

Atkins, Leah Rawls.
　The Valley and the Hills.

　Bibliography: p. 235
　Includes index.
　1. Birmingham (Ala.)—History.　2. Jefferson
County (Ala.)—History.　I. Title.
F334.B657A84　　976.1'78　　　　　80-54001
ISBN 0-89781-031-7　　　　　　　AACR2

TABLE OF CONTENTS

These boys pose on Twenty-first Street in the 1880s. Children often played with goat carts and used them to haul groceries from town. Courtesy, James F. Sulzby, Jr.

INTRODUCTION

The history of Jefferson County, like a great stream, flows from an Indian hunting ground through pioneer farms; through mines of coal and iron that produced "big, bad Birmingham," a boom town; through wars and depressions; through a cholera epidemic and racial problems; through troubles and triumphs; through sorrows and happy times. It shapes and is shaped by a community of men and women at their best and at their worst. This book garners the traditions of that community, "silent reminders of her former struggles and victories," with hope that "her wonderful history will be eagerly sought and cherished."

In the one hundred ten years of Birmingham's existence, no comprehensive, interpretive history of the Magic City and its surroundings has ever been written. In 1979 Windsor Publications approached the Birmingham-Jefferson Historical Society with the suggestion that the society sponsor such a publication. The reaction was that a first-class history of the area was long overdue. The board of trustees and the publications committee, composed of Rucker Agee, Richard J. Stockham, James F. Sulzby, Jr., Elmer Thuston, and myself held planning sessions with representatives of the publisher.

A number of historians were suggested to write the book, but Dr. Leah Rawls Atkins was the unanimous choice of the committee. A native of Birmingham, a descendant of pioneer settlers, a professional historian and university professor, Dr. Atkins knows the area and its people and loves both. Her task was "a natural," and she has succeeded in putting together the many facets of life in the valley and the hills of Birmingham and Jefferson County. "Partners in Progress," the chapter on existing businesses, educational institutions, and corporations that have played important roles in building the area and whose enthusiastic support has made the book possible, was compiled by John Bloomer, a retired editor of the Birmingham News.

The Birmingham-Jefferson Historical Society was founded in 1975 for the purpose of studying, preserving, and disseminating the history of this county, which was organized before Alabama became a state. With great pride the society presents this volume to the residents who helped build the community, to their friends and relatives, to newcomers and prospective residents who want to become acquainted with their new home, and to historians and history buffs everywhere. Dr. Atkins and The Valley and the Hills will surely engender love and pride along with a deeper knowledge of the Magic City and the county surrounding it.

Margaret Davidson Sizemore
President
Birmingham-Jefferson Historical Society

Chapter I

THE VALLEY: A HUNTING PARADISE

Though Jones Valley was a buffer zone between the lands of the Cherokee, Creek, Choctaw, and Chickasaw, the area provided an abundance of deer, bear, fox, and wild turkey for hunters from all four tribes. From a De Bry engraving in the Rucker Agee Collection, Birmingham Public Library.

As the morning mist rises slowly from Shades Valley, cars move briskly along the wide six-lane highway that rises in sharp ascent toward the cut in the mountain. Through the deep, iron-red, terraced, man-made gorge, the cars flow north into Jones Valley. The rusting hulk of the abandoned Sloss furnace is silhouetted before them against the early morning sky. The tall stacks of the furnace emit no smoke; gone is the hot-orange molten iron pouring into waiting sand molds, a remembrance for four generations of Jefferson County residents. To the west lies the city, the new city of the New South, Birmingham, a "Magic City" that rose from a cornfield upon a foundation of iron and steel. Now economically diversified, Birmingham is no longer dependent upon one industry. Birmingham, which survived depressions and racial violence, is today a city of concrete and steel pillars shooting heavenward from the valley floor, its modern cubes of multi-storied mirrored glass reflecting the sunrise back to the green hills and the red mountain.

The Valley: A Hunting Paradise

Two hundred years ago, Creek, Choctaw, Chickasaw, and Cherokee Indians sprinted silently down Jones Valley on well-worn trails that ran from Talladega to the Warrior River, from the Big Spring at Huntsville down to Tuscaloosa, from Old Town across the hills and mountain to Mud Town. There was also an Indian trail that followed the summit of Red Mountain, a route that enabled the Indians to see the campfires of possible enemies in the valley below. These Indian paths were so well planned that they became the foundations for the roads of the pioneers. The morning fog rose slowly from the valley floor then, too, but the horizon was broken only by tall pines and oak trees and the stillness was violated only by the songs of birds and noises of wild animals.

The Indians, on their way down the valley, passed several large cone-shaped mounds, relics of the prehistoric people who once lived here. Three mounds were located to the north, along Village Creek, several mounds were near Turkey Creek; and others, known as the "Talley Mounds," were to be found in the southwestern part of the valley near Jonesboro. Mary Gordon Duffee described one mound on Village Creek as "square in shape," rising some "thirty feet out of a level field" with sloping sides covered by underbrush and "massive trees" crowning the summit. The prehistoric mound-building people lived during the Indian Woodland period, between 1110 B.C. and A.D. 1100. They built temple mounds throughout the southeastern United States, and were adept at making clay pottery, carving stones, and working copper. These primitive peoples lived in Jefferson County only briefly, then moved, perhaps southward, following the Warrior and Tombigbee rivers toward Moundville.

The Indians traveled the Jones Valley trails to hunt or to journey to other villages to trade pelts and craft items. Trading was an important part of Indian life, but it was the abundance of game that attracted the Indians to the valley. Deer, bear, fox, and wild turkey were so plentiful that even with primitive bows and arrows, the Indians were able to kill the game they needed for food and clothing. On these trips the Indians would camp by the numerous springs and creeks. The Big Spring at Elyton was a favorite trading ground; and the creek bank at Jonesboro, which the Indians called "Mound Campground," became a popular camping place. Although the pottery and arrowheads found scattered through the county provide proof of Indian presence, only two permanent towns are known to have existed in the area: Old Town, on the Warrior River; and Talooehajoh, known also as Mud Town, on the Cahaba River. Both of these Creek towns were attacked by Andrew Jackson's men during the Creek Indian War and their locations were marked on his campaign map.

Early pioneers recalled that the Indians had burned the valley floor from time to time, destroying the undergrowth and leaving only the tall timbers, grass, and wild flowers. One legend proclaims that the Indians cleared these areas, usually around springs, to use as sites for annual gatherings. The Indians would meet every year to celebrate with such festivals as the "busk" or green corn dance, and to compete in games and sports. Jones Valley, close to the lands of all four Indian nations, became alternately a neutral or disputed territory. It was a buffer zone between the tribes, but sometimes became the subject of conflicting claims by the Creek and Cherokee tribes. Jones Valley was a hunting ground where Indians filled their larder, but none called it home.

Facing page, left: *This limestone effigy pipe found along the Warrior River south of Jefferson County was made by the Mound Builders who once inhabited Jones Valley and Jefferson County. It was probably used in religious ceremonies. From Moore,* Certain Aboriginal Remains of the Black Warrior River *(1905).*

Facing page, right: *Prehistoric peoples erected earthen mounds like these between 1110 B.C. and A.D. 1100 in the Jones Valley area. These mound builders constructed several other similar structures, including three along Village Creek, several near Turkey Creek, and the Talley Mounds near Jonesboro. Courtesy, Donna Peters, Alabama Museum of Natural History.*

Below: *The Creek Indians' annual green corn dance or busk was a time to renew social ties. During the festival, the Indians played games and competed in sports. From a De Bry engraving in the Rucker Agee Collection, Birmingham Public Library.*

The Valley: A Hunting Paradise

The early settlers of Jefferson County knew the Indians well, and as time passed and the Indians vanished from the valley, they shared their childhood stories of Indian legends with their children. One of the most popular stories tells of two Indian braves who were determined to fight to the death on the banks of the Warrior River. Armed with knives, they began their combat, but when one Indian lost his knife, an observer, Silent Bear, intervened and ended the fight. The victor, in a fit of rage, threw himself from the bluff into the river while the other Indian died of his wounds. The Great Spirit, so angered over this senseless duel, doomed the spirits of the two Indians to sleep during the day and at night to fish together as friends. For many years, before the dam at Lock No. 17 flooded the Heard (Hurd) Shoals near Toadvine, children would come to the banks of the river and peer into the darkness searching for a glimpse of the two Indians. Some even claimed to have seen them, springing over rocks in the shoals with their gigs and torches. Another Indian legend of the valley told of an underground river that ran the length of Jones Valley. Indian children, when they came into the white settlements to trade at the stores, would play with pioneer children and tell them stories of how they had come from a long canoe ride on this underground river.

The Indians of North Alabama lived with no awareness of white men until 1540, when De Soto came into the area. Following a southward course, his Spanish expedition entered Alabama on the Tennessee River at the northeast corner of the state, descended to the Coosa River, and proceeded on to the Alabama River. Partly because no navigable waterway flowed through Jefferson County—a geographical feature that was to affect the history of the county by isolating the region as well as protecting it—De Soto did not come into Jones Valley. But, certainly, news of the large army of pale men riding tall, graceful, and swift animals would have traveled quickly through the hills and valleys of North Alabama.

Heard (Hurd) Shoals of the Warrior River was the site of a favorite Indian legend that told of two Indian braves doomed by the Great Spirit to fish as friends after Silent Bear stopped their fight. Drawing by Mark Rikard.

According to local lore, the first white men to pass through Jefferson County were the volunteers of General Andrew Jackson's army, who came down from Tennessee to help subdue the Creek Indians after the 1813 massacre at Fort Mims. This is probably inaccurate, however. Fort Toulouse and Fort Tombecbe, first under French command and later under British, were known to have sent scouting expeditions into the interior, and Indian countrymen, trappers, and traders moved about the Alabama Indian lands during the colonial period. In the summer of 1781, a group of Tory royalists left Natchez and headed east through the Alabama Indian lands, crossing the Warrior River at the falls (probably Tuscaloosa) and ending up lost in Blount County. They may well have traveled up the Indian path through Jones Valley, but the record is not clear. In 1798 Congress created the Mississippi Territory; and in 1802 the Jefferson County area became part of this territory. Huntsville had been settled in 1805, and to the south the Federal Road had been cut by the U.S. Army by 1811, two years before the Creek War broke out. White men probably traveled the Indian trails through Jefferson County before 1813, but it was the appearance of Jackson's Tennessee militia in the valley that proved in the long run to be the most significant.

When news spread throughout the old southwest of the Indian massacre at Fort Mims, frenzied efforts were made to organize troops to subdue the Indians on the Alabama frontier. As the Creeks fought mightily to preserve their land, General Andrew Jackson, still suffering from almost fatal wounds from his duel with Jesse Benton, left his bed to march with the Tennessee volunteers. He immediately sent Colonel John Coffee to attack Big Warrior's town at the falls of the Black Warrior River. Davy Crockett was with Coffee and took part in the destruction of the abandoned village. On their return to Jackson's headquarters, Coffee, Crockett, and the militia traveled through Jones Valley. Jackson later sent troops to burn the Creek villages on the Cahaba River; Mud Town was destroyed on May 1, 1814.

Following the defeat of the Creeks at Horseshoe Bend, an uneasy peace came to the Alabama frontier. General Andrew Jackson forced the Indians to cede all their lands in central Alabama, a territory so vast that it comprised all of Jefferson County and almost half the entire state. Jackson's militia volunteers returned home, spreading the news throughout Tennessee about the green hills, with forests full of game, and the deep springs and clear creeks in a lovely long valley that lay beside a high red mountain. Many soldiers made immediate plans to move there with their families. Thus they became part of the "Great Migration" into the fertile lands of the old southwest, a migration that followed peace with England in the War of 1812 and the cession of Indian lands in Alabama.

General Andrew Jackson ended the Creek Wars in March of 1814 when he defeated the Indians at the battle of Horseshoe Bend. Jackson then forced the Creeks to relinquish their lands in central Alabama, including all of Jefferson County. From Cirker, Dictionary of American Portraits. *Painting by John Wesley Jarvis. Courtesy, Metropolitan Museum of Art, Dick Fund.*

13

Chapter II

PIONEER FARMERS IN THE HILL COUNTRY

The survey of the new Alabama Indian lands, part of the Mississippi Territory at this time, would take years to complete. Almost a decade would pass before most lands in Jefferson County were put up for sale, and settlers could acquire legal title to their land. Although federal law forbade intrusion upon the public lands, in the early part of 1815 a group of veterans of Jackson's Indian wars from Giles and Rutherford counties in Tennessee came down the trace from Huntsville to the Jefferson County area. These men were poor and land-hungry. As veteran pioneers, they understood the politics of government land sales and knew well the nightmarish pattern of speculators buying up the squatters' land and improvements. They realized that federal laws did not yet protect "squatter's rights" by preemption provisions. But regardless of this, they began to select and stake off their property in the heavy forest. They cleared fields, built fences, planted corn crops, and constructed crude cabins.

In the mid-1800s bears plagued Jones Valley farmers and many of the early pioneers in the area left "bear stories" to their families. From Special Collections, Samford University Library.

15

Pioneer Farmers in the Hill Country

One of the first settlers, John Jones, erected a shanty early in 1815 in the southern end of the valley. By local tradition, the valley received its name from him and his brother Jeremiah. During the territorial period the name "Jones's Valley" applied to the entire valley extending from northeast to southwest, and to the areas that became known as Roupe Valley and Murphree's Valley. Since most of the early settlements were in Jones Valley and the hills around the valley, for a number of years the name was also used to refer generally to what would become Jefferson County.

In May 1815, these men were joined by Williamson Hawkins who had been "detained on personal affairs" in Tennessee. He brought with him "all the supplies he could pack on one horse," and drove some cattle before him. The other men had exhausted their supplies, and they greeted Hawkins heartily, living the remaining months on his "milk and butter." After the year's crops were harvested Jones and the other early settlers returned to Tennessee to gather their families. These pioneer families traveled back down the road that had been partly cut by Tennessee troops during the Creek War. Journeying in groups, they stayed in crude inns along the trail, or camped out under the stars. On the trip into Alabama the women and children walked, rode horses, or traveled in wagons or two-wheeled carts. When they finally reached the valley, some faced disappointment. One couple, John and Sally Smith, arrived and found that another family had occupied the land that John had cleared and cultivated the previous spring. They were forced to select another location, and together they began building anew. Smith took a three-foot log, hollowed it out, attached half of a barrel head to each end, and made a "fine cradle" for their baby. Each morning they would carry the cradle with them into the field, and the baby slept while they worked together clearing and planting.

Above: *This old Jefferson County cabin has been modernized with the addition of a metal roof and a door with a window. Courtesy, James F. Sulzby, Jr.*

Below: *Veterans of the Creek Indian War built shanties or log cabins in Jones Valley. Due to the scarcity of glass, these crude dwellings were built without windows. From the Woodward Iron Collection in the William S. Hoole Special Collections, University of Alabama Library.*

The area seemed safe from Indian attacks, but the veterans of the Creek War took no chances. They constructed a crude fort in the southern end of the valley, and Fort Jonesboro became the nucleus of the first settlement. Although the fort was never occupied for protection, panic spread through the valley in the fall of 1818 when 300 Seminole Indians went on a rampage. The Indians scared a number of persons who fled up the Huntsville Road, before the Indians surrendered at Tuscaloosa. In the next decade small bands of Indians continued to roam the back country, but they came peacefully to hunt or to trade, offering the settlers oak baskets, belts, and pottery in exchange for knives, tools, and cloth.

In the summer of 1816 more people came, from Georgia, South Carolina, and Virginia, until there were 140 heads of families living in Jones Valley. They scattered settlements along the Huntsville Road, at Village Springs and around the Avondale Spring at Woodlawn, and by the Big Spring, a community first known as Frog Level, then Old Town, and finally Elyton. There were pioneer settlements at Waldrop's Mill (Toadvine), Greene's (Tarrant), Woods Station (Woodlawn), Carrollsville (Powderly), Hagood Springs (Pinson), and Crumly's Chapel. The Vines, Golden, and Williams families lived down on the Warrior River, and the Actons and Baileys filled up the Cahaba Valley. David Overton lived in a log cabin at Bald Springs. Thomas McAdory, William Sadler, and Thomas Owen built in Eastern Valley. Thomas Reeves settled at Albert Waldrop's mill. William and Rachel Burns lived in a dog-trot cabin near Woods. Elijah and John Brown, and William Pullen, a veteran of General George Washington's American Revolutionary army, constructed cabins by the Big Spring on the Georgia Road, while Stephen Hall and Elias DeJarnette selected land at the Big Spring at Elyton. Levi Reed was at Mud Creek, and William Hartgrove was over on the Shades of Death Creek. William Brown lived in Possum Valley, and George L. Greene and Bennie Tarrant had farms on the Tennessee Road. Edward Tatum, a Revolutionary veteran who fought at Guilford Court House and at Yorktown, settled on land near present-day McCalla. John Wood raised the first militia company of 100 volunteers from the valley and was elected colonel. There was enough land for all, but one pioneer recalled a bitter squabble over land ownership at the Georgia and Huntsville roads junction.

Top: *John Loveless began to construct this house on Eastern Valley Road in 1820. After his death in 1835, his widow sold the property to Isaac W. Sadler, one of the founders of Pleasant Hill Methodist Church and a trustee of Salem School. Sadler then added to the hand-hewn, one-room log structure. The Sadler house exemplifies the plantation architecture indigenous to the hill country of Jefferson County. Courtesy, West Jefferson Historical Society. Photo by Mickie H. Blackwell.*

Above: *Thomas McAdory constructed this house about 1841 with slave labor. Of the typical dog-trot design, the house has two rooms on each side of an open passageway. Six wooden hand-hewn posts support the front porch. McAdory was the grandfather of Thomas McAdory Owen who founded the Alabama Department of Archives and History. Photo by Leah R. Atkins.*

Pioneer Farmers in the Hill Country

Davy Crockett traveled through Jones Valley in the fall of 1816. He had served as a scout under Andrew Jackson during the Creek War. From Cirker, Dictionary of American Portraits. Engraved by Thomas B. Welch from a painting by S.S. Osgood.

Facing page, top: Pioneer women in the county raised cotton and used it for spinning and weaving. Each woman made clothing for her entire family. From the Roland Harper Collection in the William S. Hoole Special Collections, University of Alabama Library.

Facing page, bottom: In the nineteenth century, metal pots and pans and ceramic dishes were valuable household items because they were expensive to replace and rare to find in the isolated areas of Jefferson County. Courtesy, West Jefferson Historical Society. Photo by Mickie H. Blackwell.

In the fall of 1816 when Davy Crockett and his three friends came to the area on a hunting trip into "Creek Country," they visited several log houses in Jones Valley. Crockett came down with malaria, and stayed at three different homes while recovering, the last belonging to Jesse Jones. Mrs. Jones nursed Crockett back to good health. That same year, another Tennessee veteran of the Creek War, Richard Breckenridge, wandered lost into Jones Valley. When he finally came to the Jones's house, he was given a free bed and "supper for twelve and a half cents." Although Breckenridge considered the lands "handsome," he felt they were "too far from trade" and "of too stiff and clayed a nature," with rocks "on top of the ground" in places. Little did he realize that those boulders of brown and red iron ore, and outcroppings of limestone, would one day fuel an industrial city.

Like Breckenridge, the South Alabama planters from the rich Black Belt, who traveled through Jones Valley on their way north to Huntsville for the first meeting of the state legislature in 1819, felt only pity for the subsistence farmers they met along the Huntsville Road. (Of course neither the farmers nor the planters had any idea of the vast richness of mineral deposits that lay beneath the farmers' corn.) This road, known as the Huntsville "wagon road," or the Huntsville Pike, was the main link between Jefferson County and the outside world for many years. It ran north by "Bear Meat Cabin" (Blountsville) to Ditto's Landing, on the Tennessee River, and Huntsville. South of these points the road passed through Elyton, Jonesboro, and McMath's Spring to the falls of the Warrior River (Tuscaloosa). The people who lived along the road usually rented rooms to travelers and might greet guests with the salutation: "Light, stranger, hitch your horse and come in." The Huntsville Road was good enough in 1816 to enable James O. Crump, a Huntsville merchant, to haul 2,000 pounds of goods by a four-horse team from the "falls of the Black Warrior" to Huntsville. It took him eight days to cover the 120 miles. Crump had purchased his goods in Mobile and in St. Stephens, shipping them by boat up the Tombigbee to the falls. His cargo included "brown and Havana white sugars, coffee, rum, wine, oranges and a few dry goods." He found the road from the Warrior through Jones Valley to Huntsville in fairly good shape. Three-fifths of it was level and "the balance not much broken." He noted there were "not more than three hills of consequence," but "there had been very little labor bestowed in cutting out the road." He suggested the "winding" should be straightened. Mrs. Clement Claiborne Clay traveled the road in the 1830s, her four-wheeled stage coach pitching "perilously" over "rugged" rocks and boulders.

These years were hard ones for the pioneers. Until 1818 there was no mill and no blacksmith shop in the valley. The pioneers beat their meal in a rude mortar burned into the stump of a tree with a pestle attached. They sharpened their ploughs by heating and crudely beating them with hammers. There never seemed to be enough time to do all the work. The men would plow for half the day, then let the mule graze while they split rails and built fences. The women stayed busy cooking and washing; spinning, weaving, and sewing clothes for the family; making candles and soap; and assisting their menfolk by hoeing and picking cotton, and by working in the garden. In 1816 there was a severe drought in Jones Valley. No rain fell from June to August. Many settlers lost their entire corn crop, and the Big Spring at Elyton went dry, causing considerable suffering well into the year 1817. The pioneers survived by sharing their limited resources, and helping each other with their work.

Pioneer Farmers in the Hill Country

The large number of wild animals in the valley provided extra meat for the early pioneers, but they were also a nuisance. The deer ate the settlers' crops and the bears were a constant danger. Most of the early settlers of Jones Valley left "bear stories" indicating how extensively bears must have inhabited the valley. The *Jones Valley Times*, on April 1, 1854, published a letter from an early pioneer giving details of a confrontation between Williamson Hawkins and a bear in 1819. Hawkins had been riding his horse one mile from the Big Spring (Elyton) when he met a bear. Although he had left his rifle at home, he drove the animal as one would drive a cow. When the bear would change courses, Hawkins "would dash by," forcing the bear to change directions and "after many a zig-zag movement," he drove the bear two miles to the yard fence of the nearest settler. Hawkins forced the bear into a "nook" and then "hallowed upon the inmates of the cabin." A lady appeared, and told Hawkins that her husband was not home and their rifle was unloaded. She gave Hawkins the axe from the woodpile instead and with "a few blows the monster lay dead."

While bears were a source of immediate danger, the settlers of Jones Valley felt closer to government and to civilization after Congress admitted Mississippi to the Union and cut off the Alabama region, creating the Alabama Territory. This assured that Alabama would become a separate state, eliminated the sectional controversy and hostility between the Mississippi and Tombigbee valleys, and moved the site of territorial government from Washington, six miles east of the Mississippi River and Natchez, to St. Stephens on the Tombigbee River.

Jones Valley pioneers were concerned about the lack of churches and formal schools on the frontier. So was the Presbytery of South Carolina, which sent two missionaries into the area to help prevent the settlers of the Alabama frontier from sinking into "ignorance, superstition, and wickedness." Traveling together, James L. Sloss and Hiland Hubbard left Willington, South Carolina, in December of 1817. Crossing Georgia via Athens and Eatonton, they entered Alabama through "a wilderness of about 260 miles, almost entirely inhabited by Indians." Soon they came to the "head Settlements of Alabama" in Jones Valley where they "commenced preaching." Sloss and Hubbard described the valley as "thickly inhabited," "more closely settled than any part of the territory" through which they had traveled. They reported to the South Carolina Presbytery that there was no "individual preacher of the Gospel" in the valley, and that "most of the inhabitants who profess religion are Methodists or Babtist [sic]." Yet they believed "Presbyterian ministers might be as successful there as any other." The missionaries remained in Jones Valley six days, preaching frequently to "very large and respectable congregations."

Methodists and Baptists did indeed predominate in the county. According to some accounts, the first sermon in the area was preached at James Cunningham's house in 1818 by the Reverend Ebenezer Hearne, a Methodist minister. But there is also evidence of religious meetings as early as 1816 being held at the Frog Level Race Grounds Meeting House, which was ironically, also a popular area for horse racing. Shiloh Methodist Church (later Walker Memorial) was organized in the home of James Owen. Early Methodist churches appeared at Trussville, Tarrant, and Sweeney Branch Hollow. Cedar Mountain Church began in 1819 and Bethlehem Church was constructed at Rutledge Spring on Possum Valley Road by Reverend James Tarrant and his slave Adam.

The oldest Baptist Church in the area was Canaan, organized September 5, 1818, at the home of Isaac Brown on Valley Creek with the Reverend John B. Moore and the Reverend John Henry preaching. Oldsides Baptist Church at Hagood Springs (Pinson) also began in 1818. Ruhama was organized in 1819 at the home of John and Sarah Jacks at Rockville (East Lake). Reverend Hosea Holcombe was the leading Baptist minister in the area. He preached all over the county, but especially in the Baptist Church at Jonesboro, a church constructed of hand-hewn logs. Holcombe was aided by Job, a slave of Daniel

The Jones Valley Times of 1854 reported that one settler fired seven shots at a bear that tried to steal a hog. Only when the man's wife arrived with a pine torch was he able to see well enough to hit the bear in a vital spot and kill it. Bears frequently caused problems for farmers in the valley. From Special Collections, Samford University Library.

Pioneer Farmers in the Hill Country

Davis, who frequently filled the pulpit of the church and preached to large congregations, mostly whites. One of the leading Methodists of the county, Baylis E. Grace, whose son became a Methodist minister, recalled that Job was pious, devout, eloquent, and "truth from his lips prevailed with double sway, and those who came to scoff remained to pray." The Presbyterians organized Mt. Calvary near Clayton's Cove very early and built a church at Five Mile Creek in 1820. Shiloh Cumberland Church was constructed at Leeds the following year and a church at Elyton was organized in 1824. Until 1850, when St. John's was organized in Elyton, Episcopalians traveled to Tuscaloosa, but it would be a number of years before an ordained minister served the parish.

The scattered pioneer families found it difficult to educate their children. In 1819 William Musgrove began teaching at Elyton. At Carrollsville John Brown constructed a log house and persuaded Thomas Carroll of South Carolina to begin teaching there. The first schools in Jones Valley were one-room schools with puncheon seats and dirt floors. Boys would frequently come to school for weeks at a time, boarding with the teacher or neighbors because the trip home was too long and dangerous. In 1822 Jefferson Academy was established at Elyton, where two Connecticut sisters, Amy and Marie Welton, taught. They had come to Elyton about 1821 to teach school "in the wilderness of Jones Valley." The Salem School was established at Jonesboro under the direction of S.A. Tarrant.

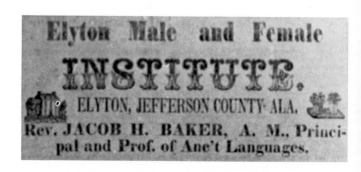

By 1850, 14 one-teacher schools, like the "Blackberry Academy" where Mr. Cooper taught in a slave cabin on the John M. Dupuy plantation, were teaching 453 children in Jefferson County. These schools were partly supported by a county appropriation of $2.40 per pupil. Public education, legally established by state law in 1854, was not developed in the county until after the Civil War. Many of the wealthy farmers in the 1860s were still illiterate. They "made their marks" instead of signing their names as they bought and sold property in Jefferson County. Having been denied an education

SALEM
Male and Female Academy:
JONESBORO', ALA.

Rev. R. PHILLIPS, *Superintendent.*
HENRY F. MEEK, Principal Teacher and Professor of Ancient Languages.

Miss SALLIE STARR, Teacher in the Female Department.
Mrs. ANNIE M. WILLIAMS, Teacher of Music.

THE FIRST SESSION of this Institution will commence on the 3d Monday in Sept. next, under the Superintendence of Rev. REUBEN PHILLIPS, who has been engaged in teaching and the government of Schools for 35 years; and whose skill and management of youth is surpassed but by few persons anywhere. His unemployed time in the government of the institution will be taken up in the instruction of the primary classes.

The male and female schools will be conducted in different buildings, some four hundred yards distance from each other, and the music will be conducted in a room in Mrs. Williams' dwelling, fitted up for the express purpose, and will be very comfortable. Great care will be exercised in carrying out the rules and regulations in reference to the pupils, in preserving their morals and their advancement in Literature.

It is believed by many that there is no location in the State so desirable for schools as SALEM, for good Springs, and surrounding forest, for recreation comfort and health. There is no location that affords fewer temptations to dissipation, vice and extravagance. No intoxicating liquors are kept by any person except for medical purposes. The institution is surrounded by a wealthy community, noted for their hospitality and love of morality and religious influence.

It is the interest of the Trustees to keep up a School of high order from year to year.

The scholastic year will consist of ten months only divided by a few days vacation at the close of five months from the time of commencement.

TERMS:
Tuition in Prep. Departm't per month, $1 60
    Higher branches, 3 00
    Ancient Languages, 4 00
    Music on Piano, and use of 4 50
Contingent expenses 20 cents per month.

Boarding per month for males at Col. James McAdory's (washing, fuel and lights included,) $6 00

In other families from $1 75 to 2 per week.
No student will be received for a shorter time than one session, or from time of entry until the close of session. No deduction from price of tuition will be made, except in case of protracted sickness.

BOARD OF TRUSTEES.
S. A. Tarrant, President.
James McAdory, Thomas McAdory,
I. W. Sadler, T. W. Sadler,
T. H. Owen, R. Phillips.
Jonesborough, Jefferson county, Ala.
August 26, 1854. 23-6ms.

by the frontier conditions of their youth, these men insisted upon a good education for their children. Those families who could afford it sent their children to one of three private academies that were established in the county by 1854: Elyton Male and Female Institute under the direction of Reverend Jacob Baker, Bucksville Male and Female High School headed by A.C. Thompson, and the Jonesboro Academy. These academies provided a classical education for those young men of the valley preparing for college, most of them planning to attend the University of Alabama, and for those young ladies of the county who were able to attend the fashionable Centenary Institute at Summerfield, Alabama. In these academies discipline was strict. The *Jones Valley Times* commented in April 1854, that "when small boys disregard sound admonition, they are whipped." By 1860 white illiteracy had declined in Jefferson County from 14 percent in 1840 to 12 percent, but the county rate remained higher than the state illiteracy rate of 7 percent.

Obtaining a valid title to their land was as important as schools were to the early pioneers who began living in Jones Valley as "squatters" on the public domain. Only the best creek bottom lands of the valley were first placed on the market at the Huntsville Land Office in 1819. Later a land office was opened at Tuscaloosa, and many residents, including the Reed, Wood, Roebuck, Hawkins, and Wilson families, went there to purchase their lands. The *Jones Valley Times* on November 3, 1854, printed an article describing the first land sales at Tuscaloosa, even before the city developed. There were only a few log cabins and the land office, which was located in a "board shanty." The sale was directed by a small man seated on a pine box. Great excitement started when a group of speculators, Simms and Company, began to intimidate poor settlers hoping to gain homes and improvements at little cost. Many pioneers saw their labor and homes taken from them, and heaped curses upon the speculators. The Jefferson County residents presented a united front and bid against the speculators, driving the amount higher to break the speculators and keep them from taking other lands in the county.

During the Alabama territorial years, Jones Valley was part of Blount County. Settlers had to travel up the Huntsville Road to Blountsville to conduct their legal business. But on December 13, 1819, just six days before Alabama was granted statehood, the legislature created Jefferson County from the southern part of Blount County. At first court was conducted in the new county in Moses Kelly's log cabin, but at the next session it was held in a building

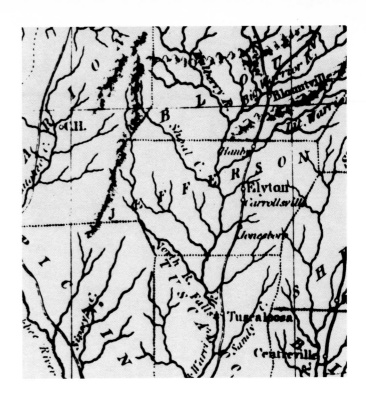

in Carrollsville. In 1821 the county seat was moved to Elyton where it remained until the founding of Birmingham.

Elyton was named for William H. Ely who deeded land to the county for a courthouse site. He was the representative of the Connecticut Asylum for the Deaf and Dumb, and was commissioned to locate and sell the township that Congress had granted for the benefit of the school. The squatters around the Big Spring were eager to gain valid title to their land and persuaded Ely to locate part of the asylum grant there. By purchasing their lands from the asylum, they were able to gain legal title before the land sales, averting the possibility of having to bid against a speculator. They deeded their "squatter's rights" to the asylum, then accepted a deed back from the asylum dated the same day.

Facing page, left: *The Salem Male and Female Academy had an excellent reputation. Boys and girls were taught in "different buildings, some four hundred yards distance from each other." Many of the students came for the session and boarded with members of the community. From the Alabama Department of Archives and History.*

Facing page, right: *The Elyton Male and Female Institute was under the direction of Jacob H. Baker who had been principal of the Salem School near Jonesboro for a number of years. Boys and girls attended class in separate buildings. During the Civil War, Wilson's raiders burned one of the buildings and for some years boys and girls went to school together, a situation that the boys recalled was the best thing about the "Yankee raid." From the Alabama Department of Archives and History.*

Above: *This 1822 map offers a distorted view of Jefferson County. Notice that Tuscaloosa is almost due south of Elyton, instead of southwest. Hamby, Elyton, Carrollsville, and Jonesboro are the only towns shown on the map. From Special Collections, Samford University Library.*

Pioneer Farmers in the Hill Country

William Ely was a devoted husband and frequently wrote to his wife from Alabama. He quickly tired of the frontier conditions he found in Jones Valley. Writing from Carrollsville on April 4, 1820, he said that he was weary of "living in the middle of Piles of Logs with no other windows than the large spaces between them (there not being a Pane of Glass to 5,000 People in the County), of living on Hog and Corn, with a few racoon. Oh how I long to return to my dear family and to a civilized & moral World." Ely also noted that deer, rabbits, squirrels, and turkey abounded in the forests and that sweet william and "a great variety of other beautiful flowers" were blooming in the woods.

Immigration into the county from Tennessee, Georgia, and South Carolina was very great from 1816 to 1820. By 1820, when the first census was taken, Jefferson County had a population of 4,114 people, which included 707 black slaves. But within 10 years there was an increase of only slightly more than 1,000 whites and slaves and 19 free Negroes — not a large growth rate when compared to other areas of the state during the 1820s, often called the "Flush Times in Alabama." An early pioneer recalled that "Jones Valley was all settled within a few years after it was open" and there was only a small increase in population until after the Civil War.

When the editor of the *Huntsville Republican* traveled through Jones Valley on his way to Tuscaloosa in 1821, he noted the "flourishing appearance of Jonesborough at the south end of the valley," and the fertile tracts of good cotton land under high cultivation. He thought the creeks in the area might produce enough water power to drive a cotton mill, and commented that there was a need for "commercial houses with a stock of goods." But he failed to report the main problem of Jefferson County — a lack of transportation, which plagued it until the 1870s.

Because of poor roads and the absence of other means of transportation, mail service was poor. Elyton and Jonesboro had the only post offices in the county in 1825, and residents constantly complained to the federal government about the poor quality of service. Horseback riders brought the mail from Huntsville once a week, but deliveries were improved in Andrew Jackson's administration when express service began from Nashville to Montgomery with Elyton a stop on the route. Much later Robert Jemison, subsequently joined by Colonel James R. Powell, began a regular stagecoach line — a four-horse coach that ran twice a week from Tuscaloosa to Huntsville — and Elyton became an important crossing place for stage routes connecting northern and southern Alabama with the eastern and western parts of the state.

Many of the early pioneers of Jefferson County brought slaves with them when they emigrated from Tennessee, Georgia, or South Carolina, but slavery was never strong in the county and most of the slaves and owners were concentrated in Jones Valley, particularly in Elyton and Jonesboro. The 1860 census showed a Jefferson County population composed of 9,078 whites and 2,649 slaves who were owned by 284 families. The largest slaveholder in the county, Williamson Hawkins, owned 107 slaves and farmed 2,000 acres on the sandy hill where Thomas now stands. Many older people in the Pratt City-Thomas area recall an elderly black, an ex-slave of the Hawkins Plantation, who assumed his master's name. He lived well into the twentieth century. Williamson Hawkins was the exception in the county. Less than 19 percent of the county families owned slaves, and more than 70 percent of these families held less than ten slaves. Only eight families owned more than 40 slaves.

As the pioneer decades passed, although some valley slaveholders did not labor with their own hands, the vast majority continued to work in the fields side by side with their slaves. The whites and blacks had a "kind of family arrangement," which was typical of the paternalism found in the antebellum South in areas where slaves were not numerous and slave ownership was small. In their personal letters, owners frequently referred to their "white family" and their "black family," commenting upon the health and activities of both. William Jemison Mims's Civil War letters to his wife at Elyton usually ended with "Kiss Ma & Babies. Give love to white and black & may God bless us continually. . . ."

John Witherspoon DuBose, who wrote the first history of Jefferson County in 1887, recalled that the "old time planters and slaveholders of Jones Valley were a peculiar class of men" who were "land locked amidst the mountains," and thus "developed a character as distinct as islanders." The planter

"differed from the mountaineers in the breadth of his education, which was liberal, in the profuse good cheer of his board, in his general intelligence and ability to rear and support his family." DuBose believed the Jefferson County planter also "differed from the great planters of the Black Belt in the simpler aspirations of life. He placed no great stress upon the fit of his clothes, the regulation of his etiquette, or the spread of his fortune. He delighted in hospitality with no thought of its exacting ceremonies." The Jones Valley planter stood "on the social 'divide' between the aristocrats of the Black Belt, and the yeomanry of the mountains." Cotton did not dominate his life. His farm was more diversified and self-sufficient. He was not as wealthy and there were less differences in economic classes in the hill country than in the south. He ate cornbread and raised hogs and cattle. His house probably had whitewashed boards over the original logs. When Francis M. Grace, son of a pioneer family, first visited South Alabama as a young man in the 1850s, he commented: "To a country boy from the mountain region of the state all this wealth in the cotton country was something oppressive."

But there was another side of slavery and another side of life in the hill country. The county was required by Alabama law to have slave patrols, as they did in other areas of the South, to control the activities of slaves. Alabama law required that all able-bodied white men serve in the patrols and assist in enforcing order. In 1849, the Jefferson County patrol was threatened by a slave of the McDaniel place. The slave fled with the patrol close behind him. Expecting no trouble, which may indicate that "trouble" was not normal, the white men were not armed. A "pattyroller" (as the blacks called the patrolers) named Pearson reached the slave first and was wounded in a fight when the black pulled a knife. The next man to reach the pair, McGuire, was "so miserably lacerated that he bled to death." The slave then broke into his owner's home and attacked him with an axe. Pearson arrived, still wounded but now with a gun, and shot the slave in the arm. The slave used his knife and committed suicide by cutting his own throat.

The hill country white families who lived on less productive land and in the more isolated regions of the county had no slaves. They farmed where they could, raising some corn, which they ate and fed to their animals, and some cotton that they wove into "homespun." Their hogs and cattle roamed the woods. Each family had a vegetable garden and chickens and a milk cow. On their infrequent trips to the mill or store, the families rode in an open wagon. Their houses were most likely of dog-trot design, rude cabins with two rooms and an open breezeway between, which gave four-way "air conditioning" in the summer. Sadly, only a few of these houses remain in the county; most that do are rotting away, covered with kudzu, and infested with rattlesnakes.

25

Pioneer Farmers in the Hill Country

The Agricultural Census of Jefferson County for 1860 suggests the variety of valuable livestock on the farms of the county, including horses, mules, cows, oxen, cattle, sheep, and pigs. The main crop was corn, but wheat, rye, oats, tobacco, peas, beans, and potatoes were also raised. Cotton was the cash crop, but the market was 50 to 70 miles by wagon down the Tuscaloosa Road to the headwaters of the Warrior River. After the completion of the Alabama and Tennessee Rivers Railroad as far as Montevallo, the valley farmers could wagon their cotton over Red and Oak Mountains to Montevallo, and haul their supplies back the same way. But in 1854 the railroad shipping rates were so high that many large planters returned to the old Tuscaloosa wagon route, which by this time had 18 miles of plank road. Colonel James A. Mudd even contracted with a freighter, Hiram Williams, to haul his cotton all the way to Selma by road. Mudd then shipped it down the Alabama River to Mobile. He reported that supplies were cheaper at Selma, and the *Jones Valley Times* noted that many small farmers (those who made only four bales of cotton) were hauling their entire crop to Selma.

In 1860 Jefferson County produced 586,785 bushels of corn and only 4,940 bales of cotton, while the Black Belt counties of South Alabama were producing between 57,000 and 63,000 bales of cotton. Jefferson County was definitely in the Corn Belt and not in the Cotton Kingdom! The increasing importance of corn was evident throughout the 1850s. The *Jones Valley Times*, noting that farmers in the area were planting less cotton and more corn and wheat, commented that the county was "not a desirable cotton region by any means, but is much better adapted to the raising of grain and stock." The only industry listed in the Jefferson County manufacturers' census of 1860 was "leather," which employed six men and produced annual products worth $4,800. There were three tanneries in the county.

Below: *On the eve of the Civil War, Elyton, the county seat of Jefferson County, was a happy southern town of 105 families where neighbors visited often and young people courted at church socials and family parties. From Harper's Weekly, January 5, 1861, Samford University Library.*

Above: *Jones Valley farmers used the cotton press to bale their cotton. Cotton was the money crop of antebellum Jefferson County even though corn was the area's main crop. From the Southern Historical Collection, University of North Carolina.*

Facing page: *Before the Civil War, this Elyton building served as an inn and stagecoach stop. The Masonic Lodge founded by Thomas Farrar and known as Farrar Lodge No. 8 often held their meetings here. From the William H. Brantley, Jr. Collection, Samford University Library.*

A.A. Condrey advertised in the *Jones Valley Times* that he "manufactured every article in the SADDLERY line," under the headline, "Encourage Home Industries." Home manufacturers had an annual value of $18,263. One ingenious man, John Thomas, known as "an eccentric bachelor," had a mulberry orchard and raised silkworms, spinning and weaving silk fabric himself.

On the eve of the Civil War, the trade center of Jefferson County was the county seat, Elyton, which boasted an academy, a masonic lodge, a post office, a hotel, several mercantile establishments, plus the county courthouse. A sleepy country town, Elyton had unpaved streets that became muddy with the rain and dusty during the dry spells. The "young chaps bathed" at "Goose Hole" near the schoolhouse on William A. Walker's place, and the older boys played at the "Elm Hole" at Dr. Joseph R. Smith's homestead. The "Big Boys" would ride off to Roebuck's mill pond on Village Creek to swim. Elyton was a Southern town of 105 families where Elias Glenn ran the county poorhouse with its five inmates. The major social events were candy pullings, prayer meetings, or visiting at Nabers' Grove or at the Worthington home. The men would sneak off to fish at Calvin Williams's place on the Warrior River at the mouth of Village Creek, go coon and fox hunting, or venture down to Cape Smith's gun shop at Waldrop's Mill. Elyton was a place where the men enjoyed racing horses at the famous Elyton Race Track and the ladies planned all-day picnics to Shades Mountain's Lintacum Springs to watch the "Balancing Rock." Carriage rides into the hills or secret meetings at the Big Spring were favorite ways to court by day; by night young couples courted by candlelight and were required to go home when the candle burned out. When the weather was bad, the old veterans of Jackson's Indian wars would gather at a mill to reminisce and spin tales about the "old days." When the circus came to town, the entire village closed and went. There were log rollings and house raisings, corn shuckings, weddings, and funerals. The men played "fives" and the women quilted. The entire county would gather together at the militia musters once a year at Massay Springs and at the revivals at the campground near Hagood's on the Clay Road. The usual "loafers' club" sat in the village square at Elyton and whittled, discussed the weather, business, religion, and politics. And in the decade of the 1850s, there was a great deal of "politics" to talk about.

Chapter III

THE VALLEY AND THE WAR

The farmers and townspeople of Jefferson County followed the political events of 1860 with intense interest. In the gubernatorial election of 1859, moderate Democrat Andrew B. Moore was opposed by William F. Samford, who bolted the Democratic Party to run against Moore because he believed Moore was not strong enough in defending Southern rights. Jefferson County overwhelmingly supported Moore, the moderate choice. Slavery, never strong in the county, seemed to many residents a poor reason for disunion. Still the election of a "black Republican" President was viewed with trepidation and the growing conflict was interpreted as an "infringement of Constitutional rights." The two towns, Elyton and Jonesboro, always more Whiggish than the hills and with a greater stake in slavery and the status quo, were more vocal in defending Southern rights. Although the majority of the county preferred not to make any precipitous decisions, they were unanimously agreed upon resisting any invasion of the state.

Many Jefferson County men were part of this Alabama regiment that marched through the streets of Richmond, Virginia, on their way to join General P.G.T. Beauregard's forces. From Harper's Weekly, *October 19, 1861, Samford University Library.*

The Valley and the War

The summer of 1860 was hot and dry in the hill country and many crops failed. The heated presidential campaign matched the weather. After all the rhetoric Jefferson County returned a 72 percent vote for Southern Democratic candidate John C. Breckinridge. This strong showing for the candidate that Alabama's secessionists supported in an area weak on secession was partly due to the long-standing Democratic loyalty of the hill country yeomanry, which dated back to the days of Andrew Jackson. The absence of cities to nourish the Whig Party precluded a large vote for the "broadcloth candidacy" of John Bell. In Jefferson County, the isolation, sparse settlement, poverty, and lack of newspapers all helped Breckinridge. William L. Barney in his study, *The Secessionist Impulse,* has concluded "Nothing short of the fear of secession and war could shake the party allegiance of the Breckinridge Democrat in the mountains" of Alabama.

In November, when the news of Lincoln's election flashed across the telegraph lines and arrived in Jones Valley by horseback from Montevallo, excitement spread throughout the county, but some people feared, as one young girl did, that it was "the beginning of woe"; just how much only time would tell.

Governor A.B. Moore called for the election on Christmas Eve of delegates to meet in convention in Montgomery to consider secession. Opinions in Jefferson County were almost evenly divided. At a large meeting held in Elyton, Probate Judge Moses Kelly was nominated as a delegate to the convention. Known as a "staunch old States Rights man," the nomination of Kelly pleased the secessionist *Montgomery Weekly Advertiser,* which commented that this "well-regarded," "prudent and conservative man" was an asset to the secessionist ticket and "his election may be regarded as quite certain." However, the South Alabama paper misjudged the sentiment of the hill country. Kelly was defeated by William S. Earnest, who ran as a Cooperationist, opposing "immediate secession" and favoring "cooperating with other Southern states in secession." The "straight-out secessionists" called the Cooperationist party "the old Federal Union Submission party under a new name," but Earnest won by more than a hundred votes. The election to the secession convention was more heated than the presidential one had been, for more men voted in this election than for presidential electors.

Top: *John Cabell Breckinridge, the Southern Democratic presidential candidate in the campaign of 1860, received 72 percent of the Jefferson County vote even though he was the secessionist's candidate. From Cirker,* Dictionary of American Portraits. *Engraved by John C. Buttre from a daguerreotype of Mathew Brady.*

Above: *John Bell, the Whig candidate in the 1860 presidential campaign, was unable to secure the votes he needed from Jefferson County. From Cirker,* Dictionary of American Portraits. *Courtesy, New York Historical Society.*

Facing page: *When Alabama issued the call "To Arms!" Jefferson County men responded, traveling down to Shelby or Tuscaloosa counties to be mustered into an Alabama regiment. From Harper's Weekly, November 16, 1861, Samford University Library.*

Earnest had represented Jefferson County in the state legislature, and in 1853 he had been soundly defeated as the Whig and mountain Democratic candidate for governor against the Democratic and Southern Rights nominee John A. Winston. Known as a "conservative citizen of substantial wealth" and good judgment, the people believed he would represent well the divided views of the county at the secession convention. At Montgomery, the Cooperationists were in the minority. During the debates, Earnest changed his views on the expediency of secession, admitting that the "majority of this convention will pass it" and "sever our allegiance from the *General Government*." When this occurred, he said his allegiance would be "due alone to the State of Alabama, and in me she shall find no laggard or lukewarm friend." His feelings represented the majority view of Jefferson County. Secession was not desired, but if Alabama went out of the Union the people's loyalty was to the state. Earnest could not bring himself to approve an act he considered treasonable, but after secession was adopted by the convention, he did sign the enrolled ordinance. Then he hastened home to the hill country to inform the people of Jefferson County that Alabama had taken her place among the free and sovereign states of the world and that the peace and happiness of their isolated valley could well be in danger.

The secession of Alabama spread excitement through the hill country. In Elyton martial spirit was high. Young boys formed a military company and drilled in the streets, while ladies fashioned blue cockades with cotton bolls in the center that became the local "symbol of resistance." A homemade cannon was fired off each time word arrived that another state had seceded. In the "quiet valley this salute was heard for miles," and all the farmers hastened to Elyton to learn the latest news that "old man Easterwood" had brought with the mail. When hostilities began in 1861 and Alabama issued the call to arms, a number of county men responded, traveling down to Shelby or Tuscaloosa counties to be mustered into an Alabama regiment. As they left Elyton someone began pulling on the old courthouse bell. This was the last reminder of home ringing in the ears of such men as Felix McLaughlin, Thomas J. Hickman, Felix M. Wood, and others as they marched off to war.

The Valley and the War

This scene of men leaving and bidding their loved ones farewell was repeated throughout the county during the Civil War. From Jonesboro the men walked to Montevallo. At Crumly Chapel, after planting a large crop of corn, the men of the community met at the Methodist Church, told their families goodbye, and walked together to Elyton to enlist and catch the stagecoach to Montevallo. Across the county at Old Mount Pinson, Thomas, Robert J., and Gideon Hagood, and Benjamin and Billy Vann, marched from Hagood's Cross Roads on August 12, 1861, as part of the Nineteenth Alabama Regiment. W.A. Worthington and John Truss bid their families at Trussville farewell and joined the Eighth Alabama Regiment. Paul H. Earle left Elyton with his black body servant Ellick, who served as a Confederate cook during the entire war. Earle's younger brother, Robert, drove his scythe deep into a tree in the yard of his parent's home by the Jasper Road and pledged to his sweetheart that his love would "last as long as this blade remains in the wood."

William Jemison Mims was typical of the Jefferson County men who went off to war. Born in Autauga County, Mims married Kate DeJarnette in 1858 and moved to a farm near Elyton. Both these people had strong family ties to South Alabama and to a plantation economy, but they opposed extremism, questioned the wisdom of secession, and doubted the Confederacy could win. Yet they were intensely loyal to the Southern cause and possessed a deep faith that with God's blessings they would somehow survive. After arranging for an overseer to look after the farm and seeing that Kate was safely delivered of her second child, Jemison Mims organized a company of Jefferson County's "hardy yeomanry" and was promptly elected captain. The company was mustered into Confederate service at Elyton on May 10, 1862, as Company G of the Forty-third Alabama Infantry.

Most of the county men who went into the Confederate army, either by volunteering or being conscripted, served with distinction, but there were many others who refused to serve. A few of these were Old Whigs intensely loyal to the Union, or hill country folk inspired by Andrew Jackson's dictum: "The Federal Union, it must be preserved!" Twenty-two men from Jefferson County served in the Union army as part of the First Alabama Cavalry. Some men were "Tories," rebelling against both Alabama and the Confederate governments, while most were plain

"mossbacks," hiding in the hills and woods "until moss grew" on their backs, avoiding all military service. These Tories and mossbacks were usually hostile to slavery and resented the slaveholding aristocracy. As if to explain this lack of support for a cause that became almost holy to whites in the decades following defeat, one historian of the hill country commented that Jefferson County was a "little world shut off largely from the other sections" and it produced "all sorts and conditions of men."

As the war continued, the people of Jones Valley became "common sympathizers," one "family group," anxiously waiting for news from the front. One Elyton resident, James E. Hawkins, was a boy during the war. He recalled that with "our fathers, brothers, and sons at the front, one could imagine the interest the mothers, sisters, and brothers and small boys felt." Elyton received mail twice a week by hack from Montevallo, but it was often delayed. Everyone in the valley was "on the alert for the trumpet sound of Simon Easterwood as he reached the crest of Shades Mountain and heralded his approach with tidings from the world. The residents of the valley would gather in, some with faint hearts and some strong with the faith that was within them, some eager to hear, and others dreading to hear." The people would stand in front of the Elyton post office and listen to the news being read from the steps. If the county companies had been part of a victory, the old homemade cannon would roar. If it was defeat then "the list of killed, wounded, and missing was reported. Imagine the scene!" After a boy was reported killed, often his "grey-haired father" would gather some supplies, hitch up a wagon, and start out toward the battlefield "to rescue the remains of a son who had sacrificed his life." The poor man did not know where to go, had no way to communicate with the company, and probably when he reached the command it would "be miles and miles from the spot where his dear boy" lay.

If it was hard on the valley to receive the news of casualties, it was even harder on the soldiers in the field. When companies were drawn from the same communities, all the men knew each other, were kin by birth or marriage, or had grown up together. Jemison Mims's letters to Kate often mentioned the "mortal wounding" of the valley men in his company and instructed her to tell the wife or mother how bravely the men fought and how his "heart was so sad" for the family. Samuel King Vann wrote his sweetheart at Cedar Grove from the ditches near Atlanta that "we lose one man from our 'Co' everytime we go on picket . . . . Oh, how awful 'tis to see friends falling about me." And later from Tennessee, Vann wrote: "Oh! You cannot have the

Facing page: The home of Dr. and Mrs. Samuel Earle was the site of a sad farewell on June 13, 1861, the eve of their son Robert's departure for war. Walking across the yard with his sweetheart Betty Dupuy, young Robert was asked by Betty if he would "love her always." He grabbed a scythe from nearby and driving it deep into a tree, shown here at left, he pledged his love would "last as long as this blade remains in the wood." Unfortunately, Earle was killed during the war. The tree was cut down in the 1930s, but the scythe remains today in the museum in Arlington. From the William H. Brantley, Jr. Collection, Samford University Library.

Below: William Jemison Mims was typical of the Jefferson County men who served in the Confederate army. He opposed extremism, questioned the wisdom of secession, and doubted the Confederacy could win, yet he remained intensely loyal to the Southern cause. On May 10, 1862, he organized a company of the county's "hardy yeomanry" which was mustered into Confederate service at Elyton as Company G of the Forty-third Alabama infantry. Courtesy, Kathleen Peacock Bruhn and Dr. Glover Moore.

Bottom: William Rose McAdory, the son of pioneers Colonel James McAdory and his wife Nancy Sadler McAdory, lived in Jonesboro. During the war he and four brothers served in the Confederate army. On November 23, 1865, William Rose was killed at Missionary Ridge (near Chattanooga). Courtesy, Bessemer Hall of History.

The Valley
and the War

slightest imagination of how many men were killed
. . . Gideon Hagood's arm was broken, Brother Billy
came out with a slight wound in breast—though well
now,—I came out without a scratch." One night,
after a fierce day of fighting at Chickamauga,
Mortimer Jordan was awakened by the body servant
of his brother, Charles Scott Jordan, who told him
that his brother was dead. Rousing himself from a
sound sleep, Jordan asked how he knew this.
" 'Cause he didn't come in with the men last night
and I gone out huntin' his body with my lantern. I
done found him and got him wrapped in the wagon.
I'm takin' him home to his Mama and I be back soon
as I kin."

Elyton was particularly stunned by the strange death
of Robert Earle, who was resting on a cot inside his
tent at Centreville, Virginia, when he was mortally
wounded by a ball that came through the top of the
tent. His father, Dr. Samuel Earle, was sent the details
of his youngest son's death by Alburto Martin, who
assured the family that the grave site was clearly
marked so that they might return and remove the
body. Later they did and today Robert rests in the
family plot of Oak Hill Cemetery. His scythe, driven
deep into the tree on the Jasper Road, remained

there, a legend and a curiosity, until the land was
cleared to make way for the apartments at Elyton
Village in the 1930s.

Throughout the war soldiers were granted furloughs
or sent home to Jefferson County to gather supplies
for the company. There was always a need for socks,
underwear, warm clothes, and shoes at the front. The
men from the county would write home, telling their
families exactly what they needed, usually sending
their letters with the returning soldier. Jemison Mims
once sent a letter home with a soldier, writing his wife
that "although I dare say this poor convalescent will
have some 200 miles to walk and about as many
letters to pack as an old U.S. Mail Coach ought to
undertake, still I cannot resist the inclination to add
this one to his load." When a veteran was ready to
return to duty, he would leave the county with one or
two mules or a wagon loaded with packages and
letters for the men in his company.

In October of 1864, the last year of the war, Samuel
Vann came home to Jefferson County on furlough.
To him, "it seemed like peace was made to see our
old Co. come marching home at the same time." But
it was sad for him to think of how many men marched

off with his company and did not come home again. "O 'tis awful to think how many noble-hearted brave men have fallen since our Co. left here. We will all form again at Old Mount Pinson in the morning where the Co. first formed at the commencement of the war." Of the 100 men who left Mount Pinson in 1861, only nine were still alive. Recent recruits brought the strength of the normal 100-man company up to 24. As the war dragged on, Confederate enrolling officers scoured the hill country looking for conscripts. In order to avoid the "odium of being conscripted," when they reached the age of 16, the young men of the valley "went forth" so that "only the women, old men, and boys were left at home." So many were serving in the army from that area that in February 1864, Jefferson County reported to the governor that it had no men available for service in compliance with a state law making men and boys from 16 to 60 liable for training as state militia reserves.

With death as a constant companion, Jefferson County soldiers had enough to occupy their thoughts at the front; yet they worried about the health of their families and the conditions of their farms in the valley. Elias Davis wrote his brother-in-law, John, "you can't imagine how I am troubled at the condition of my family; but it is out of my power to have things otherwise." Davis insisted that his wife, Georgiana, take the baby and return to her parents' home; other wives could not go home. Southern men enjoyed placing their "ladies upon a pedestal," sheltering them from many of the harsh realities of life. Now women who had never worked long in the fields began to toil from sunup to sundown. Women who had never had the responsibility of decision-making suddenly had the destinies of themselves, their children, and—for those who owned slaves, their black families—thrust into their hands. Simple questions like how many acres should be planted in cotton and how many in corn, how many hogs to slaughter, how many supplies to buy, were decisions for them alone to make. These women depended upon the loyalty and labor of their slave field hands to survive and were guided in their agricultural decisions by the elder slave leader or driver.

Although husbands assured their wives of their confidence in their ability to "make the correct decisions" and "manage," letters home were filled with advice and specific directions. Women were told to plant only the best land, to make sure and give the corn enough room, to plant more food and not so much cotton. They were advised that they were "making molasses too slowly" and "I fear you will not make enough for one white family." They were told to "kill the hogs as soon as they are fat enough

Facing page: *Confederate soldier George B. Houston (front row, left) and his friends visit with their ladies. Throughout the war soldiers were granted furloughs or sent home to Jefferson County to rest and visit with their families and to gather supplies for the county company. When the soldiers came home there was much partying and visiting. Courtesy, Bessemer Hall of History.*

Top: *Georgiana Davis was living on her farm near Trussville when her husband Dr. Elias Davis was killed while serving in the Confederate army. Davis left two sons who became beloved doctors in Birmingham: Dr. J.D.S. Davis and Dr. W.E.B. Davis. Courtesy, Sarah Lathem Nesbitt, Pioneer Museum, Oak Hill Cemetery.*

Above: *Samuel King Vann wrote often to his sweetheart, Nancy Elizabeth Neel, pouring out his heart full of love for her and sharing with her the horrors of war. Courtesy, William Y. Elliott, Sr.*

The Valley and the War

Thomas Hill Watts was a Whig and a persistent Unionist spokesman in the 1850s. He was appointed the Attorney General of the Confederacy by President Jefferson Davis in 1862, and was elected governor of Alabama in the fall of 1863. Watts tried to marshal Alabama forces to defend Jefferson County and Alabama. He opposed, however, significant military policies of the Richmond government in the last months of the war. From Cirker, Dictionary of American Portraits. Engraved by F.G. Kernan. Courtesy, Alabama State Chamber of Commerce.

and the weather cool enough,'' and not to sell them. Husbands counseled their wives not to spend any money, to ''barter anything you can spare'' for necessary articles, to hire out the Negroes, to let ''Andrew handle the field crops for he knows best,'' to keep the fences in good repair and the corn crib secure, to take great ''care of the sheep and the stock,'' and ''to save all the food you can.''

One soldier wrote his wife from Virginia that it ''pains my heart when I think of your conditions at home.'' From Tennessee, Ben Crumly cautioned his wife Arabella ''to be as saving of your corn and fodder as you can for I am afraid the time is near at hand when corn can't be bought.'' And in an undated letter Jemison Mims advised Kate: ''If you can sell Corn for $2.00 per bushel, I think what we can spare should be sold immediately.'' By 1865 corn was selling in Jefferson County for $5 a bushel, and flour throughout the Confederacy for $50 to $80 per 100 pounds. Cloth was so scarce that prices skyrocketed. A lady's black alpaca dress could not be bought for $500, a spool of black thread was $15, and men's shirts cost $100. The women in Jefferson County were urged to keep someone spinning and weaving at all times. The ''Southern Patriot's'' cry in 1860 for women to don ''homespun and calicos'' had been realized; there was nothing else to wear.

Toward the end of the war, there was little the county could send to their men in battle. Hundreds of soldiers' families were destitute. The severe drought of 1862 reduced the corn crop and by the next year affected the supply of farm animals. In 1863 Senator Robert Jemison warned the Confederate Congress in Richmond that ''thousands of families of soldiers in North Alabama have no meat.'' By December 1864, Governor Thomas H. Watts noted in his letter book that ''the cries of starving people are coming up to me almost every day'' from counties in North Alabama. State aid was sent to Jefferson County and given to ''all actually indigent.'' Poverty was due to a decrease in production, to state taxes in kind, and to impressments from the Confederacy. Fences were down, mills were not working, stores had no supplies, plows and wagons were broken. Few men remained with the skill to make repairs, and there were no available spare parts.

Jefferson County soldiers also worried about the physical safety of their wives and children at home. Bands of Confederate deserters, Tories, and mossbacks roamed the hill country pillaging and murdering. The undefended and isolated homes of Confederate soldiers were easy prey. The county and state governments could not provide protection and northern Jefferson County sheltered ''numerous squads concealed in mountains almost inaccessible to cavalry.'' In 1863 Elias Davis wrote his family that he was pleased they had ''shot those robbers, the Watsons,'' and advised that ''shooting and hanging'' deserters would stop robbing forever in their Trussville neighborhood.

But deserters and mossbacks were not the only dangers Confederate soldiers at the front feared for their families. They were tormented by the thought of Union troops invading Jefferson County and bringing the war home to their own doorstep. In 1863 rumors spread through the Confederate regiments at Chickamauga that ''Yankee Raiders'' were at Tuscaloosa. Urgent warnings were sent back to the valley. ''If you get wind of them in time, hide all you can and by all means send off the stock!'' This was one of many false rumors.

In the spring of 1863 Federal raiders under Colonel A.D. Streight crossed Blount County to the north headed for Rome, Georgia, where Confederate General Nathan Bedford Forrest forced him to surrender 28 miles from his goal. The next summer Lovell H. Rousseau led Federal troops down the state through St. Clair and Talladega counties to destroy the West Point Railroad supplying Atlanta from Montgomery; once again a major raid into Alabama had missed Jefferson County. As the new year dawned in 1865, news from all areas of the Confederate front was discouraging. Then in March 1865, the word that Yankee Raiders were coming toward the valley spread rapidly through Jefferson County. This time, it was not a rumor.

As early as February 18 the *Montgomery Daily Mail* had reported Union troop concentrations in North Alabama. On February 25 General Robert E. Lee cautioned from Richmond of the possibility of a Federal march on Selma and Tuscaloosa. On March 22 Union General James H. Wilson managed to ferry 13,480 cavalrymen across the rain-swollen Tennessee River and begin his move south toward Jasper and Jefferson County. In Mississippi General Forrest was desperately trying to defend the interior South from invasion threats at several points and was slow in learning of the Federal raid, allowing Wilson to ride into Jasper unopposed. Spies told the Yankees that Confederate forces were gathering at Tuscaloosa and Selma, so Wilson determined to move rapidly through the hill country.

Meanwhile a detachment of the Fifth Alabama Cavalry was protecting Jones Valley and manning defensive works on the Huntsville Road. The Federal forces had great difficulty fording the Mulberry fork of the Warrior River, but by the time they crossed the Locust fork, the entire valley knew Union troops were coming south down the Jasper Road. Although Wilson's order prohibiting pillaging and destruction of private property was read daily to his army, it did little to stop depredations, and the Federal advance could be followed by the smoke from burning fields and fences, barns and houses along the way. The Confederate cavalry, with Colonel Josiah Patterson commanding, hastily withdrew from the Huntsville Road. The cavalry moved west to the Jasper Road, meeting General Emory Upton's Iowa Division at Five Mile Creek. A Union soldier wrote about the meeting in his diary: "We crossed a nice Kreek called Five Mile, on its banks we discovered a newly errected works of defense. We heard afterwards that they were constructed by Negroes, and that they would fight us too."

The Federal troops had little respect for the Alabama hill country, describing it as "very mountainous," the farms and villages "poor and primitive, the yield of corn and cotton insignificant." The people were "very ignorant and poor," but with "Union proclivities," and the women "not good looking." To the Federal raiders Jones Valley, which they reached after dark, seemed an oasis in the hills. One Yankee officer recorded in his diary: "At last I think we are through the mountains, a large valley spreads before

us, it must be a beautiful looking county." The soldiers camped on the plantation of Williamson Hawkins, whom they described as "a union man, but [he] has a son in the rebel ranks." S.V. Shipman, of Madison, Wisconsin, found Hawkins to be "very cranky and insolent which will avail him little at present." General Upton's clerk, E.N. Gilpin, recorded that Hawkins was a "rich old Southerner." He wrote that they "took possession of his farm and mansion house, with a little army of Negroes, turkeys, chickens, butter, eggs, hams in the smoke house, thousands of bushels of corn in the barn, and forage of all kinds on the place, visited the wine celler," where one keg "was confiscated without delay, lest it might give aid or comfort to the enemy." Upton's men hoped to stay and enjoy Hawkins's hospitality, but at 2:00 p.m. on March 29, they were ordered to move south to capture the Cahaba River bridge and hold it for the rest of the raiders.

According to General Wilson's diary, he remained at Jasper while Upton secured the Cahaba crossing. Then on March 30, with the divisions of General Eli Long and General Edward M. McCrook, Wilson left Jasper "soon after daylight," arriving at Elyton at one in the afternoon. Wilson commented in his diary that "Jones Valley [was] fertile, forage plenty." Much later he wrote in his autobiography that "Elyton at that time was a poor, insignificant Southern village, surrounded by old field farms, most of which could

Goldsmith W. Hewitt was born in Jefferson County near Elyton in 1834. Before the Civil War he studied law in Judge William S. Mudd's office. In 1861 Hewitt volunteered for Confederate service and served in the Tenth and Twenty-eighth Alabama regiments. He was severely wounded at the battle of Chickamauga, but he recovered and later entered the field of politics. He served in the Alabama House of Representatives, the state senate, and the United States Congress. Courtesy, Harriet Smith Culp.

The Valley and the War

have been bought at five dollars per acre. . . . I was deeply impressed by the poverty-stricken and ruminating appearance of the landscape. At that time the farms and villages were poor and primitive, the yield of corn and cotton insignificant." His medical director had a better opinion of Elyton, describing it as a "very pretty village" and the land as "fertile and cultivated."

General McCrook's men took up the camp sites on the Hawkins plantation left by Upton's corps. It is uncertain just where Long's Second Division camped; records simply state "Elyton," but one local account suggests a number of Wilson's troops bivouacked on the freshly "planted crop of wheat and corn" of Dr. Nathaniel Hawkins and others on the farm of Robert H. Greene. Because of the large number of men, the raiders probably camped all over Elyton. Wilson himself made his headquarters at "The Grove," Judge William S. Mudd's home, which later became known as Arlington. He did not stay long, however, because according to his diary he left Elyton two hours after his arrival. Wilson knew that General Forrest awaited him someplace to the south. He had great respect for the brilliant Confederate general and did not wish to give the Southerner any extra time to meet his Yankee forces "First with the Most," which was Forrest's motto. At Elyton Wilson ordered McCrook to detach a brigade and send them to destroy Confederate factories and stores at Tuscaloosa and, specifically, the "military school." McCrook selected the First Brigade of General John T. Croxton.

Meanwhile, at Crumly Chapel, Yankee soldiers, in a "sulky mood," broke open all the beehives, took some honey, and spilled the rest on the ground. To the delight of the silently watching women and children, however, they were soundly stung in the process! Across the way, the soldiers visited Mrs. Sara Ann McDonald and her father Robert Crumly, but failed to locate the ham and food hidden in a hollow tree. A picture of a Union soldier tacked to the wall and sketched by a Georgia relative saved the house from being torched. At Ben Crumly's home the family hid cornbread in the attic. The raiders missed finding it, but they took a horse from the stable. When it limped the Yankees left it behind. The family later discovered that a slave had "crippled the horse temporarily." Over at King's Spring (Avondale), when the "Home Guard" opened fire on a group of raiders watering their horses, the Yankees returned their fire and Mrs. Abner Killough, who was sitting on her porch, was wounded by a stray bullet. David Hanby, coming home from a hunting trip, met Yankee soldiers on the road and was ordered to throw down his rifle. Being deaf, he was too slow to respond and was shot dead.

Official records indicate that Federal raiders were in Jones Valley about three days, but local accounts state eight days and are probably correct, since a number of companies had gotten lost and so were late in arriving. Wilson's raiders burned Lamson's Flour Mill at Black Creek on their way into Elyton, and the Oxmoor and Irondale furnaces as they were leaving. These pig iron furnaces were the most important military industries in the county. Toward the end of April Federal troops again moved through Jefferson County when General Croxton, after burning the University at Tuscaloosa, came across the back road. These troops arrived at Mount Pinson on April 20, where they burned the Mount Pinson Iron Works and a nitre works, then passed on through Trussville and Cedar Grove to Talladega. From the time of their coming until their departure, the Federal troops managed to spread fire and destruction through the valley and instill fear in the hearts of Jefferson Countians.

After the Union Army left, there was havoc everywhere. All the good horses had been confiscated. Only lame animals were left. Mary Gordon Duffee, (despite local stories of her hiding upstairs at Arlington as a Confederate spy while Wilson issued orders from the parlor below), recalled that she was in Montevallo when the raiders came through Elyton. Unable to find any transportation home, she began walking. As she came to the valley, she described the scene vividly:

As I neared the familiar scene, my heart sank at the strange stillness of the landscape—not a sound save the twitter of birds as they flew from limb to limb. Here and there a broken-down army horse searched for the tender young grass, pretty blue wild flags bloomed in the nooks and corners, the wild honeysuckle threw its spray of pink laurels against the rocks, it was all so sweet and tranquil—but so overwhelmingly lonely. At last I mustered the courage to venture on and found myself standing amid blackened ruins against the wall of the furnaces of the town.

On Palm Sunday, April 9, 1865, General Ulysses S. Grant accepted General Robert E. Lee's surrender at Appomattox Court House, Virginia. William Jemison Mims, Richard Alexander Jones, Dr. James B. Luckie, Thomas W. Reaves, J.H. Owen, and other Jefferson County men waited for their parole so they could begin the long walk home to Jefferson County. Several days later this staggering news reached Jones Valley, still devastated from Wilson's raid. One young boy recalled his mother crying, asking her husband "What are we to do?" Pointing to the hives of bees, busy rebuilding after Yankee troopers had despoiled their home, the father replied, "We, with our faith and intelligence can do the same." The good news was that the county's men would soon be coming home again—at least those who had endured the bloody conflict would be coming home.

Chapter IV

TOWARD
RECOVERY

Jefferson County's first blast furnaces were constructed at Ironton (Oxmoor). During the Civil War seventy-year-old Moses Stroup worked the furnaces day and night, forcing them to produce pig iron for the Confederacy. After General Wilson's men burned the furnaces, Daniel Pratt and Henry D. Clayton rebuilt them and Oxmoor went into blast again during the winter of 1873. From the Alabama Department of Archives and History.

The war over, Jefferson County soldiers, with paroles in hand, ragged, crippled, and weary, began the long trek home. Most of them walked, but some were able to catch rides on horses, mules, and wagons for at least part of the way. The news of Wilson's raid had traveled to the front lines and the soldiers were anxious to see how much destruction the Yankees had done to their farms and homes. The effects of the South's defeat were apparent everywhere. The men realized they faced a tremendous task of rebuilding a new life. Slavery was abolished, but most of them had never owned a slave. Under the present conditions, survival was their main concern.

Toward
Recovery

The men had been gone from home for months, some for years. When Brownlow McDonald returned, and walked up the road to his house near Crumly's Chapel, he recognized his children and asked if they knew who he was. "No," came the reply, "unless you could be our Pa." But there were many widows and orphans in the county whose "Pa" did not come home. Hundreds of widowed women and their children were destitute, and although times were hard for all, families and neighbors tried to assume some responsibility for those in need. Churches did what they could to help, but these institutions were also impoverished and their buildings badly in need of repair. The Reverend Francis Mitchell Grace, a Methodist minister of Elyton, tried to locate homes for orphaned children of the county. Merchants like Joseph B. Earle at Elyton continued to be generous with credit. But things only got worse as the crops of late 1865 failed.

The problems faced by the people of Jefferson County were overwhelming. Land worth $50 an acre in 1860 would bring only $3 to $5 in 1865. Gristmills had been burned. Gold, silverplate, furniture, carpets, and crockery had been stolen. Discharged and paroled soldiers, camp followers, and deserters from both armies roamed the countryside, and returning Confederates frequently bushwhacked loyalists or Tories in savage guerrilla warfare that continued for many months. Washington Baird, a member of the Home Service, was shot and killed by bushwhackers.

The black population of Jefferson County was small in 1860 and it decreased in the next decade. Jubilant over emancipation, many Negroes followed Wilson's troops off toward Selma and Montgomery while some drifted down to Tuscaloosa. Cities were alluring because Federal soldiers provided some protection and rations. In Jefferson County there were no towns of any size and no garrisons of soldiers. The black migration out of the county was so great that between 1860 and 1870 the black population declined 3.5 percent. Many of those who stayed left their old plantations and, affirming their independence, moved around the county searching for a new life. Some blacks simply remained, at least temporarily, as tenants with their former masters.

Alabama was without any legal government for several months following the surrender of Southern troops, but local officials of Jefferson County continued to assume political responsibility during the interim until a loyal and legal state government could be organized. The county was little affected by the politics of Radical Reconstruction in which local

A Prospective Scene in the "City of Oaks," 4th of March, 1869.

The September 1, 1868 issue of the Tuscaloosa Independent Monitor *warned carpetbaggers and scalawags to keep out of the town or else face the wrath of the Ku Klux Klan. From William S. Hoole Special Collections, University of Alabama Library.*

and state governments were taken over by Yankee "carpetbaggers" and Southern Republicans, called "scalawags." A check of county officials shows that, with very few exceptions, men who held positions before or during the war continued to hold office after the Radicals took control of the state government. Only for a few months in the summer of 1868 were any Federal troops stationed in the county, and carpetbaggers avoided the poor, hilly, isolated areas. When Confederate soldiers were disfranchised, Union Whigs and Union Democrats emerged as the political leaders of the county. For the most part they were descendants of pioneers, well-known and respected.

Two excellent examples of the quality of leadership of the county during Reconstruction were William S. Mudd and William A. Walker. Before the war Mudd, a Whig, had been elected judge in a Democratic circuit. He remained on the bench from 1856 until 1883, when he resigned because of ill health. In 1865 he was selected as the Jefferson County representative to the constitutional convention, where he served as chairman of the important committee to restore Alabama to the Union and to repeal the ordinance of secession. William A. Walker, the son of an old county pioneer family, represented the county at the Radical Constitutional Convention of 1867. Both men have been variously identified as "conservatives," "the better class," or as "scalawags" or Republicans. Mudd did receive the Republican nomination for circuit judge in 1868 and 1874. On April 23, 1874, the Birmingham *Weekly Iron Age* printed a complimentary article on Mudd saying he was "a model judicial Officer," was "Impartial, honest, able, and fearless." The paper said Mudd holds "the scales of Justice with even hand. His judicial robes are without spot and his private character without stain." The *Montgomery Weekly Advertiser* identified Walker in 1867 with the Republican party; however, the people of Jefferson County knew and trusted him. Both these men were regarded as practical and honorable men and the odium associated with "scalawag Republican" was not applied to them by their home county where the Republican vote was large among native whites.

Under the direction of General Wager Swayne at Montgomery, the Freedmen's Bureau was organized in Alabama the summer of 1865 and took over the responsibility of regulating and feeding the ex-slaves. In January of 1866, a bureau representative made a trip to the hill country and reported to Swayne that certain portions of Jefferson County were "very destitute," that there were "frequent applications for relief from that county," but that the poverty was mostly among the white population. Since there was

William S. Mudd is best known in Birmingham as the man who built Arlington. Mudd called Arlington "The Grove." In 1856 he was elected on the Whig ticket as judge of the circuit court. Mudd opposed secession and after the war he became active in Republican Party affairs in Alabama. He was respected throughout Northern Alabama and stayed on the bench until poor health forced him to retire in 1883. During his political life he was known as a Whig, a Republican, and a Democrat, a fact that reflects the political turmoil of the Reconstruction period. From DuBose, Jefferson County and Birmingham, Alabama (1887).

no Freedmen's Bureau office in the county, Swayne detailed the responsibility of disbursing rations to the bureau headquarters in Montevallo, which created an agency in Elyton. Provisions were shipped by rail from Selma to Montevallo and then hauled by wagon to Elyton. From May to August 1868, the bureau operated the Elyton agency under C.C. Barlett. Jefferson County had no Freedmen's hospital; blacks and refugees needing medical care could obtain it at Huntsville or Talladega. Nor were there any Freedmen's schools in the county. The thirst for learning was high among the ex-slaves, and this was no doubt one reason why blacks emigrated to towns that provided black education. Later a number of Northern missionaries and preachers opened small schools in the county, but Southern white approval waned when Negro schools became centers of Loyal League and Radical political activity.

Toward
Recovery

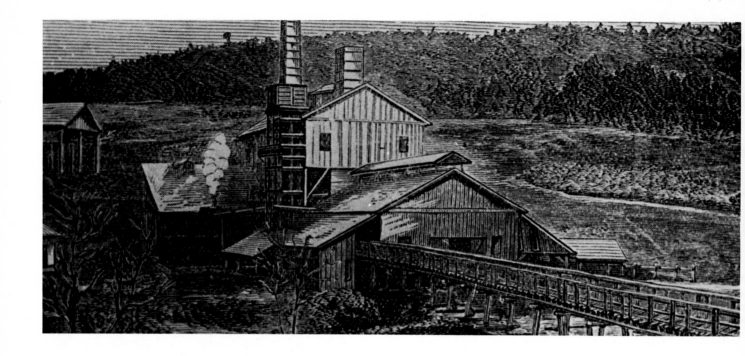

Wallace S. McElwain's Cahaba Iron Works looked like this in 1863. Two years later Union troops led by General James Wilson burned the furnace and buildings. McElwain immediately left for Ohio to obtain funds to rebuild the furnaces. When McElwain put the furnace back into blast in 1866, it was the only blast furnace in Alabama producing pig iron. From the Alabama Department of Archives and History.

In the fall of 1865, with state government in chaos, the old patrol organizations were being used to maintain order. Soon the Tennessee-born Ku Klux Klan spread into Alabama. Although not the only white vigilante group, the "Ku Klux" became the most commonly known. Solomon Palmer, from the northern part of the county, noted that during the winter of 1870-1871 "there were a great many kluklux (a secret disguised klan) who ride of a night and profess to execute laws—they visit our town frequently and are a source of terror to all negroes and radicals." Julius C. Greene recalled a childhood incident after the war when armed blacks came to his house while his father was away. The blacks soon "were surrounded by men on white horses and dressed in long white robes and white hoods." They took the blacks to Sam and Tom Truss's tanyard, whipped them, put them on the road north, telling them never to return to Pinson Valley. Two did return and one was killed, but Greene insisted that the men who whipped the blacks "came from Blount and St. Clair counties." Although a federal marshal from Huntsville came down and "arrested every man from Hagood's Cross Roads to Five Mile Creek" and took them to Elyton jail, none was ever tried for the murder.

According to testimony before the joint congressional committee investigating violence and regulator organizations in Alabama, "unknown persons in disguise" were responsible for five murders and six beatings in Jefferson County between 1867 and 1871. Judge William S. Mudd of Elyton testified that the usual reasons given for whipping blacks were "bad conduct," "stealing cotton," "being impudent," and once for voting the "radical ticket." (Jefferson County Klan terrorism was not directed solely at blacks. One man, a white stranger, came through the county and make the mistake of publicly stating that there was not "a virtuous woman in the world." For this he was whipped.) Mudd could recall no cases of "voter intimidation" in the county similar to those in counties to the south, however. The small black population made more widespread intimidation unnecessary. In 1867 there were 1,366 whites and 430 blacks registered to vote in Jefferson County.

Confederate hero Isaac Wellington McAdory fought with the Army of the Tennessee from the battle of Shiloh to General Joseph E. Johnston's surrender in North Carolina in 1865. After the war, McAdory began Pleasant Hill Academy, one of Jefferson County's most outstanding schools. Though once a member of the Ku Klux Klan, he opposed violence. Courtesy, Henry and Betty McAdory.

In the spring of 1871, a public meeting was held in the county and "all the respectable citizens denounced" the violence of the Ku Klux Klan. For "some time there were no demonstrations, no acts of violence perpetrated," and Solomon Palmer rejoiced "to see the organization cease to exist." But by September Klan activities had resumed. Judge Mudd insisted that it was impossible to gain convictions for these offenses because no witnesses could ever be found who would testify, adding that "the best man, I think, in the country would not be disposed to do it through fear of personal violence, or fear for their property from the hands of some of these men." Stanley Horn, in his study of the Reconstruction Klan, tells the story of a black Jefferson County resident who was arrested for stealing cotton. When he told his lawyer that the Klan had already interrogated him and, convinced of his guilt, beaten him, his lawyer went into court demanding his client be released on the constitutional grounds of double jeopardy since the Klan had clearly already tried the black on the offense. Whether it was the audacity of the theory or the logic, the black man was released.

Although the present was gloomy, the impoverished farmers and landowners of Jefferson County viewed the future with some optimism. The demands of the Southern war economy for iron had encouraged the Confederate government to develop the mineral resources of the area. The iron ore, or "red-dye rock," of the county had been commonly used by the Indians for staining leather and cloth and for war paint, and by the pioneers to color woolen and cotton fabrics, but the crude efforts of the early blacksmiths to utilize the ore had not been successful. In 1844 Baylis Grace became convinced that the outcropping of dye rock on his farm at Grace's Gap (Spaulding) was quality ore. He dug a wagon load and sent it down to Bibb County, where it was made into blooms and distributed to blacksmiths in the valley.

Professor Michael Tuomey of the University of Alabama was appointed the first state geologist in 1848. Six years later the legislature appropriated funds to finance his geological survey, but in the antebellum period, the red mountain of ore remained virtually untouched, considered "good to dye breeches, not to make iron." The six-horse stagecoach carrying passengers and mail from Montgomery to Huntsville continued to cross Red Mountain and "the iron tires of the wheels and the iron shoes of the coach horses," along with countless "farm wagons and cattle," crushed the surface iron ore of the roadbed, "exposing its dazzling red dust to view, but seldom exciting a serious inquiry" about its long neglect. Only when the military necessities of war, a war primarily being fought to protect planter interests, forced the Confederate government to subsidize the building of a railroad into the mineral district and the construction of blast furnaces to supply the Confederate arsenal at Selma would something be done about the transportation needs and industrial possibilities of Jefferson County

In 1862 there was only one crude water blast forge and foundry in all Jefferson County, McGee's Mount Pinson Iron Works on Turkey Creek, which forged farm tools and shod horses. But with Confederate support, in 1863 the Red Mountain Iron and Coal Company was organized by Frank Gilmer and John T. Milner, who purchased Baylis Grace's Red Mountain iron ore lands on the west side of Grace's Gap. Under the direction of Moses Stroup, pioneer ironman of Tannehill furnaces on the Bibb-Tuscaloosa county line, two furnaces were constructed at Ironton (Oxmoor). When they went into blast they produced 20 tons of charcoal iron a day. The next year Wallace S. McElwain and W.A. Jones organized the Cahaba Iron Works. With Confederate support they built a stone stack off the Montevallo Road in Shades Valley. Using Shades

45

Toward Recovery

Creek for water power and red ore from his Helen Bess Mine, McElwain sent 10 tons of charcoal pig iron a day to the Confederate ironworks at Selma. McElwain also experimented with using coke as fuel and produced the first coke pig iron in Alabama. Because of difficulty obtaining coal, however, he returned to charcoal.

Facing page: *The Tannehill furnaces, located on the Bibb County-Jefferson County line, were constructed on the ruins of a forge built by Daniel Hillman in 1830 and operated by Ninion Tannehill from 1836 to 1855. Hillman opened up the Goethite brown ore mines, but when Moses Stroup built the new stone furnaces shown here, he experimented with red iron ore from Red Mountain. It was the first time Red Mountain iron ore was used. Stroup operated the furnaces until 1862 when he sold them to his partner and moved to Oxmoor to operate furnaces for Frank Gilmer and John T. Milner. From the Department of Archives and Manuscripts, Birmingham Public Library.*

Below: *Jefferson County blacksmiths tried to use the local iron ore, but were unsuccessful. From the William S. Hoole Special Collections, University of Alabama Library.*

But the great potential of these Jefferson County Confederate blast furnaces was never realized because of inadequate railroad transportation and the difficulty of maintaining timber supplies for charcoal production. Since the state government was dominated by cotton planters, antebellum railroad development in Alabama reflected planter needs and interests. In 1850, to quiet the long rivalry between North and South Alabama, the planter legislature proposed linking the state together by a railroad joining the navigable waters of the Alabama and Tennessee rivers; however, this railroad by-passed Jefferson County, but reached Montevallo, the Shelby County mineral district, and Talladega by 1854.

When Gilmer and Milner negotiated their contract with the Confederate government in Richmond, it included not only the erection of blast furnaces and rolling mills, but also a railroad to Red Mountain. Such a railroad, called the South & North, had been surveyed by Milner for Governor A.B. Moore and the Alabama legislature in 1858, but the cotton planter interests opposed Milner's route through hill country, which the planters described as "so poor that a buzzard would have to carry provisions on his back or starve to death on his passage." Milner's report was printed, but the railroad was not constructed. In 1863, with a Confederate government subsidy, Gilmer was able to complete the railroad from Calera only as

far as Brock's Gap, but he was not able to cut through the 60 feet of solid rock of Shades Mountain without powder. Although he graded the roadbed to Grace's Gap in Red Mountain, iron from the Oxmoor and Irondale furnaces was slowed considerably because it had to be sent by wagon to the railhead at Brock's Gap and then by the Alabama & Tennessee Rivers Railroad from Montevallo to Selma.

Coal was another great mineral resource of Jefferson County, yet early iron production used charcoal rather than coal for fuel. During the pioneer period the wealth of coal deposits of the area was well-known. The blacksmith shops of Jones Valley used bituminous coal from coal beds on Five-Mile Creek, hauling it in wagons to the smithy. Underground digging was not necessary, because the coal was exposed in the beds of streams and could easily be pried loose and raised. A large amount of coal was located in the bed of the Warrior River. Levi Reid and James Grindle took Warrior coal down the river in the late 1820s. By the 1840s Jonathan Steele and David Hanby were shipping coal to Mobile, and James A. Mudd, Elyton merchant and brother to Judge Mudd, opened a coal yard there in 1850. But the first Alabama coal to commercially compete with Pennsylvania and English coal was dug from the Cahaba field in Shelby County instead of Jefferson County. This was because in the late 1850s Shelby County coal could be shipped by railroad from Montevallo to Selma, and then by riverboat to Mobile. Although coal had been mined for more than 40 years, and coke was produced in Tuscaloosa by 1854 and commonly used in British as well as Pennsylvania blast furnaces, the Red Mountain Iron Company shipped coal to various places in the South during the Civil War, but continued to fire their blast furnaces with charcoal. Even the little locomotive that hauled the entire iron output of the Oxmoor and Irondale furnaces to Selma was a "broad gauge woodburner." Timber supplies were dwindling, but there was all that coal which could be made into coke.

As the war ended, the potential of Jefferson County coal along with iron ore, remained virtually untouched. Yet there were men with confidence in the district who realized its wealth could only be exploited with adequate transportation. A railroad would bring the minerals of the hills—coal and iron ore—to the limestone valley to be manufactured into pig iron products, and a railroad could transport this iron and its products to the world. John T. Milner had a dream that a great city would grow at the foot of Red Mountain. It was a fine dream, but the first step toward its realization was the completion of the railroad.

The old Northeast & Southwest Railroad Company, organized in the late 1850s to construct a railroad from Meridian, Mississippi, to Chattanooga, Tennessee, surveyed a line straight through Jones Valley. By 1865 only 27 miles of track from Meridian to York, had been completed. But more than 200 miles, most of the route through Jefferson County, had been graded. Only capital was needed to complete the road. Willing financiers appeared in the form of two carpetbagger brothers, John C. and D.N. Stanton of Boston. Unknown to the company directors, the Stantons had no funds; what they did have was a grand scheme to use the credit and taxes of the state of Alabama to finance the railroad and to line their pockets as well.

The Stantons reorganized the old Northeast & Southwest Railroad Company as the Alabama & Chattanooga Railroad, and John Stanton began to lobby the Alabama legislature. He was successful. The first legislative session under the Radical constitution of 1868 authorized the governor to endorse railroad bonds at $16,000 per mile after five miles of track were complete. Stanton, described as a "red-headed, hustling rascal" by one account eventually was able to acquire from the state of Alabama $4,720,000 in endorsed bonds and loans for the Alabama & Chattanooga Railroad in transactions so fraudulent and illegal they are mind boggling. Meanwhile John T. Milner and Frank Gilmer had procured a special state endorsement of $22,000 a mile for the old South & North Railroad, and construction from Decatur southward and northward from Montgomery was progressing rapidly toward Jefferson County. At long last Jefferson County would have transportation beyond the valley and the hills. The railroad was coming—not just one railroad—but two.

Chapter V

THE BIRTH OF A MAGIC NEW SOUTH CITY

As construction on the two railroads rushed toward Elyton and Jones Valley, the dreams of John T. Milner for a great city approached reality. Gone was the Old South; its chivalric and idyllic plantation society of cotton and magnolias vanished in the smoke of a thousand Shilohs. The agrarian ideal was discredited, defeated by the iron and steel of an industrial society. From the ashes of the old, a New South would emerge. In Jefferson County there was a limestone valley beside a mountain with iron ore between three immense fields of coal, the mineral foundations for a heavy industrial economy. Surely, at the junction of the Alabama & Chattanooga Railroad and the South & North Railroad, a great New South city would rise.

The Morris Hotel, 1903. Josiah Morris began construction of an office building in 1888 on the southeast corner of First Avenue and Nineteenth Street. The building was designed by the French architect Edouard Sidel in the Renaissance style. After the Caldwell Hotel burned, the Morris building was converted into a hotel. It developed a reputation for elegance. From the Department of Archives and Manuscripts, Birmingham Public Library.

The Birth of a Magic New South City

But opposition to building the South & North Railroad into Jones Valley came from planter interests in South Alabama who desired a competing Montgomery-to-New York railroad to ship their cotton, and from Chattanooga investors who wished to monopolize the iron ore and coal traffic from the mineral district. In a lengthy game of cat and mouse, South & North president Frank Gilmer was defeated by Montgomery's John Whiting, who represented South Alabama planters and had connections with New York financial agents tied to John C. Stanton. When Whiting became president of the South & North, this faction insisted that the S & N route be changed to go directly from Calera to Chattanooga. Whiting died suddenly, however, and Gilmer was able to locate enough proxy votes in November of 1869 to be reelected president. At least for the time being, the South & North route into the mineral district of Jones Valley and Milner's dream of a city were saved.

Evidently there was a great fight among the Jones Valley landowners over the opportunity to sell land for a city. The *Elyton Sun* published an editorial on May 13, 1870, calling for a mass meeting of citizens to demand that the railroad junction be made at Elyton. The editor commented that land prices at Elyton were too high compared to those two miles "above Elyton," and warned the "older and more interested citizens" of the consequences to Elyton of losing the crossing. On August 12, 1870, the *Sun*

printed a Biblical parody, "Titas Brick's letter," written by Alburto Martin, which told the story of "John, the son of Stanton, and John, the son of Milner" and their land deal. According to this tale the people of Elyton wanted the junction located at Elyton; William Jemison Mims and Mitchell T. Porter tried to get the crossing west of Elyton; Baylis Grace and Alfred Roebuck pushed for the Village Creek deal; and William S. Mudd and Sylvester Steele were manipulating and trying to make sure their land was part of the city.

Meanwhile John Stanton was trying to complete his Alabama & Chattanooga line. In order to push construction, he hired 1,000 coolie laborers from Western railroads and housed them in a tent village near Elyton. The appearance of a thousand Chinese in Jones Valley caused considerable talk since most residents had never before seen an Oriental. On Saturday nights when the railroad construction crews came to town in nearby Elyton, the quiet village turned rowdy to the consternation of the local population. Afraid of shoplifting, Elyton merchants like Hawkins and Earle stationed a guard at the door of their stores and allowed only one Chinese at a time to enter.

John Turner Milner dreamt of building a great new industrial city in Jones Valley where the Alabama & Chattanooga and South & North railroads crossed. From DuBose, Jefferson County and Birmingham, Alabama *(1887).*

The traditional story of the founding of a city in the Jones Valley cornfield is that John T. Milner suggested to Stanton that they acquire for their respective companies the land where their two railroads would cross. Milner selected a site for the city on 7,000 acres of land near Village Creek, and he and Stanton negotiated options on it. Then one April morning in 1870, Milner and Stanton's chief engineer, R.C. McCalla, were camped at Alfred Roebuck's (today the intersection of the Huntsville and Stout roads beyond Oak Hill Cemetery), staking off streets and blocks. Baylis Grace and Tom Peters rode up and said that Stanton had ceased construction on his Alabama & Chattanooga line, had taken up land options for himself alone around Elyton, and had backed out of his Village Creek agreement. Ethel Armes relates that Milner then surveyed 15 to 16 different crossings (although the Milner family tradition has it as five crossings). This confused Stanton and caused him to give up his Elyton land options. These option-deeds ran out at Josiah Morris's bank in Montgomery on December 19, 1870, Stanton's third day of grace. According to the Armes story, Milner then told Morris to purchase Stanton's options because he planned to cross the South & North with the A & C in Stanton's area.

This is surely not the true story. In the first place, why would Milner, who knew every hill and dale of Jefferson County and shared the confidence of the landowners in the valley, invite Stanton, a dishonest, wheeling-dealing carpetbagger to become part of a land deal at the railroad's crossing? Milner knew from Stanton's work with the Alabama legislature during the summer of 1868 that he was not to be trusted. He recognized that Stanton was behind the scheme of 1869 to alter the South & North to by-pass the mineral district, and it was well-known throughout the state that Stanton had fraudulently acquired state-endorsed railroad bonds. Furthermore there was no doubt that the Alabama & Chattanooga Railroad would be in operation through the valley before the South & North Railroad could possibly be constructed beyond Grace's Gap. Although Milner's route through the mountain gaps was circumscribed, once he reached the valley floor, his survey was only limited by his ability to acquire right of way. Milner could plot the South & North to cross the Alabama & Chattanooga at whatever point he wished; therefore he held the trump card from the beginning. From the sources available, it may never be possible to completely understand the motives and actions of these men during the summer and fall of 1870. Who deceived and double-crossed whom may never be known.

But we do know that some 4,000 acres of valley farm lands were deeded jointly to John Stanton and to Montgomery banker and South & North Railroad supporter Josiah Morris during this period. These deeds, from Jefferson County landowners William F. Nabers, William S. Mudd, Sylvester Steele, Thomas Peters, Robert N. Green, William W. Brown, Alburto Martin, James M. Ware, William A. Walker, Sr., and Benjamin P. Worthington, were never recorded; but they transferred a two-thirds interest to Stanton and Morris on condition that the South & North and Alabama & Chattanooga railroads intersect each other "at what is known as the Walnut tree crossing," or "some other point east of Elyton." The landowners agreed to transfer their remaining one-third interest to an "incorporated company . . . with the view and . . . purpose of effecting the building of a city on said lands." Evidently these deeds were held in escrow by Alburto Martin, who witnessed several of them and delivered the documents at Josiah Morris's bank on Commerce Street in Montgomery in December of 1870.

Alburto Martin was very much involved in the land deal which led to the founding of Birmingham. He held the Valley landowner's deeds in escrow and delivered them to Josiah Morris' bank in Montgomery. From DuBose, Jefferson County and Birmingham, Alabama (1887).

While it has been reported that these were "Stanton's options," which he took up behind Milner's back, the deeds in the Elyton Land Company papers clearly prove that Morris and Milner were equally involved in the original land options on the 4,150 acres upon which the Elyton Land Company built Birmingham. To make matters more interesting (and confusing), Morris had in his possession, long before December 19, second deeds from these same landowners conveying to him alone full interest in the properties. These second deeds failed to mention any land company, but the deeds filed later in probate court did. Stanton had no funds to complete any real-estate transaction at this time, because in January 1871 his failure to pay the interest on the Alabama & Chattanooga-endorsed railroad bonds caused a financial panic for the state of Alabama and resulted in a special session of the legislature to investigate his fraud and corruption. Thus it seems logical to assume that Milner brought Stanton into the land deal more to buy time and control Stanton; but regardless of his motives, Milner, with the financial support of Josiah Morris, outmaneuvered Stanton. Although the wily A & C president had failed to block the birth of the proposed new city in the valley, he would later come dangerously close to strangling the city in its infancy, thus evening his score with Milner.

Even before Josiah Morris paid the Jefferson County landowners some $100,000 for their property, an association was organized on December 8, 1870, called the Elyton Land Company. The initial stockholders were Josiah Morris, James R. Powell, Samuel Tate, Campbell Wallace, Henry M. Caldwell, Bolling Hall, James N. Gilmer, Benjamin P. Worthington, William F. Nabers, and William S. Mudd. They met at the Morris Bank, elected five directors, and selected Colonel James R. Powell president of the company. (Powell was a Virginian, who came to Alabama in 1833, settled in Montgomery, and became a partner in the stagecoach firm of Jemison, Powell, Ficklen, and Company.) After suggestions that the town be named Mudd Town, Powellton, Milnerville, and Morriston, Colonel

Powell, who had recently visited the great city of Britain's industrial midlands, suggested Birmingham.

On February 28, 1871, Josiah Morris and his wife deeded the Jones Valley acreage to the Elyton Land Company, and Colonel Powell left to inspect the city site. With him as he rode over the rough terrain were Milner and the newly appointed city engineer and surveyor, Major William P. Barker. Milner's young son, Henry, recalled riding over the area on horseback with his father: "The place was cleared of stumps and trees, but not under cultivation at the time. It was just an old cornfield, all overgrown with weeds and briers." Since there were no landmarks to interfere with Barker's survey, he was able to lay off straight and square blocks between 100-foot-wide streets. As Major Barker began staking off lots down Twentieth Street, which was from the beginning the central boulevard of the city, Colonel Powell hired the young farmers of the valley to grade the streets, offering them lots in the city in lieu of payment, but he had few takers. Most of the people in the valley doubted the city would grow or amount to much, and the farmers, who had their own land, preferred cash to lots staked off in a cornfield. William Dobbin, whom a newspaper reporter called "the man who struck the first lick for Birmingham," remembered having to "cut through trees and muscadine vines to get across the railroad" tracks when the only visible signs of habitation were his three tents pitched about where the corner of First Avenue and Twentieth Street later was located.

With tremendous energy Colonel Powell began writing to newspapers, organizations, and friends across the state and nation announcing an auction sale of lots in the new city on June 1, 1871. At this time when the name of Birmingham failed to appear on the map of Jefferson County, when there was no "inn for the entertainment of visitors," and when there was no dependable railroad into the city, the riches of Birmingham were being advertised across the United States and Europe.

Facing page, top: *Usually identified as the first house in Birmingham, this structure was built by William F. Nabers in 1869, before the city existed. It was used at different times as a storage area, blacksmith shop, tool shed, and wagon wheel works. In 1890, the Steiner brothers purchased the land, tore down the house, and built the Steiner Bank Building which is still standing. From the William H. Brantley, Jr. Collection, Samford University Library.*

Facing page, bottom: *Looking down Seventh Avenue from Nineteenth Street in Birmingham, 1874. This photo, one of the earliest of the city, is the work of Colonel A.C. Oxford. From the William H. Brantley, Jr. Collection, Samford University Library.*

The Birth
of a Magic New
South City

Top: *Colonel A.C. Oxford took this photograph of Birmingham from the courthouse. It is one of the earliest photos made of the city. The center house is where Phillips High School now stands. From the William H. Brantley, Jr. Collection, Samford University Library.*

Above: *Albert Fink, railroad executive and general superintendent of the Louisville & Nashville Railroad, saved the budding city of Birmingham when he took over the South & North Railroad and paid off its debts. From Cirker,* Dictionary of American Portraits. *From a painting by Benoni Irwin. Courtesy, the Filson Club.*

Meanwhile John C. Stanton and the Chattanooga group made one final attempt to destroy Birmingham before it was born. They purchased the bonds of the South & North Railroad from New York investors. In April of 1871, Vernon K. Stevenson and Russell Sage appeared at the Exchange Hotel in Montgomery and demanded that the South & North Railroad immediately pay all back interest or transfer complete control of the railroad to the Nashville & Chattanooga Railroad Company. This would mean the "murder of the new city in cold blood," and John T. Milner believed it was the "most critical and dangerous period in the history of Birmingham." The directors of the South & North refused even though they knew it was impossible to raise the cash. They realized it was only a matter of time before the Chattanooga bondholders would foreclose. Suddenly Colonel James Withers Sloss, president of the Nashville & Decatur Railroad, appeared and convinced Albert Fink, president of the Louisville & Nashville Railroad, to absorb the South & North, pay off the bondholders, and make the S & N part of the L & N System. This corporate takeover saved Birmingham, gave the L & N a route to the Gulf Coast ports, and opened up the Alabama mineral district to the L & N. Thus began the close involvement of the Louisville & Nashville Railroad with the industrial development of the Birmingham district.

Henry Milner recalled that when he first saw the cornfield where Birmingham would grow, there were "a couple of Alabama & Chattanooga section houses alongside the railroad tracks," and these no doubt became Birmingham's first hotel. Although there were two boarding houses, the Eureka House and the Nabers House, as well as the Elyton Inn in nearby Elyton, the little town was considered too far away to accommodate the company men and the workers, so the Elyton Land Company converted one of the A & C section houses into an office, another into sleeping quarters, and installed a black woman, known simply as Aunt Nancy, as cook and housekeeper in an adjacent log cabin. This complex was called the St. Nicholas and existed until December 1871, when a new complex was completed. Kevin St. Michael Cunningham described the section houses as "two-roomed, vertical pine board shacks, battened on the outside" and remembered the food had "coal dust mixed in the gravy" and "iron ore in the soup."

The Elyton Land Company realized that better accommodations were essential to house the curious as well as the serious speculators who were flocking daily into the city. They arranged to build an L-shaped, two-story frame building named the Relay ouse, and leased it to Mr. and Mrs. William etcham. Located on the north side of the railroad acks at Nineteenth Street, the hotel opened in ecember of 1871 and was locally known as Ketcham Hotel." The next spring the Relay House as praised in a letter to the editor of the Montgomery Daily Advertiser for its "nice beds" and great variety of eatables and elegant dinners." But hat was considered elegant to Alabamians failed to npress the well-known Irish leader and member of ne British Parliament, Charles Stewart Parnell, who isited Birmingham with his brother in the fall of 872. Parnell described the Relay House as a "small, irty wooden hotel, full of adventurers who had come here in the hope of getting work on the railroad and n the] mines. The hotel was a miserable place and ery crowded, and we were constantly in dread of aving five or six not too cleanly strangers sleeping in he same room." When James Bowron visited the Relay House in 1878 he commented on the "tin bowl nd dipper outside on the porch for anybody to wash." Dr. Edward Palmer of the U.S. Bureau of Ethnology stopped in Birmingham in January of 1884 to survey the Indian mounds in the valley, but left complaining about the quality of his 75-cent lunch at the Relay House. Regardless of how visitors felt, though, beginning with the grand ball on opening night, the Relay House, with its wide porches, rocking chairs, excellent food, large dining room, and spacious parlors, became the pride of the city and the social center of early Birmingham.

Colonel James R. Powell, first president of the Elyton Land Company, inexhaustibly promoted the new city. He placed advertisements in newspapers all across the country. This one appeared in The South in 1873. He audaciously invited the New York Press Association to hold its meeting in Birmingham, a city so new it could not be found on the map. The Press Association thought it was a joke and accepted, intrigued by the thought of meeting in a wilderness. The town rolled out the red carpet for the easterners and gave them a reception at Sublett Hall, tours of Red Mountain, the water works, planing mills, coal mines, and a train trip to Blount Springs. From the Alabama Department of Archives and History.

BIRMINGHAM,
The IRON CITY of Alabama.
GREAT SALE OF LOTS
AT AUCTION,
On WEDNESDAY, JUNE 18th, 1873.
TITLES WARRANTED.

OFFICE OF ELYTON LAND COMPANY,
BIRMINGHAM, ALA., April 16th, 1873.

The Elyton Land Company will sell at auction on the 18th of June next a large number of lots in this city and on their property adjoining.

Suburban lots will be sold in sizes to suit purchasers, not exceeding twenty acres in any one lot.

Titles will be guaranteed without restriction as to time of erecting buildings or making other improvements.

Terms of sale, either cash, or one fifth cash, one fifth in six months, one fifth in twelve months, and balance in eighteen months.

The sale will be conducted on the premises.

J. R. POWELL, President.

The Birth of a Magic New South City

Birmingham, in stark contrast to Alabama's antebellum cities of Mobile and Montgomery, was born during the height of the "Wild West" era. Texas cowboys were herding longhorns up the Chisholm trail to Marshall "Wild Bill" Hickok's Abilene; "Doc" Holliday and Wyatt Earp were drinking and gambling at the legendary Long Branch Saloon in Dodge City; and Jesse and Frank James were spreading a Robin Hood legend across the plains as they robbed banks and stagecoaches in Missouri and Iowa when Birmingham's "boom town" period began. In these years the city was "as wild as a Comanche Indian," more like a frontier Western town than a city in the genteel and decorous Old South. The Birmingham *Weekly Iron Age* on June 11, 1885, reported that "Everything that ever got loose that was in the least wild flocked to Birmingham." At this early period saloons abounded and violence frequently flared among the rough adventurers who came to seek their fortune. There were fights and shootouts every day and some saloons never closed. Many of the young men who came were from families who had lost all their property and wealth during the war, forcing them to seek opportunities elsewhere. Men looking for investments and laborers seeking work rubbed shoulders with the sons of old Jefferson County families, people the newcomers called "Old Mossbacks." Although lumber was scarce, houses seemed to spring into being overnight. It was a young city filled with young men; there were so few eligible unmarried ladies that each had many beaux and her pick of a dozen escorts for every ball or party.

To the rest of the state, Birmingham was "a new young braggart" that represented the industrialism of the enemy. As Frank O'Brien recalled, the city was "the target of the boorish wit and sarcasm of the surrounding territory." The antagonism of the older Alabama cities was marked and "Little Birmy" was "slurred, slandered, and laughed at." The city's growth or imminent death were popular subjects for newspaper editorials across the state and a topic of conversation throughout the South. The *Mobile Register* suggested that one wear asafetida around the neck when visiting the city "to guard against the contagion" of the boom town, a condition the newspaper called "the Birmingham fever." Although the South Alabama paper believed the town would "probably remain in status quo for some years," J.J. Watson wrote his brother from Ruhama on April 27, 1871, stating that "Birmingham is a fix of a town, Elyton is gone up the spout." The *Shelby Guide* warned its readers in Columbiana in September 1871 that "those of us who think Birmingham a myth are mistaken." The paper then described a city of 57 wooden houses, 18 brick stores, two planing mills, with a first-class 25-room hotel, the Relay House, almost completed.

Throughout 1872 the city continued to thrive. Writing from Trussville in the spring, R.J. Waldorf described the rapid growth of the city, speculating that "in less than ten years Birmingham would be the 'Atlanta' of Alabama." In the fall the Elyton Land Company began construction of a waterworks and in December the city celebrated its first birthday with a large banquet where the citizens presented Colonel Powell, the "Duke of Birmingham," with an expensive knife.

The year 1873 opened auspiciously with a victory for Birmingham. The Elyton Land Company and the founders of Birmingham had long coveted the county seat. When the courthouse burned at Elyton, a few old-timers claimed "Birmingham had done it." Although a new courthouse had been constructed at Elyton, Colonel Powell, always eager to take advantage of an opportunity, secured a legislative act calling for an election the first Monday in May to allow the voters of the county to determine where they wished the courthouse to be located: Elyton or Birmingham. The act named as election commissioners J.C. Morrow, B. Gully, James O. Conner, S.H. Dupuy, and John L. Ellison.

The contest was heated. Families were divided and jobs were lost or won on the issue. Francis M. Grace found it necessary to leave Elyton Academy after he took the side of Birmingham in the courthouse fight.

Facing page: *The Florence Hotel, located at Nineteenth Street and Second Avenue, was Birmingham's first elegant hotel. Courtesy, James F. Sulzby, Jr.*

Top: *Though this old, ivy-covered Jefferson County farmhouse has not been positively identified, this photograph was found with pictures of the old Williamson Hawkins plantation cemetery. Jefferson County's early residents were called "old mossbacks" by the new citizens of Birming-*

ham. Many of them laughed at the prospect of anyone building a city in that "ole worn out cornfield." From the Harper Collection, Special Collections, Samford University Library.

Above: *The Star Saloon was located at Twenty-second Avenue South and Twentieth Street. The churches bitterly opposed the presence of saloons and worked to regulate, segregate, and abolish them. Courtesy, James F. Sulzby, Jr.*

The Birth
of a Magic New
South City

Above: *The Birmingham Foundry and Machine Shop circa 1875. It was one of the earliest foundries in the city. From the William H. Brantley, Jr. Collection, Samford University Library.*

Bottom: *Located on First Avenue and Fourteenth Street, the Birmingham Foundry and Machine Shop and the Linn Iron Works and Machine Shop were representative of two early Birmingham industries. Courtesy, James F. Sulzby, Jr.*

Facing page, top: *The Elks Club was a strong organization in early Birmingham. One of its first meeting halls was located above Ed Warren's and Jack Biddle's cycle shop at the corner of Twentieth Street and Fourth Avenue. From the Perkins Collection in the William S. Hoole Special Collections, University of Alabama Library.*

Facing page, bottom: *President of both the Elyton Land Company and the Caldwell Hotel Company, Henry M. Caldwell wrote* History of the Elyton Land Company. *From DuBose, Jefferson County and Birmingham, Alabama (1887).*

But Elyton never really had a chance. Alabama was still under Radical rule and blacks voted regularly without any challenge to residency. Colonel Powell, determined to win the courthouse fight for Birmingham, arranged to have the railroads run free excursion trains into the city where he prepared a giant barbecue on the grounds of the proposed courthouse site and had Brewer's Band playing. Powell met each train. He was riding a calico pony, sitting tall and erect, his white hair lending dignity and his drawn, fancy sword, authority. Word passed among the black passengers that this was General U.S. Grant who wanted them to vote for Birmingham. As Powell greeted the new arrivals, he shouted: "Vote, my friend. Vote for God and your native land!" Sallie Harrison Pearson recalled that many of the "country men and Negroes thought they were voting for God." In any case the result was an overwhelming victory for Birmingham and an intense feeling of indignation among the people of Elyton, many of whom had ridiculed the idea of a city in a cornfield.

In the next 12 months, however, a cholera epidemic struck the city and it was almost destroyed. Early summer brought the first tragedy of 1873. On June 12 Dr. Mortimer Jordan treated a Negro man who had just arrived from Huntsville. Suspecting cholera, he called in Dr. James B. Luckie. Soon there were other cases, especially in a section of the city called "Baconsides," a low swampy area with open sewers and contaminated water along Second Avenue North between Eleventh and Fourteenth streets. By the first of July cholera was epidemic in the city. Colonel Powell lamented that it would ruin the town. When an excursion train took a group of citizens to Blount Springs for Fourth of July picnicking and dancing, a number of people were ill when the train returned to Birmingham at 8:00 p.m. By the next morning seven were dead of cholera. The little city of 4,000 was "helpless to cope" with such

an emergency for there were many poor and the city was so young that it was a town of strangers who were not able to give each other support.

The acrid odor of burning tar filled the downtown area as pots were burned on every corner to disinfect the air. All business was suspended. No one went into the city streets unless it was absolutely necessary. People panicked and crowded into every train leaving town. Those who had farms or summer houses in the country moved their families there. Those who had homes, property, or relatives in other parts of the state also left. Those who remained in the stricken city were either too poor to leave, or had investments or responsibility that held them. Willis J. Milner, secretary and treasurer of the Elyton Land Company and head of the new waterworks, wrote that it was "a great strain to go through the daily routine trying to look cheerful and to keep each member of the family from getting panicky." The city's population fell to about 2,000.

A few "brave and noble ones who were not afraid to face danger" remained to nurse the sick and bury the dead. Elizabeth Kerr Terry died, leaving her husband John with six young children to care for. Doctors Jordan, Luckie, Sears, Taylor, Crawford, and Parker worked for days with little rest and without even changing clothes. George Allan, G.W. Narrimore, the Presbyterian minister W.L. Kennedy, Dr. T.H. Davenport of the First Methodist Church, and Father McDonough of St. Paul's Catholic Church worked day and night nursing the sick and relieving their suffering. For many years Birmingham remembered Frank O'Brien attending the victims until he too became so ill that a coffin was ordered for him from Montgomery and his obituary appeared in the newspaper. Dr. Luckie came down with cholera and he, like O'Brien, read his obituary in the paper, but lived to talk about it.

One of the favorite stories of the Birmingham cholera epidemic concerned Louise Wooster, a madam who turned her brothel into an infirmary. She told Dr. Luckie to send her any of the ill who had no one to care for them, and she went about the town giving food and comfort to the sick, buying coffins, and preparing the dead for burial.

Lou Wooster came from a prominent Mobile family that was embarrassed by her profession. When her memoirs, *The Autobiography of a Magdalen*, were published in 1911, her family tried to purchase all the copies. She became a legend in early Birmingham and stories abounded about her. She lent her huge American flag to the Elks each year to use in their

grand parade; she discreetly purchased tickets for all charity functions and then returned the tickets to be resold or distributed to the poor; and when she died a long line of empty carriages followed her coffin to the cemetery, the gentlemen of the town wishing to pay their respects but propriety forbidding their presence. Lou Wooster had often wondered why she remained in Birmingham during the cholera epidemic when she had the means to leave. She decided that she was "determined to stay and help nurse the poor and sick and suffering ones who needed me."

The disease killed the young and the weak quickly. Each day black hearses, carriages, and wagons slowly made their way up Nineteenth Street to Oak Hill, the new city cemetery which was then considered far out of town. So much property was vacated that values plummeted, but still there were no buyers. Henry M. Caldwell, later president of the Elyton Land Company, wrote that "Bats and owls were the sole occupants of many buildings which had been rented by anxious tenants and occupied almost before they were finished, only a year and a half before."

The Birth of a Magic New South City

Across the nation reports indicated that "Birmingham was dead of cholera." The reputation of the city suffered, and although 128 people died, the country imagined 10 times that many had perished. The cholera epidemic, however, accomplished some good. It forced the city to deal with the problems of clean water and adequate sanitation. There was no cholera at the Relay House or other houses serviced by the newly organized Birmingham Water Works, proving to all the necessity of a pure water supply. Colonel Powell, backed by the city aldermen and the board of health, began cleaning up the city, improving sanitary drainage, and increasing the capacity of the Birmingham Water Works.

The second tragedy of 1873 hit Birmingham just as the cool weather of fall was helping to dispel the cholera. On September 18, 1873, the country was electrified by the news that Jay Cooke and Company, considered an unshakable pillar of the nation, had failed. There had been apprehensions that the economic condition of the country was not good, but this news sent the New York Stock Exchange into panic. Banks closed and a succession of business failures followed. A feeling of gloom settled over Birmingham. The expected industrial development had not materialized and the construction industry

had collapsed. Birmingham remained only a real-estate boom town at a railroad crossing. The city had no established industry to create sufficient jobs for the residents and many were forced to leave. It was a long, hard climb from the very bottom for those who remained. Episcopal Bishop Richard H. Wilmer, preaching at the Church of the Advent, warned that Birmingham "had all the staves of society but the hoops had not been driven on tightly."

In these hard times, retrenchment and rigid economy were the order, but civic leaders refused to give up. Charles Linn, founder of the National Bank of Birmingham, forerunner of the First National Bank, had just completed his three-story building on the northeast corner of Twentieth Street and First Avenue. Called "Linn's Folly" by the skeptics who thought the "skyscraper" out of place in the little town, the building was the scene of Birmingham's most famous New Year's Eve party. To celebrate the opening of his bank, as well as Birmingham's survival from the cholera epidemic, Linn invited 500 people to a Calico Ball. At 9:00 p.m., James T. DeJarnette's band from Montgomery started playing and the citizens of Birmingham began dancing away their cares, optimistic that 1874 would be a better year.

Facing page, top: *Dr. James B. Luckie, a hero of the cholera epidemic, contracted the disease and became so ill that he read his own obituary in the newspaper. Fortunately, the doctor lived to talk about it. From DuBose,* Jefferson County and Birmingham, Alabama *(1887).*

Facing page, bottom: *Charles Linn's son Edward owned this house which has been identified as the first brick house in Birmingham. Much later it became a boardinghouse. From the William H. Brantley, Jr. Collection, Samford University.*

Below: *This three-story building located on the northeast corner of First Avenue and Twentieth Street was the tallest building in Birmingham when Charles Linn completed it in 1873. Jefferson County residents called it "Linn's Folly." Courtesy, James F. Sulzby, Jr.*

Chapter VI

OF MINES, MEN, AND COMPANY VILLAGES

Miners working at Blossburg old Number 8 Coal Mine pause in 1898 to be photographed. In 1890, the areas around Adamsville began to boom when a four-foot coal seam was discovered in the hills. Coke ovens were then built all along the hollow to turn coal into coke. Courtesy, Eddie Smith.

The fortunes of Birmingham were tied to the successful exploitation of the mineral resources of the district. The Cahaba Iron Works at Irondale was able to resume production in 1866 after Wallace S. McElwain had obtained Northern financing. The only blast furnace in Alabama at the time, it produced pig iron that was used for casting domestic utensils and small railroad parts. In rebuilding the Iron Works, McElwain not only improved his furnaces, but doubled their capacity. He also constructed a foundry, machine shop, commissary, boarding house, corral, and employee houses, Negro quarters, and stables—the first "company village" in Jefferson County. Company villages like the Cahaba Iron Works would become commonplace because of the county's sparse population, physical isolation, and lack of transportation.

Of Mines, Men and Company Villages

When the McElwain Furnaces went into blast, they would blow a large "Big Jim" whistle that was described as waking up Shades Valley, bringing people from miles around just to watch. The iron was still being hauled by ox team to Brock's Gap where it was loaded on freight cars. Although the first few years of operation were very profitable, by 1873 a shortage of funds, the cost of transportation, the falling price of pig iron, and McElwain's poor health convinced him to sell his furnace.

But McElwain's success had encouraged the owners of the Oxmoor property to rebuild. In the summer of 1871 the stockholders of the Red Mountain Iron and Coal Company met to discuss the reconstruction of the furnaces. Daniel S. Troy tried to enlist Northern capital, but failed. Then Daniel Pratt, probably the richest man in Alabama at that time, and Judge Henry D. Clayton of Eufaula agreed to advance most of the money needed to construct two 25-ton charcoal furnaces at Oxmoor. Pratt acquired a controlling interest in the company, (now called the Eureka Mining Company), and turned the supervision over to his son-in-law, Henry Fairchild DeBardeleben. Pratt was too old to see the project through, but he believed something should be done to develop the mineral resources of Alabama.

DeBardeleben had never been to the mineral district and knew nothing about mining iron ore or coal, nor the manufacturing of pig iron, but he was destined to become the most important industrial leader of Jefferson County. Historian Ethel Armes described DeBardeleben as "savagely energetic, restless, impatient," and always seeming to have one foot "in the stirrup, and to be itching to mount and be off and away"—usually upon his pet mule, Roadey. On May 13, 1872, Pratt and DeBardeleben arrived to inspect Oxmoor with Joe Squire, their engineer, and gave directions to rebuild the furnaces. Pratt was able to see Oxmoor go into blast early in the winter of 1873 before his untimely death in May.

In the months ahead the Oxmoor furnaces were plagued with difficulties. The furnaces could not exceed 10 tons a day. "Jay Cooke's Panic" caused the price of pig iron to fall from $40 to $8 per ton. Furthermore DeBardeleben's ignorance of the iron business caused him to make numerous mistakes. He resigned and the furnaces were shut down. At the beginning of 1874 development of the Birmingham district had all but ceased. The lack of industrial growth caused the L & N Railroad, which was hard-pressed for cash, to be criticized for its expansion into the Alabama mineral lands. There was not enough Birmingham traffic to run even a train a day. When

Top: *Henry Fairchild DeBardeleben has often been described as the first big money man of the Birmingham District. He once said: "There's nothing like taking a wild piece of land, all rock and woods, ground not fit to feed a goat on, and turning it into a settlement of men and women, making payrolls, bringing the railroads in, and starting things going. There's nothing like boring a hillside through and turning over a mountain. That's what money does, and that's what money's for. I like to use money as I use a horse—to ride!" From Cruikshank, A History of Birmingham in the Department of Archives and Manuscripts, Birmingham Public Library.*

Above: *This building was once part of the commissary for the Oxmoor furnace community. Due to the isolation of the mines and furnaces, the companies built almost self-contained communities with stores, houses, schools, and dispensaries. Courtesy, James F. Sulzby, Jr.*

John T. Milner happened to meet Albert Fink, the railroad president, in Montgomery, Fink practically shouted at him: "You have ruined me, you fool, me and the Louisville and Nashville Railroad Company. The railroad [to Birmingham] will not pay for the grease that is used on its car wheels! Where are those coal mines and those iron mines you talked so much about . . . where are they? I look, but I see nothing. All lies!—all lies."

Milner returned to Birmingham, later recalling he was "determined to open the Newcastle mines in self defense." He sank a slope mine in the Warrior field and began producing 70 tons of coal a day. In the new few years another mine was opened by the Jefferson Coal Company, and J.T. Pierce made improvements on his Warrior mine on the Worthington property.

The Eureka Company made one more attempt to produce iron at Oxmoor, this time with an experienced ironman, Levin S. Goodrich, as superintendent. The furnace, however, was still using charcoal, the county timber resources were depleted, and Goodrich could not produce charcoal iron profitably. The success of the Birmingham iron industry depended upon making iron with coke from Birmingham coal. Judge William S. Mudd acquired the Oxmoor property temporarily in a settlement of a timber debt, and then the furnaces were silent. Land values dropped and people continued to leave.

In 1877 the Eureka Company offered the furnaces to anyone who could prove that coke pig iron could be made in the Birmingham district. John T. Milner called a meeting at the Elyton Land Company office for all those "interested in the success of Birmingham." Judge Mudd chaired the meeting and plans were made to organize the Cooperative Experimental Company to see if coke pig iron could be produced. Benjamin F. Roden, John T. Milner and his brother, Willis J. Milner, Judge Mudd, and Frank O'Brien were selected to negotiate with the Eureka Company. Mudd advanced $30,000, and Colonel James W. Sloss, Charles Linn, and Mudd were elected as a "board of managers." Levin Goodrich was appointed superintendent. O'Brien began building five Shantle-style coke ovens; the coal mines furnished the coal; the L & N Railroad contributed free transportation; the Eureka Company donated the iron ore; and Goodrich, with master ironman, John Veitch, began restructuring the furnaces from charcoal to coke firing.

To succeed, a good coking coal was needed. Surprisingly it was found in a load supplied by

William Gould from a small hole he had dug in the Warrior field. "Uncle Billy" Gould had spent a lifetime in the Alabama coal industry, first at Montevallo where a seam in the Cahaba field was named for him, and then with J.T. Pierce at Warrior. Gould had discovered what was later to be known as the Pratt seam, a thick mother lode of coal that eventually would fuel the industrial development of the Birmingham district.

Top: *These Jefferson County coke ovens turned coal into coke to feed the blast furnaces. The first good coking coal in the county came from a Warrior field seam, later called the Pratt seam. From the Harper Collection, Special Collections, Samford University Library.*

Above: *A train enters a Woodward Iron Company camp. From the William S. Hoole Special Collections, University of Alabama Library.*

Of Mines, Men and Company Villages

On February 28, 1876, coke pig iron was first made at Oxmoor. Ethel Miller Gorman, in her novel of early Birmingham, *Red Acres*, describes the scene this way:

> The crowd pressed as close as they dared while the fiery soup rushed down the main sow and spread out into the dozens of pig beds. The keeper, a white man red from the intense heat, directed the flow of sizzling liquid into the sow while two Negro helpers walked about on the wet sand with pointed hoes, opening clogged runways and leading the iron. . . . Off to one side slag skimmed from the iron rushed by gravity toward the great slag pots lined up on railroad cars on the lower side of the wall. This wall, called the cinder pit track, stretched above the wide mouths of the eight-foot high cauldrons which were filling rapidly with the waste material from the furnace. When full, the boiling pots would be pulled off to the top of the growing mountain of slag and dumped over the sides in a torrential river of fire.

And a man shouted: "Some fireworks! . . . Like the Fourth of July in hell!" Sloss and James Thomas quickly organized a company backed by Cincinnati and Louisville investors. It was a great day in the history of Jefferson County.

In January, 1878, DeBardeleben, Sloss, and Truman H. Aldrich purchased extensive coal lands in Jefferson County and organized the Pratt Coal and Coke Company. These three men became the big names in the Birmingham district. DeBardeleben had a South Alabama cotton gin background and Daniel Pratt's money. Sloss, from Limestone County, had made a fortune in land speculations, the mercantile business, and railroads. Aldrich was a talented New York mining engineer who had arrived in Alabama in 1871 and later leased the Montevallo coal mines. With a mining and civil engineering degree, Aldrich knew more about coal and minerals than anyone in the district. He was the first to accurately assess the Pratt coal seam, and was the dynamic force for two decades behind the district coal business. Until this time, most of the coal had been shipped for use as fuel, but the Pratt Company was interested in fueling iron furnaces. They built a railroad from their Pratt mining camp to Birmingham, and DeBardeleben put his entire fortune behind the company.

Taking the place of Colonel Powell, DeBardeleben became the booster for Birmingham and the man most responsible for bringing in investment capital.

Top: *Truman H. Aldrich, a graduate of Van Rensselaer Polytechnic Institute in Troy, N.Y., was the first trained mining engineer to work in the Alabama coal fields. When he leased the Montevallo mines after the Civil War, he said he "knew as much about practical coal mining as a horse about holy water." Nevertheless, he put his men to work digging coal in the summer. This act was unprecedented, for coal had never been dug in the hot Alabama sun. The coal kept piling up but no one bought any of it. Then, when the frosts came, the demand for coal soared and Aldrich had cornered the market. From the Department of Archives and Manuscripts, Birmingham Public Library.*

Facing page, top: *Sarah Latham Jowers, seen here with her grandchildren, was the wife of Theophilus Calvin Jowers, otherwise known as the "ghost in the Sloss furnace." On September 9, 1887, Jowers was killed when he fell into the Alice furnace. Supposedly, his ghost appeared there for many years and when the Alice furnaces were dismantled in 1927, the ghost began appearing in the Sloss furnace. Courtesy, Billy and Becky Strickland.*

Facing page, bottom: *The Oxmoor furnaces as they appeared over a decade after the Cooperative Experimental Company made coke pig iron. Eventually, these furnaces became part of the Tennessee Coal Iron and Railroad holdings. Courtesy, James F. Sulzby, Jr.*

Augustine Smythe explained: "It's many a man has been lured upon the rocks of Alabama by that siren tongue of DeBardeleben." While addressing a group of potential investors, DeBardeleben once exclaimed: "I knew a coal mine, gentlemen, in the Birmingham District where nature herself has driven the main entry for clean a hundred miles." And they invested on the spot. Llewellyn Johns said that DeBardeleben "has a way about him that takes! He's a regular play-actor when you get him started." Milton H. Smith, president of the L & N Railroad, once said that DeBardeleben was "the darndest man I ever knew in my life! Why, I've spent thirty million following that man!"

With the Pratt Company organized, DeBardeleben then turned to the construction of a rolling mill and a furnace. Enticing new investors into the district, he was the impetus behind the Birmingham Rolling Mill, which opened in July of 1880 and manufactured sheet, bar, and plate iron. Recalling his failure at Oxmoor, DeBardeleben was convinced he needed an experienced ironman to develop a furnace, so he negotiated a deal that brought the grandson of pioneer Tannehill ironman Daniel Hillman to Birmingham.

Of Mines, Men and Company Villages

Alice furnaces. With improvements and additions, remnants of these Sloss furnaces still stand. Now abandoned, silent, and grass-overgrown, their rusting hulks are a reminder of the by-gone days of Birmingham's golden iron age.

Although the rolling mill and blast furnaces were important in the economic development of Jefferson County, it was coal that got the economy moving. Milner said that only when Pratt coal hit the market in February 1879 was there "any sign of life in Birmingham." The great iron boom of the 1880s was on!

"Born and bred in a blast furnace," as Armes put it, Thomas T. Hillman directed the construction of the Alice furnaces at Fourteenth Street and First Avenue on land donated by the Elyton Land Company. "Little Alice," the first furnace in Birmingham, went into blast November 30, 1880, "Big Alice" followed in 1883. In 1881 DeBardeleben encouraged Colonel Sloss to cut his ties with the Eureka Company and organize the Sloss Furnace Company. Sloss began construction of two blast furnaces at Twenty-sixth Street on the opposite end of First Avenue from the

In the next decade coal and ore lands, railroad tracks and rolling stock, mines and mills, camps and villages, furnaces and company stock changed hands so rapidly it was difficult for banks to keep up with which men were authorized to draw payrolls. In 1883 DeBardeleben with William T. Underwood of Nashville, Tennessee, developed the Mary Pratt furnace. Then the next year, exhausted and believing he had tuberculosis, DeBardeleben suddenly sold his interest in the Pratt Coal Company to Colonel Enoch Ensley for $1 million and headed West to regain his

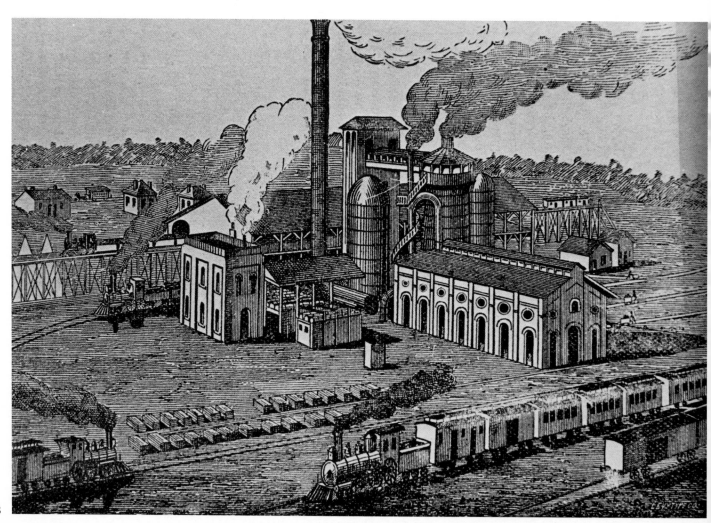

health. Ensley was a Memphis man who was "bred to the law," but "liked swapping horses better." He had inherited a fortune from his father and came to the Relay House "looking for something in the way of a coal mine." Ensley's down-payment check to DeBardeleben was exactly six times the capital stock of the Berney Bank where it was deposited, and caused a sensation in downtown Birmingham and in the Alabama coal and iron business. Ensley then began acquiring majority control in the Alice Furnace Company and the Linn Iron Works.

In 1885 Charles P. Williamson and James B. Simpson incorporated the Williamson Iron Company and built a furnace south of First Avenue and Fourteenth Street. Stimpson Hersey Woodward, West Virginia ironman, as well as the Thomas family, Pennsylvania ironmasters, had been acquiring mineral lands in the county during the 1870s, but had not developed them. Woodward kept sending one of his sons down to Birmingham to check things out, and the Thomases were doing the same thing. When the boom came in the 1880s, both men felt the time was right to move into the district. The Woodward brothers came to Birmingham with $400,000 cash, and the Woodward Iron Company's first furnace went into blast in 1883 on the Fleming Jordan farm where the town of Woodward was located. The Williamson Hawkins plantation became the site of the Thomas furnace and the town of Thomas. How things had changed from the pastoral days of the antebellum period! Woodward's blast furnace was in Mrs. Jordan's rose garden and two of the Hawkins's former slaves, still living in their old slave cabin, complained to Thomas that his miserable furnaces, slag piles, and pig iron had ruined their watermelon patch.

By 1885 Debardeleben was back in Birmingham, rested and recovered. He organized the DeBardeleben Coal and Iron Company with David Roberts, and sent Dr. Frank M. Prince to purchase thousands of acres in the western area of the county around old Jonesboro. DeBardeleben, inspired by the growth of Birmingham and other Alabama iron boom towns, established a city honoring Sir Henry Bessemer, the British inventor of the Bessemer process of steelmaking. Although no steel had yet been produced in the state, it was the dream of the future. The Bessemer Land and Improvement

Top: *Colonel Enoch Ensley, who had recently purchased DeBardeleben's interest in the Pratt Coal Company, shipped this solid eleven ton lump of coal to New Orleans to be exhibited at the New Orleans Commercial Exposition. Ensley, who attended the exposition, believed the coal lump was a good advertising promotion for Birmingham coal. The coal lump was shipped, without any breakage, by L&N Railroad flatcar. From the Auburn University Archives.*

Middle: *This candid shot of Joseph Hersey Woodward on the streets of Birmingham was taken soon after he and his father organized the Woodward Iron Company in 1881 during Birmingham's boom period. Notice the covered sidewalk and horses. Courtesy, James F. Sulzby, Jr.*

Above: *A train leaves the Woodward ore mines. A.H. "Rick" Woodward drove his own locomotive on his own tracks. From the Woodward Collection in the William S. Hoole Special Collections, University of Alabama Library.*

Facing page: *In 1883 Henry F. DeBardeleben and William T. Underwood developed the Mary Pratt Furnace Company, named for DeBardeleben's daughter. They purchased thirty acres off First Avenue near Avondale from the Elyton Land Company and the new furnace went into blast in 1883, making it the tenth important coal and iron development in the city. Courtesy, James F. Sulzby, Jr.*

Of Mines, Men and Company Villages

Company, with considerable British capital, was incorporated in 1887 and by the spring town lots in the boom city of Bessemer were selling for $18,000 an acre.

The city of Bessemer grew rapidly. Within three years the population reached 4,544 people. R.M. McAdory was the first mayor and T.Y. Huffman, J.A. Hall, J.B. Cosby, and L.H. King served with him as aldermen. The Charleston Building, Palmetto Building, Grand Hotel, and the Bessemer Rolling Mill were completed in a construction boom. To encourage investment the Bessemer Land and Improvement Company donated 80 acres to a St. Louis, Missouri, firm and the completed plant was the forerunner of U.S. Pipe and Foundry. The Bessemer Fire Brick Company also contributed to the growth of the city.

For Jefferson County the most momentous event of 1886 was the entrance of the Tennessee Coal, Iron and Railroad Company (TCI) into Alabama. The Tennessee Company, founded in the 1850s, had been operating in middle Tennessee. Its move into Jefferson County developed from a conflict between Birmingham capitalists T.T. Hillman (who disliked being a minority stockholder to Enoch Ensley) and Tennessee Company stockholder Colonel Alfred M. Shook, who had been frozen out of TCI in a reorganization. Although it took two years to complete the $2.25 million stock deal, the Tennessee Coal, Iron and Railroad Company swallowed up the Pratt Coal and Iron Company. Hillman was "square with Ensley and Shook was reinstated." In the next 15 years TCI continued to consolidate its holdings, but a lack of capital and a board of directors who sat in New York and were more concerned with fluctuating stock values on Wall Street than in long term capital gains, greatly limited the development of the company's assets.

The reorganization of TCI brought Nat Baxter, Jr., James Bowron, and George B. McCormack, three able leaders of the iron and coal industry, to Birmingham. Colonel Ensley was made president. Ensley had a dream of building a new industrial town, and because of his large block of stock, he was able to secure 4,000 acres of TCI land for the Ensley Land Company as a site for his town. As Ensley told Colonel Shook: "I intend to fill this valley, from the foot of the chert ridge yonder to the Pratt Railroad, with manufacturing plants. I'm going to build four big blast furnaces and a steel plant. The whole of this chert ridge I'll use for residences, and the day the work is begun I'll agree to pay $200 a foot for this corner lot, and here I will build the bank of Ensley."

The land company was incorporated by Ensley, Hillman, Thomas D. Radcliffe, and William A. Walker. Although the land was surveyed and a hotel built, delays and problems forced the company into receivership. It was another decade before Ensley's vision materialized into a town in Possum Valley called Ensley.

In 1891 Nat Baxter, Jr., TCI president following Ensley's resignation, negotiated a grand merger. According to Ethel Armes, he convinced DeBardeleben "to exchange $10,000,000 worth of good stock [in the DeBardeleben Coal and Iron Company] for $8,000,000 worth of Tennessee Company's securities." Unknown to DeBardeleben, TCI was almost broke and the securities virtually worthless. The consolidation of the DeBardeleben interests with the Tennessee Coal, Iron and Railroad Company gave the Tennessee Company unbelievable assets and a staggering monopoly on the Birmingham district. From here on, if Alabama was a one-crop state, Birmingham was a one-company town.

The industrial boom of the 1880s set off another dizzy period of speculation in Jefferson County real estate. People came to Birmingham on every incoming train with bank drafts to buy property, thinking they would make a fortune before the week was over. Hotels and boarding houses stayed full. The Florence Hotel opened in 1884 in time to provide better accommodations, but it was July of 1889 before the elegant Caldwell Hotel was completed. Unfortunately the Caldwell lasted only five years

before being destroyed by fire. Henry M. Caldwell, in his *History of the Elyton Land Company*, records that the "young and old, male and female, merchant and clerk, minister and layman—everybody seemed seized with a desire to speculate in town lots." Conservative citizens who looked on predicting disaster as land prices doubled, joined the speculation themselves when prices rose 200 and 300 percent.

Facing page, top: *The city of Bessemer grew rapidly. The Charleston Building, on Second Avenue between Eighteenth and Nineteenth streets, was completed during the construction boom of the first few years. Bessemer was founded by Henry F. DeBardeleben who saw that there was money to be made from town building as well as from iron furnaces and coal mines. Within three years, Bessemer's population reached 4,544. From the Department of Archives and History, Birmingham Public Library.*

Facing page, middle: *The Grand Hotel, completed soon after the incorporation of Bessemer in 1887, housed Tillman's Shoe Store and the Bessemer Shoe Palace on its ground floor. From the Woodward Iron Collection, University of Alabama Library.*

Facing page, bottom: *Colonel Alfred Montgomery Shook became associated with the Tennessee Coal Iron and Railroad Company in 1866, and later became vice-president and general manager. When a Wall Street syndicate purchased controlling interest in TCI, W.M. Duncan virtually forced Shook out of office. When TCI moved into the Birmingham district and absorbed the Pratt Coal and Iron Company, Shook was reinstated. Though his home and financial headquarters was Nashville, Tennessee, Shook stayed in Birmingham frequently for long business visits and is associated with the industrial development of the city. From the Department of Archives and Manuscripts, Birmingham Public Library.*

Below: *Enoch Ensley dreamed of building a new industrial town around blast furnaces. He said: "I intend to fill this valley, from the foot of the chert ridge yonder to the Pratt Railroad, with manufacturing plants. I'm going to build four big blast furnaces and a steel plant." From the Department of Archives and Manuscripts, Birmingham Public Library.*

Of Mines, Men and Company Villages

"Wilder and wilder the excitement grew. Stranger and resident alike plunged into the market, hoping to gather in a portion of the golden shower which was now falling in glistening sheets upon the Magic City." In his autobiography Willis J. Milner recalls the 1886 real-estate boom:

> Almost the entire adult population, young and old, male and female, became involved in the wild craze. Nor can any class of citizens claim exemption from its influence. Staid old bankers, men of affairs, professional men of all classes, were drawn into it, not alone those living in Birmingham, but those coming in from other cities were even worse demented than our own citizens. After the orgy had passed someone said to a highly honored and respected old citizen, "Colonel, did you lose your head, too?" "No," was the reply, "but I loaned it to my son." And so with most of us. If we did not lose our heads, we loaned them out to our friends.

The Elyton Land Company office was crowded each day with speculators eager to buy any parcel of land. Sometimes newcomers would purchase property on the street before reaching the Elyton Land Company and sell it before sundown for a profit. When Margaret O'Connor purchased five lots on the northwest corner of Fourth Avenue and Twenty-first Street from the Elyton Land Company in 1874, she paid $120 for each lot. When three of these same lots were sold in 1886 they brought over $1,300 each. The Elyton Land Company sent its stockholders in 1886 a Christmas greeting card and a dividend check, which represented a 340 percent return for the year. The city's growth was so exciting that in February 1885 the *Iron Age* discussed the "tide sweeping the state to make Birmingham the capital city." The park at the top of Twentieth Street was still called "Capitol Park," waiting for Colonel Powell's dream of the capitol building of the state of Alabama to materialize.

Fortunes may have been won and lost in Birmingham during the boom times, but for many the "big boom" meant only survival. They were the workers upon whose labor it all depended. They were the ones who went down into the dark to dig the black coal or red iron ore, or labored in open pits stripping the brown ore from the land. They were white and they were black. Most had left poor lands and tenant farms ravished by the boll weevil, and had given up sharecropping in favor of eating. Many were foreign-born. Life was hard for all of them. Ellis Lockridge

Top: *James Bowron came to the United States from England as a representative of his father's British coal and land company. In 1882, the British company merged with the Tennessee Coal Iron and Railroad Company with Bowron as treasurer and later vice-president. He resigned in 1901 due to his opposition to a policy of paying stock dividends with borrowed money. Courtesy, Paul Bowron.*

Above: *During the 1880s iron boom, speculators eager to buy anything crowded the Elyton Land Company office each day. Sometimes newcomers would purchase property on the street before reaching the land company office and sell it for a profit that same day. Courtesy, James F. Sulzby, Jr.*

recalled that "picks 'n shovels were the tools used to dig out coal in the 'hardspat' mines," and lanterns and lunchpails were "passed on at sunup and sundown." Too little money was invested in safety technology and too little time spent in safety education. Mine disasters took many lives. In 1891 Pratt Mine No. 1 had an explosion that killed 11; in 1898 four men were killed at Blocton; at the Banner mine in 1911, 123 convict miners were killed. But the greatest disaster to the district was the coal dust explosion in February of 1905 that became known as the "holocaust of the Virginia Mines." John D. Hanby, superintendent of Sloss mines, and William Herbert, superintendent of Belle Ellen Mines, brought over a rescue crew of expert miners. Others also rushed to the scene, volunteering to go down and try to save the injured. But only the bodies of 112 men were found. Relief funds were immediately established. The Birmingham Commercial Club raised $26,000 for the widows and orphans, and Bessemer citizens responded with equal charity. The Virginia Mines used union labor, and such bitter feelings existed between union and non-union miners that even during the rescue operations, there was conflict between the two groups. The *Bessemer News* actually blamed the disaster on the unions, suggesting that if the owners "had been left to their freedom" the catastrophe might not have occurred!

Miners in Jefferson County lived and worked at mining camps, little more than a collection of tents with wooden floors, shacks, and board shanties. They were scattered across the hills of the county and had

colorful names like Coalburg, Coketon (later known as Pratt Mines), Coaldale, Magella, Cardiff, Palos, Couglar Hollow, Blossburg, Brazil, Belle Tona, Dolomite, Horse Creek (Dora), Brookside, Henry Ellen, Gurney, Adger, Blue Creek, Iron City, and Red Ore. As profits increased the camps were elevated to company towns or villages. Crude bathhouses flanked the mine entrance, and houses, offices, and storerooms were clustered beside muddy roads. Company commissaries provided a convenient place, sometimes the only place, to exchange cash or "clackers" (purchasing against earnings) for staple goods. There was a small infirmary or dispensary where the contract doctor treated accident victims and the sick. The company employed a doctor who was on call 24 hours a day and lived in the mining camp. The miners were cut over their payroll for the doctor's services for a flat fee.

A small, one-room school housed one company-employed teacher and all the community children. Little attention was given to health or sanitation. Outdoor toilets were often higher than springs or wells that provided water, and typhoid, malaria, and

Children heading for an all-day outing at East Lake board the East Lake Steam dummy at First Avenue and Twenty-second Street North circa 1890. The Caldwell Hotel, opened in 1889, can be seen in the background. Courtesy, James F. Sulzby, Jr.

Of Mines, Men and Company Villages

complicated by several factors. Four distinct groups worked in the Jefferson County mines. Of the employed miners, about 35 percent were native-born whites, 20 percent were immigrants, and the rest were blacks. The fourth group of miners were convicts leased from the state, and they were mostly black. Although state, city, and county prisoners had been sent to the mines earlier, the Tennessee Coal, Iron and Railroad Company won an exclusive contract in 1888 to lease state prisoners. A large prison was completed at the Pratt Mines and by 1894 the Tennessee Company was working almost 1,000 prisoners. The presence of convict miners took jobs away from free miners with families to support, hurt union organization because convicts could be used as strike breakers, and remained a point of friction until the state finally abolished the system in 1928.

Between 1879 and 1900 a number of strikes over low wages, working conditions, and convict labor shook the coal industry in the Birmingham district. The spring of 1894 brought a four-month strike. After violence flared at Horse Creek, Governor Thomas G. Jones called out the National Guard. The soldiers were stationed at a makeshift camp in Ensley provided by TCI and named Camp Forney. The encampment was located very near the furnaces and the rural boys from South Alabama were obviously uncomfortable in their industrial surroundings with the furnaces roaring and glowing all day and all night. They addressed their letters home: "Ensley City, near hell." Informed at midnight that there was violence at Blue Creek mining camp, the governor himself, who

dysentery were endemic. Yet a committee that investigated Jefferson County mines in 1897 found that white miners were "men of intelligence," who had a "patriotic interest in the success of the mine" and appreciated the excellent school facilities and improved living conditions that were "better than farming."

Upgrading conditions at the mining camps was

happened to be in Birmingham then, led the soldiers to the fray on a special L & N train. But they found only sleeping men, women, and children. The "Battle of Blue Creek," as it was called, was followed by real tragedy. Strikers attacked "scabs" at Slope No. 3 of the Pratt Mines and killed three "blacklegs" and one company guard. The companies had brought in Negroes from as far away as Kansas, were using convict labor against the miners, and had ordered all miners evicted from the company houses.

The miners managed to stay out through the gubernatorial elections in August, hoping that a Kolb victory would somehow help them. Reuben F. Kolb was the reformist Jefferson-Democratic (Populist) candidate, and he was strongly supported in Jefferson County, especially among the workers; but William C. Oates, the old line Bourbon-Democratic candidate, combined the support of Birmingham's industrialists, the middle class, and the Black Belt political aristocracy and won. The strike was settled. Although the miners received some increase in wages, it was no victory for either side.

Thomas A. Hendricks, Vice President of the United States, visited Birmingham in 1885 and crowds turned out to cheer as he rode to look at the Alice furnace. In 1890 there was more excitement when the Liberty Bell came through town on its way to the New Orleans Exposition and was exhibited briefly on a flatcar by the Relay House. Rube Burrow, Alabama's own desperado who had robbed trains from Alabama to Texas, also came through town in 1890—at least his body did. Burrow had been shot by detectives in Linden, Alabama. His body, bound for his hometown Sulligent, came into Birmingham on the 3:30 a.m. train. Hundreds stayed up all night to view the remains of the bandit. Another celebrated criminal of the era was Richard Hawes, who committed what the newspapers labeled "the crime of the century" when he murdered his two little daughters and his wife. He threw one body in East Lake and the other two in Lakeview. Hawes was captured by Birmingham police at Union Station aboard a train from Columbus, Mississippi, where he had just remarried. The sordid affair shocked the city and swept it into a frenzy. Two thousand irate men stormed the Birmingham jail and, when they refused repeatedly to halt, Sheriff Joe Smith ordered his deputies to fire into the mob. Eleven were killed and 21 wounded in the fusillade. Many citizens blamed saloons and whiskey for the crimes and violence of "Bad Birmingham," and pressure increased to close down saloons such as Ruby's, the Rabbit Foot, Brown's, the White Elephant, the Dude, and many more.

For Birmingham the last two decades of the 19th century were gilded with iron. The boom period provided just a living for most, made fortunes for some, and left promises to many. It did provide opportunities for business leaders like Edward H. Tutwiler, John H. Adams, George B. McCormack, Edmund W. Rucker, John C. Maben, James W. McQueen, and James Hillhouse. But it could not have happened without the talents of expert furnacemen like James Shannon, John Dowling, Harry Hargeaves, F.B. Keiser, and J.H. McCune; or the abilities of mining engineers or mining foremen, such as Llewellyn Johns, Jones G. Moore, Erskine Ramsay, Charles J. Hager, John McClary; chemists Albert E. Barton, Dr. William B. Phillips, William Herbert; and Dr. Eugene A. Smith, the state geologist. But, more importantly, no dreams could have been realized without the labor of thousands of workers, now forgotten to history. But there is more to a city than industries and business, more to a county than mines, mills, and men.

Facing page, top: *Dr. Herndon Gaines Owen, who finished medical school in Mobile in 1908, began his practice with the Pratt Consolidated Coal Company at Maxine Mine and later moved to Wegra Mines, Flat Creek, and Praco where he retired. Often, mining companies contracted physicians to provide medical care for the miners and their families. Courtesy, Emily Owen Hager.*

Facing page, bottom: *The DeBardeleben Coal Company's store was a place where one could purchase almost any necessity. Its pot-bellied stove was a gathering place in the winter and its porch steps provided a place to sit and visit during the good weather. Courtesy, Jackie Dobbs, Old Birmingham Photographs.*

Above: *Because of the difficulty in reaching isolated mine and mill locations, the iron companies provided housing for their laborers. This is a picture of the Negro company housing provided by the Woodward Iron Company at Dolomite. In the center, to the rear of the houses, can be seen the commissary. It sold canned and fresh foods, shoes, fabrics, clothes, household items, and patent medicines. When the men went on strike, the commissary was closed to them. When there were hard times, the company would issue "clackers" which were a draw against their wages or "pity slips" which would allow credit. From the Woodward Collection, William S. Hoole Special Collections, University of Alabama Library.*

Chapter VII

SENSE OF PLACE, SENSE OF FAMILY

The South is most often thought of in terms of the old plantation myth of white-columned mansions, fields of shining cotton, and fragile belles dancing on moonlit verandas. Writers of fact and fiction have recognized that part of the South's regional distinctiveness is a rural tradition where people have roots in the land. An agrarian philosophy fosters individuality, self-reliance, strength, and pride, and Southerners are from a special place and have a heightened sense of family, and moral and religious values. Although Jefferson County does not historically fit into the Southern pattern of the romantic myth of the Old South, and Birmingham did not rise from an agrarian base, both the county and the city have been influenced by Southern agrarian traditions. A sense of place and of family remain strong in the people who live in the valley and the hills.

Mr. and Mrs. James Bowron stand with three of their children: James, Paul, and Edgar. James Bowron, born in England, came to Birmingham as an executive with the Tennessee Coal Iron and Railroad Company. He became a leader of the Southern Club and the YMCA. Mrs. Bowron worked for women's suffrage and the YWCA. From the James Bowron Collection, University of Alabama Library.

Sense of Place,
Sense of Family

In the Gilded Age Jefferson County was a man's world and Birmingham was a man's town. The mines and mills were run by the sweat of men's brows as much as by machines. The capitalists and politicians were all men. But as Howell Vines so beautifully wrote in his short story about Jefferson County's Toadvine, "The Mustydines Was Ripe": "No man's ever been won to a place 'cept by some woman." It was the women who gave the men a sense of place and a sense of family, who insisted upon churches, missionary societies, and Sunday schools; who supported public education, art, music, and drama; who brought culture into their homes and raised a rough frontier town to a true city of the New South. In Vines's story, the main character, Benny Freeland, who had "strolloped on foot" from Georgia and "been gaddin' about" for five years, passes through Birmingham on his way to Toadvine, falls in love with Patsy Tucker, and determines to make his home in Jefferson County. As he explains: "It takes love for a woman to make a man feel at home in a place. Without that a man never can be nothin' more'n a stranger on top of the ground in any country."

There are many Patsy Tuckers in the history of Jefferson County and Birmingham; regrettably, most of them are recalled only by their families. Their place in history, like that of many miners, clerks, and workers, has been lost to the historian. Even much about Amelia Peters Henley has been lost. As wife of Birmingham's first mayor, Robert H. Henley, she may technically be called "the city's first first lady," but we know little else about her. Perhaps the honor really belongs to Mrs. William Ketcham, who for many years was the gracious hostess of the Relay House. After her husband died in 1877, "Miss Jane" was the first lady hotel manager and was "almost a mother to the large crowd of young men" filling Birmingham. Jane Ketcham brought dignity to the rough new city. She was once described as like "one of the colonial dames of the olden times in the stateliness of her bearing as she greeted one and all." She was a woman "of great dignity and kindness" who left a "broad minded and beneficient" imprint upon the city. She and her daughter, Margaret Ward, were active members of the Church of the Advent.

Birmingham was only a "wide crossing in the road" when Lizzie Taylor Berney arrived and began to influence the town with her refined presence. A staunch Presbyterian, Mrs. Berney had been reared in Montgomery and was a strong supporter of "uplifting" cultural activities. Sallie Harrison Pearson had left her South Alabama home much against the wishes of her family. They felt it highly improper for a refined, unmarried Southern belle to live and work in the new city. Only because of the unimpeachable reputation of Mrs. Ketcham and the Relay House did they allow her to come to Birmingham. Sallie was a lively, determined, and popular young lady. Scores of gentlemen vied for her attentions and were "kept away from many of the evil influences" of the city by her "gracious kindliness and entertaining powers." Gustrine Key Milner was important in keeping down "any who might be inclined to be rude and lawless." In church activities and the social world of early Birmingham, "amid the discouragement and discomforts of a new world," Mrs. Milner kept "her light burning brightly, showing to the strangers who were thrown with her" that Birmingham was "not without people of the highest type."

In later years Elyton Methodist Church was named Walker Memorial for Corilla Walker, whose Christian devotion was an inspiring example. Mrs. R.D. Johnston founded the Boys Industrial School at Roebuck; Mrs. S.D. Weakley, the girls' Home of Refuge; and Mrs. C.B. Spencer, the Mercy Home for young girls. The United Daughters of Charity was organized in 1884 by Mrs. Joseph R. Smith and Mrs. A.O. Lane. Later Mrs. J.W. Pierce, Mrs. John C. Henley, and Mrs. Samuel J. Ullman worked toward establishing a charity hospital that opened in 1888 as the Hillman Hospital.

Mrs. William Hardie promoted the first women's literary club, the Cadmean Club, in 1887. Three years later the North Highlands Chautauqua was organized. Mrs. Sam Blake, Lillie Palmer Bell, and Mrs. Rivers Copeland began the Twentieth Century Literary Club, and in a burst of women's club activity in the 1890s the Highland Book Club and Clioian Club were founded. Birmingham's black women, particularly under the leadership of Mrs. Arthur McKimmon Brown, Clara Wilson, and Margie Gaillard, organized a number of women's clubs. The Semper Fidelis Club was led at one time by Mrs. A.H. Parker and Mrs. A.M. Walker. Vivian Bell was a leader of the Climbers Club, and the Sinovadad Club was founded by Mrs. B.G. Shaw and Mrs. R.M. Neely. The Negro Federation of Women's Clubs sponsored a day-care center. At one time the Sojourner Truth Club was a very important black women's club, and later the Periclean Club, under leadership of Myra Bryant, was most influential.

Women began the Birmingham Art League in 1891 and were admitted to the Mendelssohn Club in 1888. Mamie Fogarty, who was known for her landscapes, still lifes, and portraits, was a favorite artist, while "Miss Hannah" Elliott, a famous miniature artist, taught three generations of youth how to paint. Carrie Hill, Martha Beggs Elliott, A.L. Bairnsfather,

Facing page, top: *The Earle, Munger, and Montgomery children of Birmingham gathered around the Christmas tree at Arlington when Mr. and Mrs. A.C. Montgomery lived there. Celebrating Christmas at Arlington is now a public tradition in Birmingham, with the presiding mayor greeting the visitors at the door. Courtesy, Mrs. A.C. Montgomery.*

Facing page, middle left: *Martha Gordon Nabers was a young girl during the Civil War when a handsome wounded Alabama cavalryman was brought to her parent's Tennessee home. She nursed him back to health and they fell in love. When he left, he assured her he would return for her after the war to make her his bride. Months went by and there was no word from the man—Francis Drayton Nabers of Jefferson County. Finally, he came and took her to his father's plantation near Elyton. Here she raised a large family during Birmingham's early days. Courtesy, Dr. Hugh Nabers.*

Facing page, middle right: *Robert H. Pearson, a Barbour County native, came to Birmingham soon after the city was founded. He was a lawyer and soon was chosen city attorney. He courted Miss Sallie Harrison (and wed her) and together their home became one of Birmingham's early social centers. Pearson was active in Democratic politics and as a senior warden at the Church of the Advent. From the Department of Archives and Manuscripts, Birmingham Public Library.*

Facing page, bottom: *A traveling photographer made this snapshot of Robert, Leita, Harold, Jack, Lottie, Frances, and Lois Hood of Bessemer. Many Birmingham families had their pictures taken by door-to-door photographers, some of whom carried little goat carts to use as props. Courtesy, Mickie H. Blackwell.*

Above: *Robert H. Henley, Birmingham's first mayor. Failing health forced him to retire after one year and he died shortly thereafter. He is buried at Oak Hill Cemetery with the epitaph: "Here lies the first mayor of Birmingham." From the William H. Brantley, Jr. Collection, Samford University Library.*

Sense of Place, Sense of Family

Top: *Birmingham women were leaders in the Alabama Equal Suffrage Association, which opened an office on Second Avenue North about 1913. Here Patti Ruffner Jacobs, Lillian Roden Bowron, and others fold literature advocating approval of women's suffrage. Despite their hard work, Alabama never approved the suffrage amendment. When the Nineteenth Amendment was added to the Constitution, Birmingham women finally received the right to vote. From the Department of Archives and Manuscripts, Birmingham Public Library.*

Above: *Patti Ruffner Jacobs (Mrs. Solon Jacobs) was a leader of Birmingham society, a member of Independent Presbyterian Church, and president of the Alabama Equal Suffrage Association. She worked tirelessly for the abolition of child labor, for compulsory school attendance laws, for the appointment of women to boards of education, for equal pay for equal work (for women), and for the abolition of the convict lease system. She wished to show through all her suffrage work that "suffragist" and "Southern lady" were not conflicting terms. From the Department of Archives and Manuscripts, Birmingham Public Library.*

and Lucile Douglass were other significant artists. The Philharmonics and the Apollo Club sponsored musical programs and concerts by Birmingham musicians, but the most important music club after 1900 was the Music Study Club organized by Mrs. Oliver Chalifoux and Julia Neely Finch. Daisy Rowley trained Birmingham singers and imported famous singers as leads in the operas she produced. Opera singer Herman Posner, a German immigrant, stayed in Birmingham and married Nancy Lee. After 1883 the most popular band was that of Professor Fred L. Grambs. Birmingham's best-known author was Mary Johnston, who published a number of novels before 1900, including *To Have and to Hold* and *Prisoners of Hope.*

Although there were a number of Birmingham women such as Amelia Worthington and Mrs. W.L. Murdoch associated with the "liberal" cause of women's suffrage, the most active, well-known, and indefatigable worker was Pattie Ruffner Jacobs (Mrs. Solon Jacobs). Women's involvement in patriotic societies was more acceptable, less controversial, and more widespread. The United Daughters of the Confederacy had many chapters in the county, and Mrs. Chappell Cory was a tireless worker for the UDC. Mrs. J. Morgan Smith, a significant national leader in the Daughters of the American Revolution, convinced the DAR to establish a quality academic school in the isolated mountains of North Alabama, later named the Kate Duncan Smith school after her. Mrs. John C. Henley organized the Pioneers Club on June 13, 1914, the 100th anniversary of the birth of her father, Charles Linn. The purpose of the club was "to preserve the recollections of the early days in Birmingham." Membership was limited to those ladies who were living in Birmingham during 1872 and 1873. The club collected and later published remembrances of early Birmingham.

The importance of religion in Birmingham during its early period has sometimes been neglected, overshadowed by tales of saloons and fist fights; but churches were always a significant part of Birmingham life. The Elyton Land Company donated city lots to churches, but even before buildings could be erected, interdenominational services were held in the Bryant Building on First Avenue. This cooperation between the pastors and congregations of different churches, and even different faiths, continued to be an important aspect of the religious history of Birmingham and Jefferson County. Such cooperation remained despite periods of religious intolerance. As early as 1874 free Bibles could be obtained from the Birmingham *Iron Age* office. Sunday blue laws prohibiting card playing, sports, or hog and cattle driving were enacted by the city.

The Presbyterians were the first denomination to select a lot from the Elyton Land Company; because they dismantled their church at Elyton and hauled it by wagon to Birmingham, they were also the first to occupy a church building in the city. The Presbyterian Ladies Society was very active and its minister, the Reverend L.S. Handley, was much beloved throughout the city. He was the guiding hand behind the construction of the Gothic brick building completed in 1889 that still stands on Fourth Avenue and Twenty-first Street.

The Methodist Church was organized in Birmingham in February of 1872 by the Reverend T.G. Slaughter of Elyton. But after a building was constructed, Reverend T.H. Davenport filled the pulpit. In 1891 the Methodist Church began a financial drive to raise $160,000 for a new church of Early Romanesque design. Mr. and Mrs. T.T. Hillman donated $30,000 which they had saved to build themselves a new house, to the church drive. Later, when the church was unable to clear a debt at the bank, the bank refused to extend the loan and threatened foreclosure. Only when W.P. Brewer, a leading manufacturer of the city and a large depositor, threatened to withdraw his total deposits, did the bank agree to extend the loan.

In 1871 the Home Mission Board of the Southern Baptist Convention appointed the Reverend John L.D. Hillyer as missionary to the city, and Baptist church services were first held in homes. Lucy Miles recalled one of the first baptisms in the city "when the First Baptist Church had about 50 people to

baptize and no place to baptize them. So one Sunday, they went down to Linn's Park, the marshy spot on First Avenue between Nineteenth and Twentieth streets that Charles Linn had beautified, and dammed up the stream there and baptized them all." Initially the congregation used both the Methodist and Presbyterian churches for services, but in 1885 they rented O'Brien's Opera House until their new sanctuary could be completed. On June 4, 1885, the Birmingham *Weekly Iron Age* commented on the novel scene of baptism at the opera house. The Reverend D.I. Purser delivered a sermon on "Sin and Its Effects," and the stage was turned into "a charming woodland scene" with a pool in the center surrounded by rocks and flowers. Reverend Purser baptized Mrs. S.C. Moore, Mary Slade, and M.P. Lewis, and the choir ended the service singing "In The Sweet Bye and Bye."

A large number of Catholics, mostly Irish and Italian railroad construction workers and miners, settled permanently in Birmingham in its first decade. Father William J. McDonough came from Tuscaloosa to

Below left: *J.L. McKinney, minister of the First Baptist Church of Trussville, baptized David Barr, Eugene McDanal, and Daisey McDanal in the Little Cahaba River around the turn of the century. Rural baptisms were common in the county until after World War II. Courtesy, Frances Hamilton.*

Below: *Kate Duncan Smith was born in Cusseta, Alabama, in 1844. She served as regent of the Alabama State Society, Daughters of the American Revolution for eight years. In 1919 the Alabama society honored Mrs. Smith by naming their school on Gunter Mountain the Kate Duncan Smith (KDS) School. It has greatly improved the quality of life for the rural people of North Alabama. Courtesy, Harriet Smith Culp.*

Sense of Place, Sense of Family

celebrate, in the Michael Murray Cahalan home, the first Catholic mass. Thirty-one people were present, including the Frank O'Briens, the Patrick McAnnallys, and the James Fogartys. A small church with an altar of undressed lumber was later erected. In the late 1880s Matthew T. Smith, Frank O'Brien, Charles Whelan, and James O'Conner petitioned the Bishop of Mobile for financial help in constructing a new church because, they said, the members were "poor mechanics and laborers" who could not afford "to build anything like a suitable church edifice capable of accommodating all." But it was 1893 befo St. Paul's was completed. The dynamic leader was the Reverend Patrick O'Reilly. Meanwhile Father James A. Meurer began Our Lady of Sorrows, a parish for German-speaking Catholics in a little wooden church where German Bibles were used and the sermon was delivered in German. Fathers John J. Browne, James P. McCafferty, and Patrick O'Reilly—all Irish priests—were popular in the city and noted for their clever wit and entertaining storytelling.

The Episcopal Church of the Advent was organized as a mission of St. John's parish in Elyton, but was soon the more important church. A chapel was completed in early 1873 with the Reverend P.A. Fitts as the first rector. One of the Advent's most loyal supporters was the Reverend James A. Van Hoose, who served as rector for only several months before poor eyesight forced him to leave the ministry; he remained in Birmingham, however, where he became an important political leader and wholesale grocer. In 1894 Van Hoose, promising to clean up vice and close saloons on Sundays, was elected mayor as head of the Citizens' Reform ticket. Although his opposition claimed he would "close barrooms and open prayer meetings," he was not able to control the city aldermen and his reform proposals were not enacted.

The oldest black church in the area was the Green Springs Baptist Church, but soon the most important black churches became the Sixteenth Street, Sixth Avenue, and Shiloh Baptist Churches. By 1896 other churches had been organized: Sardis, Spring Street, St. James, Bethlehem, Bethel, and Vernon. There were also a number of African Methodist Episcopal churches in the city, with St. John's the largest, and one Congregational church. The black church was very significant in the cultural life of the black family. Women's church organizations were often the only form of social activity for black women and the black minister was a prominent community leader. Ministers were frequently pioneer businessmen, founding early black companies. The most important black leader was the Reverend W.R. Pettiford of

Sixteenth Street Baptist Church, who established the Alabama Penny Savings Bank. The Reverend T.W. Walker of Shiloh began the People's Home and Insurance Company.

The pioneer Jewish families in Birmingham were the Henry Simons, Samuel Marxes, and Isaac R. Hochstadters, with the Schuesters, Wises, Foxes, and Jacobs arriving later. The first observance of a Jewish holiday was held in the Henry Simon home, and in 1882 the Jewish community established Congregation Emanu-El, arranging to have a rabbi come for the High Holy Days. The historian of Jewish life in Birmingham, Mark Elovitz, says that "the first public service ever held in Birmingham was conducted on the Friday evening preceding Rosh Hashanah, September 1882 in the Cumberland Presbyterian Church located on Fifth Avenue." Frank O'Brien arranged the music for the occasion and served in the choir, which also included Mrs. George R. Ward, Mrs. Robert H. Pearson, Nellie Cobbs, and Mrs. Elias Gusfield. Professor Fred Grambs played the organ. This group, popular throughout the area, was in great demand for funerals and wakes, and were rather interdenominational, being composed of "one Methodist, one Catholic, one Baptist, two Episcopalians, and one Hebrew." It was a promising beginning for the Jewish community for the

"hallmark of Congregation Emanu-El in its association and interaction in the life of Birmingham" was to be interfaith cooperation. Two of the most beloved early Jewish leaders were Samuel Ullman and Rabbi Morris Newfield, who served Emanu-El from 1895 until his death in 1940.

Revivals and "protracted meetings" were popular religious events with both women and men, and were always interfaith gatherings. When Sam Jones preached a revival at the Winnie Davis Wigwam in 1893, 8,000 men showed up for "men only" night, a

Facing page, top: The Reverend W.R. Pettiford of the Sixteenth Street Baptist Church was probably the most important leader of the black community. He served as president of the National Negro Business League and began the Alabama Penny Savings Bank in 1890. At one time the bank was the largest black bank in the United States in terms of depositors and amount deposited. Over 1,000 homes were built for blacks with construction loans and mortgages from the bank. Courtesy, Birmingham Branch of the Association for the Study of Afro-American Life and History.

Facing page, bottom: Located at the corner of Fourth Avenue and Nineteenth Street was the second Methodist church built in Birmingham. The Methodists occupied three churches until the early 1890s when they permanently settled in their new stone church. Courtesy, James F. Sulzby, Jr.

Below: Tent revival meetings were frequently sponsored by evangelical churches and were important events within the community. This meeting took place at the First Baptist Church in Tarrant City about 1938. Courtesy, Jackie Dobbs, Old Birmingham Photographs.

Sense of Place,
Sense of Family

**THE CELEBRATION OF MY
67th BIRTHDAY**
WILL TAKE PLACE AT
LINN PARK
Saturday, June 11th, 1881
Commencing at 8 o'clock P. M., where all my friends are invited.

ON ENTERING THE PARK, THE "LOVERS BOWER" WILL BE FOUND ON THE LEFT WHERE SEATS WILL BE PREPARED FOR THE LOVING ONES. THE "BACHELOR'S RETREAT" WILL BE FOUND TO THE RIGHT, WHERE SEATS WILL BE PREPARED FOR THE DESOLATE ONES. IN THE CENTER SEATS FOR THE LADIES AND CHILDREN.

Programme

1. MUSIC BY THE JEFFERSON CORNET BAND, "KISS ME BY MOONLIGHT." ALL WILL PROMENADE ON THE GRASS AMONG THE TREES.
2. A HEARTY WELCOME, AND LEMONADE FOR ALL.
3. SPEECH BY C. LINN, SUBJECT: "THE NATIONAL BANKING ASSOCIATION IS CHARTERED FOR THE BENEFIT AND GOOD OF THE MASSES."
4. ICE CREAM FOR LADIES AND CHILDREN, AND LEMONADE, LITTLE DASHED WITH WINE, IF ANY LEFT, FOR MEN.
5. PREMIUM WILL BE PRESENTED TO THE BEST LADY HOUSEKEEPER IN THIS CITY.
6. MUSIC, "THE COUNTRY WE LIVE IN."
7. CONCLUDING WITH THE ECLIPSE OF THE MOON, WHICH WILL BE SEEN SHORTLY AFTER 12 O'CLOCK.

IN CASE OF RAIN, THE ABOVE WILL BE POSTPONED UNTIL MONDAY FOLLOWING.

Tickets at the gate--Entrance Fee, "Good Behavior."

C. LINN

Above: *Charles Linn celebrated his birthday several times a year "without regard to family records or the calender [sic]." He came to Birmingham in 1871 and organized Jefferson County's first bank. Until the establishment of the National Bank of Birmingham, county residents either had to depend on merchants for credit or had to travel to Tuscaloosa or Mobile to do their banking. Linn also organized the Linn Iron Works and was involved in building the district's first coke ovens. From the Department of Archives and Manuscripts, Birmingham Public Library.*

Facing page, left: *Braxton Bevelle Comer, daughter of Governor Braxton Bragg Comer, sits on the steps of her home with beau Dr. Frank E. Nabers, whom she later married. Behind her is one of her sisters, who by tradition had engagements for evening worship services at First Methodist Church booked eleven weeks in advance. Dr. Nabers was the grandson of Francis Drayton Nabers upon whose cornfield the city of Birmingham was built. Courtesy, Dr. and Mrs. Hugh Nabers.*

Facing page, right top: *When the Red Mountain Church near Bessemer changed its name to the South Highland Baptist Church in 1916, members posed in front of their building. Picnics, all-day sings, and dinners on the church grounds provided the main social life for many Birmingham and Jefferson County residents. Courtesy, Mickie H. Blackwell.*

Facing page, right bottom: *This interior view of the Hellenic Orthodox Church of the Holy Cross was taken in 1939. Birmingham's industrialization and the arrival of immigrants produced a rich religious diversity in the city. From the Auburn University Archives.*

significant number since the total population of the city was about 26,000. DuPont Thompson was there and had to stand up, recalling that Sam Jones "hit everyone from the preachers to the lowest sinner." Dwight L. Moody preached twice on October 29, 1894, with 18,000 people in attendance. Some people rode special "excursion trains" to Birmingham from crossroad towns and mining villages. But DuPont Thompson believed George R. Stuart, preaching at the Wigwam in 1916, was the most effective. Thompson wrote: "I have seen a buzz-saw cut up logs; I've seen a man fight bees and kill snakes, but never until tonight have I seen a man preach like he was doing all three."

In Birmingham and Jefferson County church activities were important social events as well as religious duties. Singing was considered a social grace and many marriages resulted from courting at choir practice. Sunday was the day for family reunions, the gathering of the clan for a big dinner under a brush arbor, when every lady brought her favorite dish and tried to outcook her relatives. Sunday afternoon groups of young people would hike out to the North Birmingham reservoir to pick flowers or ride horses out to Red Mountain to sit upon the "Rock House" and view the valley. For short walks couples would stroll out to Oak Hill Cemetery or to Linn's Park and sit upon the benches or hide away in one of the two summer houses—"Bachelor's Retreat" and "Maiden's Bower"—where they would recite poetry to each other. Sunday night was a popular dating night. Baptist belles always had escorts to church, but the unofficial record was held by Sallie B. Comer, a belle at First Methodist Church, who had "engagements" for evening worship booked 11 weeks in advance. One of the most popular houses in Birmingham at this time was the Edward Fields Lee home, which stood where Phillips High School stands. The Lees had seven beautiful daughters who were constantly courted by the city's most eligible bachelors.

The most popular place of amusement in the county was the so-called Crystal Palace at Naber's Spring. Although nothing like Queen Victoria's glass building for which it was named, Birmingham's Crystal Palace was an open pavilion with benches along the sides and a 10-foot stage running the width of the building. At the Crystal Palace Colonel Powell told prospective buyers all about the great promise of Birmingham; it was always crowded for political rallies, barbecues, dramatic performances, skating parties, and band concerts. Summer dances were popular and favorite steps were the Dixie reel, quadrilles, and the minuet. The Herma Vista Club

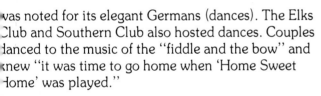

was noted for its elegant Germans (dances). The Elks Club and Southern Club also hosted dances. Couples danced to the music of the "fiddle and the bow" and knew "it was time to go home when 'Home Sweet Home' was played."

Although the evangelical churches looked with increasing disfavor upon dancing, it was 1890 before its propriety became a controversial community issue. In order to raise money, the ladies of the Church of the Advent sponsored a Kirmess, an outdoor festival from Holland that featured the dances of many countries. The event was attacked by Methodist, Baptist, and Presbyterian ministers who felt it was inappropriate for a church to raise funds in this way. In the controversy that followed, families were often divided. Of the affair, the *Birmingham News* dryly remarked that "Birmingham seems to be the most wicked and the most pious city in Christendom."

Like dancing, prohibition became a contested subject in the late nineteenth century. Jefferson County, where the evangelical churches predominated, favored prohibition while the city itself was divided. Its more liberal Catholic, Lutheran, Episcopal, Greek Orthodox, and Jewish populations opposed state interference. When they had the opportunity to be vocal, women generally supported prohibition and

opposed "demon rum." Throughout the 1890s, the city was divided into political factions that called themselves "Moral Elements" and "Liberal Elements." They fought battles in the newspapers and at the ballot box. Leadership for the "Moral Element" came from the Birmingham Pastors' Union, the Women's Christian Temperance Union, the Christian Endeavor Society, and after 1906, the Anti-Saloon League. The "Liberal Element," which drew its support from ethnic groups like the Irish Democratic Club and the German Political Union, favored "orderly saloons" but opposed stricter regulation or blue laws.

The education of their children was an important priority of Birmingham families. In December 1872, the Elyton Land Company donated land free for a white public school. The next year Colonel John Terry raised enough money to build a schoolhouse there, and in 1874 Powell School opened. Mary Ann Cahalan became the most beloved and best-remembered teacher at Powell and for 30 years instilled the principles of honor and patriotism in the youth of the city.

Birmingham's black community, led by Alfred Jackson, petitioned for a free black school. The city agreed to assist in maintaining the school that city

Sense of Place,
Sense of Family

blacks had already organized. Teachers were Viola M. Binford, Lucy B. Smith, and B.H. Hudson. Later Julia Scott served as principal of the Free Colored School. Five years later Hudson, George Turner, and H.C. Crawford began a drive for more city-supported black schools; gradually, through individual initiative by parents, black schools in the city increased. The Lane School had six grades by 1890; B.H. Hudson's school on Fifteenth Street was expanded and named the Slater School; and the Cameron School was started. The East End Negro School was still being conducted in the basement of St. John's Methodist Episcopal Church in 1890, however. The next year the Thomas School was completed but it burned down a few years later and the children returned to the basement of the church.

The Birmingham school system achieved rapid growth after 1883, when John Herbert Phillips became superintendent. A new Powell School was completed in 1887; Paul Hayne School began serving the southside; and a separate high school was established. In 1902 the Ullman, Lakeview, and Alberto Martin schools were built. Five years later South Highlands School and Barker School were opened, and New Central High School was occupied the fall of 1906.

Black parents demanded their own high school in 1899, and the next fall Principal A.H. Parker opened one in a room of the Cameron School. Influenced by the educational philosophy of Booker T. Washington, the school was called the Industrial High School. Although trade and occupational subjects were stressed, the large number of graduates who embarked upon professional careers proves the quality of the education. In 1910 an old two-story Negro theater, Lane's Auditorium, was rented by the Board of Education and the high school moved there. Although there was widespread white support for better Negro schools, such as the *Age-Herald*'s condemnation in October 1903, of crowded and unhealthy conditions at Thomas School, little improvement in black facilities resulted. But poor as conditions were for black children in Birmingham, they were much superior to those in rural areas of the county. It was 1921 before Jefferson County owned a single black public-school building. Educational opportunity was an important factor drawing black families from the farms of Alabama to the city of Birmingham.

Above: *Paul Bowron grew up at his parents' home on Twentieth Street where tennis was an important sport. His father, James Bowron, was active in the Birmingham Athletic Club. From the James Bowron Collection, University of Alabama Library.*

Children in Jefferson County were educated in schools provided by mining companies or in private academies (an Old South tradition) and both were subsidized, although very little, by the county. In the

1890s a number of these one-professor, tutorial schools existed. F.M. Grace for some years operated the Greene Farm High School, and Isaac Wellington McAdory taught at the Pleasant Hill Academy, one of the best and most popular schools in the entire area. Other schools were scattered across the hills and hollows of the county: Trussville Academy; Poplar Springs or Deer Lick School, which was located on land donated by Levi Black in 1880; Union Grove School; Rocky Ridge School; Oak Grove Academy; and Dr. J.B. Stagg's one-room school at Shady Grove.

Many parents still opposed having their daughters attend coeducational schools, so the Birmingham Female Seminary was established in 1881. Uncle Dick Jones College for Girls and Young Ladies was

Above: *These boys were part of Brother Blackwelder's class at West End Baptist Church in 1913. Courtesy, Billy and Becky Strickland.*

Left: *Regardless of how much church and social work women did, their children were their most important responsibility. The Williams children, Japhet Isaiah, Arthur Elish, and Callie Mabel, pose in their Sunday best. Notice that Arthur is barefooted. The old Southern tradition of going barefoot was fostered sometimes by poverty, but more often by choice. The warm southern weather discouraged the children from wearing shoes. Courtesy, Mickie H. Blackwell.*

Sense of Place, Sense of Family

Top: *Alice Sadler and Isaac Wellington McAdory were living in this house near McCalla when their first son, Wellington Prude, was born in 1875. McAdory was one of the most famous teachers in Jefferson County and his Pleasant Hill Academy had a reputation for providing excellent academic preparation. Courtesy, Henry and Betty McAdory.*

Above: *Members of an Allen School art class drew a classmate in 1908. The Allen School for young ladies was started in Birmingham in 1884 by sisters Ruth, Willie, and Beff Allen. The Allen sisters were cultural leaders in Birmingham and active in the woman's literary club movement. The school stressed Latin, music, the classics, and Shakespeare. It later became known as the Margaret Allen School. Courtesy, Jackie Dobbs, Old Birmingham Photographs.*

founded at Jonesville in 1889; the Pollock-Stephens Institute in 1890; and the Margaret Allen School in 1906. Two girls' colleges were opened in Birmingham in the 1890s, but both were ill-fated. The East Lake Atheneum operated for 10 years, but the Southern Female University lasted only one year at the Lakeview Hotel; when the facility burned, the school moved to Anniston. There was a German school; two Catholic parochial schools; and one Episcopal school for blacks, St. Mark's Academy. Blacks attended the Tuggle Institute, founded by Carrie Tuggle; Lauderdale College; or Miles College.

In 1887 East Lake convinced the Baptists to move Howard College from Marion to Birmingham by promising land and money, although a large portion of the amount promised was never delivered. Professor A.D. Smith, chairman of the Mathematics Department, took temporary charge of the college after the president, James T. Murfree, refused to move to Birmingham. When Professor Smith arrived he found only two unpainted wooden structures. "They have outfigured us," he said. Although Howard College began classes in October of 1887, it was 1892 before the East Lake campus was completed. In 1896 the North Alabama Methodist Conference accepted land from Rose Owen, and the next year a building was begun on Flint Ridge in Owenton. Officially named the North Alabama Conference College for Men, the school was commonly called Owenton College; later, when the Methodists moved Southern University from Greensboro, it was named Birmingham-Southern College.

The Birmingham Conservatory of Music and the Birmingham College of Music were established in 1895, and the Birmingham Dental College and the Birmingham Medical College in the same decade. Montezuma University opened in Bessemer in 1896. Named for the Mexican building DeBardeleben purchased from the New Orleans Cotton Exposition and reassembled in Bessemer, the school had an undergraduate school as well as a medical college. Unfortunately the structure burned in 1900 and the college eventually disbanded. Three business colleges—Massey, Wheeler, and Spencer—trained whites; a fourth, Eaton, supplied the demand for black secretaries and bookkeepers.

Education often provided an entree to "society" in early Birmingham, but there were conflicting attitudes toward this social order. Mrs. S.M. Mims, writing from South Alabama in 1893 to her young granddaughter in Birmingham, approved of Maud Mims's new teaching career for "it is the entrance into the best society, and by that I don't mean the

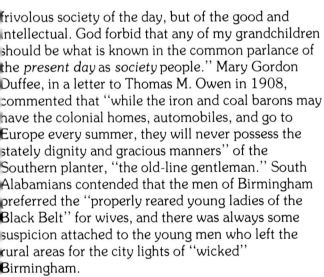

frivolous society of the day, but of the good and intellectual. God forbid that any of my grandchildren should be what is known in the common parlance of the *present day* as *society* people." Mary Gordon Duffee, in a letter to Thomas M. Owen in 1908, commented that "while the iron and coal barons may have the colonial homes, automobiles, and go to Europe every summer, they will never possess the stately dignity and gracious manners" of the Southern planter, "the old-line gentleman." South Alabamians contended that the men of Birmingham preferred the "properly reared young ladies of the Black Belt" for wives, and there was always some suspicion attached to the young men who left the rural areas for the city lights of "wicked" Birmingham.

Although the old Jefferson County aristocracy remained important within the county, the businessmen, Northerners, and Europeans who moved to Birmingham were unaware of any social discrimination. James Bowron, an English steel executive with TCI, was impressed by the city's society, which he felt was "based more upon what an individual accomplished than who his parents were." But soon even those "recent immigrants" to the coal mines and ore mines, as well as Yankee entrepreneurs and British capitalists, came to be "Southernized," imbued with a sense of family and a sense of place.

Above left: *Judge William S. Mudd's daughter Miss Susie Mudd, who was raised at her parent's home "The Grove" (Arlington), resented being so far from the Birmingham social scene. So, her parents sold the house and moved to the city. Miss Mudd later married and became Mrs. J. Rivers Carter. As a young matron she was active in the social scene of the city and in civic and literary clubs. From the Department of Archives and Manuscripts, Birmingham Public Library.*

Above: *Jesse Boring Wadsworth and his wife, the former Margaret Mc-Coy, were leaders in the Birmingham community at the turn of the century. Mr. Wadsworth was connected with the First National Bank of Birmingham and the Swansea Coal Company. Margaret Wadsworth's father, Dr. W.C. McCoy, was a well-known Methodist minister and her brother was Bishop James H. McCoy. Wadsworth was active in fraternal orders and commercial clubs and his wife engaged in work for the Methodist Church. The family later moved to Gadsden where Wadsworth founded the Etowah Trust and Savings Bank. Courtesy, Clare Gillam.*

Chapter VIII

TWENTIETH-CENTURY PROMISES

Birmingham's exhibit at the 1904 St. Louis World's Fair was this iron statue of Vulcan which was exhibited inside a building. Created by the Italian sculptor Guiseppe Moretti, the statue was cast in iron by the Birmingham Steel and Iron Company. Courtesy, Gary Dobbs.

The most severe depression of the nineteenth century shook the country in 1893. Banks failed, furnaces were put out of blast, scrip went into general use, and unemployed men tramped from town to town seeking jobs. Braxton Bragg Comer, who began the Western Grain Company in 1888 and later bought out the City National Bank, advanced the Tennessee Company $19,000 worth of grain and flour. Each day Comer would drop by to see TCI General Manager, Truman Aldrich, inquiring, "Going to bust today?" And Aldrich would reply, "Not today, Mr. Comer, but I can't tell about tomorrow." Joshua H. Foster, Jr., wrote to friends that Jefferson County had suffered grievously, and that miners and workers "were starving to death." In Birmingham R. DuPont Thompson recorded in his diary that he "began the New Year under inauspicious circumstances" with $8 in his pocket "and little prospect of increasing it. The night is cold, the fire almost out for want of fuel, the lamp is fast going out and there is no more oil in the house."

Twentieth-Century Promises

Top: *Spanish-American war hero Captain Richmond Pearson Hobson spoke to the students, alumni and faculty of Birmingham College in June 1906 as part of the college's semi-centennial celebration. In 1918 Birmingham College merged with Southern University in Greensboro to become Birmingham-Southern College. Hobson was an alumnus of Southern University. Courtesy, James F. Sulzby, Jr.*

Above: *The Bessemer Rifles was one of the first of many Jefferson County militia companies to volunteer for military duty in the Spanish-American War. The Rifles left Birmingham in 1898 for Mobile. Courtesy, the Bessemer Hall of History.*

Facing page: *A horse-drawn funeral procession begins outside the undertaker's office in the Watts building. The cortege would make its way up Twentieth Street to Capitol Park, over to Nineteenth Street, and up to Oak Hill Cemetery. Courtesy, James F. Sulzby, Jr*

Birmingham had been knocked down, but not out. James Bowron, a steel executive who lived on the South Highlands, recalled in his autobiography that the city reminded him "of a great big beetle turned over on its back, kicking very hard to get on its feet, but really quite uninjured." Comer's mill and bank, and Aldrich's TCI all survived. By 1895 a measure of recovery had begun, and the economic demands of the Spanish-American War, beginning in 1898, brought a degree of prosperity to Birmingham and Jefferson County, as well as to the nation at large.

In the war with Spain, the county responded well to the call for men, and a number of local militia companies volunteered. Colonel Elijah L. Higdon commanded the Woodlawn Light Infantry, known as "Higdon's Hobos," and Captain Hughes B. Kennedy, Leon Schwarz, and Walter Gardner led the Jefferson Volunteers. The Bessemer Rifles, the Birmingham Rifles, the Huey Guards from East Lake, and the Clark Rifles from Pratt City completed the county groups in the all-white First Alabama Regiment. The Third Alabama was a "colored regiment," and Birmingham's contribution was Company F, led by Lieutenant Dabney Luckie. On May 1, 1898, these men met at various armories in the county, then assembled in downtown Birmingham. With bands playing they paraded to the L & N Station. At First Avenue and Nineteenth Street they passed a group of aged Confederate veterans in faded gray uniforms standing at attention beside a large American flag, which spoke more for the passing of an era than the turn of the century. The Jefferson County troops joined their regiments at Mobile, then were transferred to Miami, where summer heat, typhoid, and dysentery depleted their ranks. Peace was declared before the men could leave for Cuba, but this did not dampen the spirit of the jubilant crowd that welcomed them home to Birmingham in the fall.

As the twentieth century opened, the future of Birmingham was indeed bright with the promises of tomorrow. Developments in the iron and steel industry were more than encouraging, and industrial prospects were optimistic for the Birmingham district. Using the Henderson process of open-hearth production, the Henderson Steel and Manufacturing Company had produced, in 1888, the first steel ever made in Alabama. The next year Andrew Carnegie made his first visit to the city. The Pennsylvania steel magnate must have been impressed with his competitors, because after touring the district he remarked, "The South is Pennsylvania's most formidable enemy." But he had no immediate worry. Henderson Steel was woefully underfinanced—a problem for the entire district—and its furnaces were never fully developed. In 1895 Albert E. Barton,

working at TCI's Alice furnace, successfully cast a basic pig iron, which was sold and shipped to the Carnegie steel mills. If Carnegie could produce quality steel from Birmingham basic pig iron, then it could be done in Birmingham. But it would be four years later, on Thanksgiving Day, 1899, before TCI cast steel at its new mill at Ensley. For three decades boomers and barkers had boasted of Birmingham as "the Pittsburgh of the South." Only now, at the turn of the century, was the district ready to accept the challenge.

The city itself had achieved remarkable growth in 30 years. Many of those who had laughed and called Charles Linn's three-story brick bank building "Linn's Folly" were alive in the twentieth century to marvel at Birmingham's skyscrapers. In 1902 William Henry Woodward built the first steel-frame building, the 10-floor Woodward Building. On the other corners of the intersection of Twentieth Street and First Avenue, which came to be known as the

"heaviest corner on earth," were the 16-story Brown-Marx Building, finished in 1905; the 16-story Empire Building (City National), built in 1909; and the American Trust and Savings Bank Building (John Hand) of 20 stories, completed in 1912. The third skyscraper built in Birmingham, the First National Bank Building, was located at the northeast corner of Second Avenue and Twentieth Street. This 10-story building was also financed by Woodward. For many years the Jefferson County Savings and Loan (City Federal) Building on Twenty-first Street and Second Avenue was the tallest building in the city. Eugene F. Enslen built this 25-story skyscraper after he succeeded his father, Christian F. Enslen, as president of the bank. In 1914, after George Gordon Crawford complained that there was no hotel in Birmingham elegant enough to entertain visting Northern board members of U.S. Steel, Robert Jemison, Jr., put together a financial group and built a new hotel. It was called the Tutwiler, named for Edward Magruder Tutwiler, the major stockholder, and a much-beloved man in Birmingham business circles.

Twentieth-Century Promises

Birmingham entered the twentieth century with electric and gas lights, paved main streets, and a telephone exchange. The Birmingham Water Works completed a new filter plant at Shades Mountain and North Birmingham in 1903 and began chlorine treatment in 1914 to insure bacteria-free water. A good system of intercity trolley cars made Jones Valley practically one city. Towns such as Bessemer, Ensley, North Birmingham, Woodlawn, East Lake, Avondale, Graymont, Jonesboro, Brighton, Elyton, Pratt City, Gate City, Thomas, Kingston, Powderly, West End, Wylam, and Fairview were tied to Birmingham with street railway transportation. And Birmingham wished to annex them all.

Three daily newspapers, the *Birmingham Age-Herald,* the *Birmingham News,* and the *Birmingham Ledger* kept the citizens informed, generally reflecting a business-oriented outlook. The weekly *Labor Advocate,* established in 1890 by Jere Dennis and later edited by J.H.F. Mosley, presented the working man's view. The *Alabama Christian Advocate,* founded by Birmingham Methodists in 1883, was widely read by many, and *The Alabama Baptist,* purchased by Frank William Barnett in 1901 and sold later to the State Baptist Convention, was located permanently in Birmingham after 1919. The *Birmingham Reporter* became the most important black-edited newspaper, and Oscar W. Adams, Sr., the most significant black editor.

Two well-remembered tragedies struck the city early in the century. On March 25, 1901, a fierce tornado-spawning storm swept across the county, striking Ensley and Pratt City, then Birmingham. At the James Van Hoose house, the first floor "was blown into kindling wood." Nineteen people were killed in

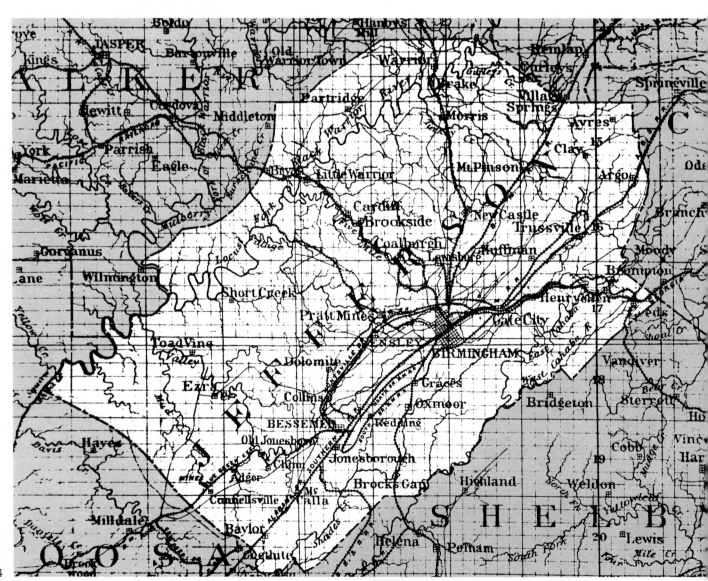

the southside area and more than a hundred injured. The second disaster occurred the next year when the National Baptist Convention was holding its annual meeting at Shiloh Baptist Church. On the night of September 19, Booker T. Washington, president of Tuskegee Institute, was to deliver the main address; an hour before, the church was filled to its 3,000-seat capacity. The staircases were crowded and the vestibule packed. Usher John H. Bunn warned people to stay back, but many began pushing forward to hear Washington. His speech expressed his life's philosophy, the theme that both white and black must learn to live in peace and harmony together with mutual respect. He was given a standing ovation. At the front of the church, when a man stood, a woman took his seat; he stepped back and sat down upon her lap. There was "an exchange of words." Another lady cried "fight," which the throng mistook for "Fire!" and a stampede for the doors began. Reverend T.W. Walker, the church's minister, desperately tried to calm the crowd. The choir sang "The Trumpet Blast," but the mad rush for the door continued. Women and children fainted, and men rushed over them. (One woman, Ora Bell Nolums, arriving too late to get inside, walked away disappointed. Annie Bradford had left the church before Washington finished. Both their lives were spared.) One hundred and twenty people died and it took 12 hours to clear the bodies from the church. Booker T. Washington never recovered from the incident. As a result of this tragedy, many Birmingham-area churches designed extra doors and police-enforced ordinances to keep aisles and exits clear.

The twentieth-century promises of the Birmingham district were stressed by the Birmingham Commercial Club, which had been organized in 1887 to encourage trade and create more economic diversification. This group later developed into the Birmingham Chamber of Commerce. One of the significant successes of the Commercial Club was the organization by Braxton Bragg Comer, with the club's support, of the city's first and most important textile mill. Comer, a banker, miller, and cotton factor, founded Avondale Mills in 1897 and developed a village of 120 houses around his factory. By 1920 the mill had adopted a comprehensive welfare program that included a community house, with a gymnasium and two swimming pools. Although Avondale Mills supported an infirmary and resident doctors, they operated no schools as did TCI. Avondale was located in the city, and the children of mill families attended Cunningham School in the Birmingham system. The mill employed both men and women, as well as some children. When Comer was elected governor in 1906, the anti-

Facing page: *This 1892 Jefferson County map shows the old communities and mining villages of Old Jonesboro (Jonesborough), Toadvine, Mt. Pinson, Brock's Gap, Cardiff, and Brookside. In 1887 J.W. DuBose said "All Alabama roads lead to Birmingham." Special Collections, Samford University Library.*

Above top: *These Birmingham firemen were photographed outside Fire Station Number 7 in Behrens Park in 1911. The Birmingham Fire Department has always been a close-knit organization priding itself on professionalism. Courtesy, Billy and Becky Strickland.*

Above middle: *This fire truck was the pride of Behrens Park Fire Station Number 7. Samuel Merritt earned $80 a month driving the truck and fighting fires. Although the Birmingham Fire Department owned trucks by 1911, it was still using a few horse-drawn wagons. Courtesy, Billy and Becky Strickland.*

Above: *A South Highlands-Jonesville car connects with the Red Mountain dummy in front of the Braxton Bragg Comer house, circa 1895. The northern terminus of the line was located at Jonesville, a community centered around Wesley Chapel, UDJ College for Girls and Young Ladies, and the Richard A. Jones farm. Courtesy, James F. Sulzby, Jr.*

Twentieth-Century Promises

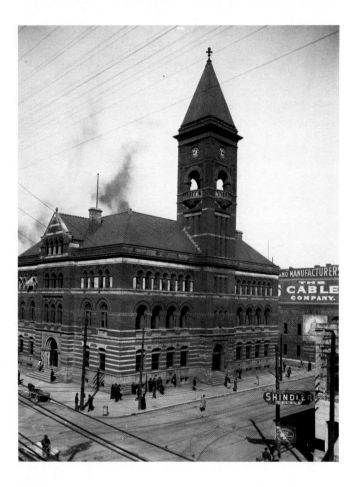

Top: *When the famous American photographer Lewis Hine visited Birmingham in November 1910, he went to Governor Braxton Bragg Comer's Avondale Mill to take pictures and see if children were employed there. Most children who worked refused to admit their real age, insisting they were fourteen. From the Lewis Hine photographs in the Edward L. Bafford Photography Collection of the University of Maryland, Baltimore County Library.*

Above: *The United States Courthouse and Post Office were located on the corner of Second Avenue and Eighteenth Street. Courtesy, Library of Congress.*

child-labor movement was at its height and he was sensitive to charges that Avondale Mills exploited child labor. The Selma Manufacturing Company was the only mill in Birmingham besides Comer's, but neither Avondale nor Selma did any cutting or sewing operations.

In 1899 the Sloss-Sheffield Coal and Iron Company was formed by the consolidation of 12 firms, and Republic Iron and Steel Company entered the Birmingham district by purchasing the Thomas properties. The Continental Gin Company, organized in 1896, resulted from several mergers and benefited from Robert S. Munger's inventions and able management. Soon it was the largest cotton-gin manufacturing company in the world. Birmingham also became a center of cotton trade with storage warehouses, cotton compresses, and three mattress factories. By the turn of the century, coal-byproduct ovens were converting burning coal into tar, ammonia, gas, and other products. Within 10 years Birmingham became the center of the cast-iron pipe industry in America. In 1900 J.K. Dimmick built a plant in North Birmingham and in 1905 Charlotte Blair, her brother, J.W. Blair, and John Joseph Eagan of Atlanta organized the American Cast Iron Pipe Company and built the largest pipe plant in the city. William H. Stockham left Chicago and established a foundry in 1903 in a ramshackle barn on Tenth Avenue. Stockham, who directed his company with vision and industry, made simple castings of manhole covers, car wheels, brake shoes, and later cast-iron soil pipe. In 1904, James Ransom McWane began the Birmingham Steel and Iron Company. Four years later he joined Eagan at American Cast Iron Pipe Company. In 1922 he left ACIPCO and organized the McWane Cast Iron Pipe Company. Through the years McWane invented and patented many new foundry processes. Cast-iron pipe became one of Birmingham's most important products, soon amounting to half the value of foundry and machine-shop products.

The wholesale lumber and grocery trade were other important Birmingham businesses. Retail stores were dominated by Yieldings (founded in 1876), Blach's (1885), Burger-Phillips (1895), and Pizitz (1899). E.E. Forbes began selling pianos in 1889, and the same year R.B. Broyles started peddling in the mining communities. The Bromberg family of Mobile opened a Birmingham store in 1900 and sold diamonds, as did Jobe-Rose and the Ash brothers. By 1899 Loveman, Joseph and Loeb advertised they were the "Leaders, We Expect Imitations and Defy Competition." But Caheen Brothers, Saks, and older concerns were not discouraged, and Pizitz opened a branch store in Bessemer the next year. While

Loveman's is no longer in business, most of the older concerns survive as competitors. Probably the most influential black businessman of this period was C.M. Harris, who founded the Davenport and Harris Funeral Home and the Protective and Industrial Life Insurance Company. The first black Birmingham millionaire reputedly was Andrew J. Beard, an ex-slave from a farm at Mount Pinson, who later owned an 80-acre farm near Center Point, worked for the Alabama & Chattanooga Railroad, and patented, with the help of Birmingham mayor Walter M. Drennen, a number of mechanical inventions—improvements in rotary engines and a railroad car coupling device. He also operated Beard's Jitney Line.

For 10 years the nation and the Birmingham district enjoyed economic prosperity. Then suddenly, in March 1907, the stock market declined, railroads went into receivership, 13 New York City banks failed, and there were job layoffs and business failures. Birmingham's largest corporation, the Tennessee Coal, Iron and Railroad Company, was in acute financial distress. President Don H. Bacon, a mining man, made numerous improvements in TCI's plant facilities after 1902 and established new production records, but the debt only increased. In 1906 a New York investment group purchased a majority of the stock and named John A. Topping president. Topping was experienced in steel manufacture and continued to borrow money for new plants and equipment. When the Panic of 1907 came, TCI had a combined debt of over $5 million. Although appraisers estimated it would take another $20 million to make the plants profitable, when the Harriman railroad lines ordered 150,000 tons of TCI open-hearth rails, the steel world riveted its attention on Birmingham.

Meanwhile the New York City banking firm of Moore and Schley, which held TCI stock as loan collateral, was being pressured financially by the panic. The firm

needed to sell the TCI stock to save its corporate life. Grant B. Schley approached J. Pierpont Morgan, suggesting that the United States Steel Company purchase their Tennessee Company stock. There were two days of secret meetings, which included a special consultation at the White House between U.S. Steel representatives Judge Elbert H. Gary and Henry C. Frick, and President Theodore Roosevelt in order to gain Roosevelt's support and the government's acquiescence that such a purchase would not be prosecuted as a violation of antitrust laws. United States Steel agreed to purchase TCI's $1 billion assets for $35,317,632 only as a "public service" to "prevent a panic and general industrial smash-up."

Top left: *James Ransom McWane organized the Birmingham Steel and Iron Company in 1904 and directed the casting of Vulcan, the city's exhibition at the 1904 St. Louis World's Fair. In 1908, McWane became associated with American Cast Iron Pipe Company and in 1922 left ACIPCO to establish McWane Cast Iron Pipe Company. Through these years, he invented and patented many new foundry processes and became one of the city's industrial leaders. Courtesy, James R. McWane.*

Top right: *The Robert S. Munger house was located on the southwest curve of Five Points South. Munger was so concerned with the noise from the dummy railroad that he put his house on rollers and moved it across the alley to the lot next door. Still longing for the quiet of the countryside, however, Munger purchased the old William S. Mudd house, Arlington, and moved his family there in 1902. Courtesy, Mrs. A.C. Montgomery.*

Above: *The backyard of the Robert S. Munger home was designed with stable and carriage barns but these were quickly converted into automobile garages when Munger became one of the first people in the city to own a motor vehicle. In this picture the family members are seen in a 1903 Winton (left) and a 1902 Winton (right). Courtesy, Mrs. A.C. Montgomery.*

Twentieth-Century Promises

Top: *The Winter-Green Drugstore, on the corner across from the Terminal Station, was a busy place. It provided refreshments at the soda fountain and medicines for travelers leaving or arriving by train. Grover Winter, who operated the drugstore, is seen in this 1913 photo in the center with Amzi Walker on the left and Frank Winter on the right. The soda jerk is unidentified. The Winters were famous for their Winter Smith Chill Tonic patent medicine for malaria. Courtesy, Mildred Winter Barber.*

Above: *William Jennings Bryan, who came to Birmingham on several occasions, is seen outside of the First Cumberland Presbyterian Church following a Birmingham speaking engagement. Though he unsuccessfully ran for President three times, he later was named Woodrow Wilson's Secretary of State. From the Department of Archives and Manuscripts, Birmingham Public Library.*

The stock purchase was hailed in the Birmingham district as the salvation for Birmingham's underfinanced steel industry and as adding 25 percent to the value of all property in Jefferson County. U.S. Steel would bring "money mixed with experience," which was "all that the Birmingham District needs for fullest development." Arguments that such a purchase violated the Sherman Anti-Trust Act were brushed aside. Later a committee of the United States Senate investigating the affair reported that the merger gave the giant steel corporation control of the nation's open-hearth rail production, its iron ore supply, "practical monopoly of the iron and steel trade in the South, and the elimination of a strong and growing competitor."

Lawyers, judges, historians, and economists have argued long about whether U.S. Steel's advent into the Birmingham district was the greatest possible boon for Birmingham or the most catastrophic economic disaster, whether U.S. Steel's corporate decisions and investment capital pushed Birmingham development forward or retarded it in favor of Pittsburgh plants. But even such pricing scales as "Pittsburgh plus" and "Birmingham Differential," which artificially raised the price of Birmingham steel and cut the district's competitive edge of low production costs, did not deter Alabama supporters of U.S. Steel. In Birmingham criticisms of the giant steel corporation were rarely voiced publicly or loudly. Perhaps this was due to a first-hand awareness of the district's economic advances after the arrival of U.S. Steel, or an appreciation for the increased standard of living that U.S. Steel brought to Birmingham through its continued investment at TCI; or, it may have reflected the monopoly which U.S. Steel came to have over the voices of the community. In any case United States Steel's TCI Division was the largest employer, the greatest landowner, and the most politically and economically powerful corporation in Jefferson County, a power that the corporation was never shy about wielding.

After acquiring control of TCI, United States Steel Corporation, in a masterful decision, selected Southern-born Georgia Tech graduate, George Gordon Crawford, as president. Crawford had worked briefly as a draftsman for Sloss-Sheffield in Birmingham and knew the reputations of many men had been destroyed in the attempt to make steel in the district. He was not eager to come. Once here Crawford faced two problems: the technical problem of converting Birmingham's low-grade iron ore into steel, which was more easily solved than the human factor of Birmingham's inefficient and unreliable labor force. The Tennessee Company had a 400 percent employee turnover, which was partially

due to the poor living conditions in the mining and mill communities. Men were reluctant to bring their families into the area and stayed only for short periods of time. Sickness and poor health caused excessive absenteeism. Crawford immediately began a program of company welfare, creating new villages with streets, proper drainage, playgrounds, tennis courts, and sometimes even a swimming pool. New homes were built, along with schools, clinics, dispensaries, community recreational houses, and homes for teachers and resident doctors. Usually two villages were built: one for blacks and one for whites.

Crawford hired Winifred Collins, a Chicago social worker, to head his Department of Social Science. Collins recruited a large number of college-educated teachers from the northeast to teach in the TCI schools. At this time most public school teachers in the county had only a high-school education, but TCI's salary subsidy allowed Miss Collins to seek the best-trained and most-dedicated teachers. The outstanding TCI schools were models for the county and the state. Besides strong programs in the fundamentals, there were art, music, and health classes. There were also courses in domestic arts and home demonstration. TCI Negro schools had an excellent black heritage program 50 years before the subject was in demand across the nation.

To improve the health of TCI employees, as well as to increase the number of work days and improve worker efficiency, Crawford recruited Dr. Lloyd Noland from Dr. William Gorgas's staff at the Panama Canal Zone. Noland investigated the health conditions of TCI employees and presented a first-

year budget of $750,000—a dramatic figure considering the entire Alabama state public health budget was only $25,000. TCI's program eventually included dental care, first aid, sanitation improvements, and one of the best hospitals in Jefferson County, making TCI a pioneer in industrial health medicine.

The standards established by TCI through the work of Miss Collins and Dr. Noland, influenced other Jefferson County corporations, as well as the city and county boards of education and the county board of health. The standard of living for employees in the district improved. In 1912 the Alabama Coal Operators Association held its state meeting at Docena, a model TCI village, and adopted the concept: "Health is essential to good work." Though these paternalistic programs decreased union support among the working force (no doubt part of the corporation's motive), they were mainly instituted to

Above left: *After the United States Steel Corporation acquired its southern subsidiary, the Tennessee Coal Iron and Railroad Company, it selected George Gordon Crawford, a southern-born, Georgia Tech graduate, as president. Crawford, who had worked briefly in Birmingham for Sloss-Sheffield, realized the technical problems of converting Birmingham's low-grade iron ore into steel and the problems of the district's inefficient and unreliable labor force. He was determined to conquer both. From the Auburn University Archives.*

Above right: *The ore mining village of Fossil appeared quite peaceful in October of 1916 as plans were being made to build an outdoor theater at the site. The name of the village was later changed to Wenonah to match the Indian names of its companion villages of Ishkooda and Muscoda. From the William S. Hoole Special Collections, University of Alabama Library.*

Twentieth-Century Promises

Top left: *Miss Winifred Collins, a graduate of the University of Chicago and an experienced social worker, was hired by George Gordon Crawford to head his Department of Social Science of the Tennessee Coal Iron and Railroad Company. Miss Collins had her main office in the executive offices of TCI in the Brown-Marx Building. At one time, she held what was probably the most prestigious executive position of any woman in Birmingham. One man said, "When Miss Collins spoke, she moved mountains!" She was able to attract a number of the best trained teachers with degrees from eastern and midwestern universities to teach in the TCI schools. From the Auburn University Archives.*

Top right: *To improve the health of TCI employees, George Gordon Crawford recruited Dr. Lloyd Noland from Dr. William Gorgas' staff at the Panama Canal Zone. Noland investigated the health conditions of TCI employees and presented the first year budget of $750,000, a dramatic figure considering that the entire Alabama state public health budget was only $25,000. Noland's health work in the Birmingham district was recognized when TCI named its hospital after him. From the Knox Collection, Auburn University Archives.*

Above: *The children at both the white and black TCI schools would take part in tooth brush drills as part of the health education classes. On the playground, the children would line up and brush to music in unison. From the Harper Collection, Special Collections, Samford University Library.*

increase productivity and profits. In these expanding years TCI built the coal-mining villages of Docena and Edgewater, created Bayview Lake to increase its industrial supply of water, built the first coke-byproducts ovens, constructed a steel-wire plant, and created a new industrial city in Possum Valley called Corey, later named Fairfield. This community was a different concept in industrial paternalism. Although TCI conceived the idea of the city and provided the land, the real-estate firm of Robert Jemison, Jr., directed the planning, hired a New York designer, and built moderately priced houses to encourage workers to buy their own homes.

The social and health programs pioneered at TCI were occurring during the Progressive reform movement that swept across the nation during the first two decades of the twentieth century. Birmingham's philanthropic efforts were reflected in the organization of the Mercy Homes, industrial schools for both boys and girls, orphan homes, and the Hillman and St. Vincent's hospitals. A black board of directors, headed by the Reverend W.R. Pettiford, founded the Alabama Colored Orphans and Old Folks Home with the Federation of Colored Women's Clubs later assuming responsibility for its operation. In 1908, four black fraternal organizations established the Carrie Tuggle Institute as a school and orphanage with strong white financial support. Attorney Hugo Black and the Reverend James A. "Brother" Bryan served on the advisory board, and in 1915 City Commissioner Arlie K. Barber addressed an integrated mass meeting to raise money to meet a school debt. A Boys' Club was begun in 1903 and a Children's Aid Society in 1911. All these efforts, however, were inadequate to serve the needs of a growing urban population.

The Birmingham Humane Society for the Prevention of Cruelty to Children and Animals was established in 1910. Mrs. W.N. Wood was an active supporter and under her leadership the society passed out information in both English and Italian. This bilingual treatment indicated the extent of Italian immigration to the city. By 1910 Italians were the largest foreign-born group in Birmingham, surpassing both the British and the German populations.

Birmingham was the second city in Alabama to have a women's suffrage association. Growing out of the progressive indignation over child labor, its leaders were Patti Rufner Jacobs, Lillian Roden Bowron, and Amelia Worthington. Mrs. W.L. Murdoch was not only a suffragist but also was active in the anti-child-labor movement. In 1910 the Anti-Tuberculosis Association of Jefferson County was organized with B.M. Allen as president, and the next year the group

opened a sanatorium on Red Mountain. G. Bowden Settle supervised a tent and shack camp (the forerunner of the Lakeshore tuberculosis facility) where 12 sick people were isolated and nursed back to full health.

As the Progressive reformist winds swept across the nation, in Jefferson County they blew strongest in the prohibition movement. Maybe it was because of the great abundance of saloons in Birmingham, and their all-too-pleasant ambience. When DuPont Thompson was a young lawyer in the Birmingham of the 1890s, he was more than impressed by their ubiquity and appeal. He put it this way:

> Bars, man, bars. Bars everywhere; one couldn't keep out of 'em. It was so easy to make a mistake and the first thing you'd know you were right spank in one. Bars with real brass rails to rest your feet on, and nice mahogany counters to put your elbows on, and a big looking glass in front of you, and a gent in front in a white apron and a smile softly purring, "Well, gents, what'll it be?"

Birmingham increased the saloon license fee from $500 in 1906 to $3,000 in 1911, forbade Negro saloons, and restricted Birmingham saloons to a heavily policed central section of the city. In 1902

Students of the St. Elias Arabic School pose for the camera in the early 1900s. At the beginning of the twentieth century a large number of Lebanese emigrated to Birmingham. The St. Elias Catholic Church established an Arabic School, one of the earliest of its kind in the city. Literature and poetry were taught in Arabic to young children. For many years, Khattar Wehby, educated at the National College of Lebanon, taught the children the Arabic language without monetary compensation. Courtesy, Josephine Wehby Sharbel.

Lem Motlow, the nephew of Tennessee's famous Jack Daniels, operated the Motlow Distilling Company of Avenue B under the name of Jack Daniels Distillery. When Jefferson County went dry in 1907, the distillery was closed, but it reopened after the county went wet again in 1911. After the Alabama legislature voted statewide prohibition in 1915, Birmingham was dry once more, and the Motlow distillery closed for good. But there was always a strong moonshine market in the city with Walker, Winston, and Shelby residents adding their talents to the local expertise. Throughout the 1920s, those who knew where to look could find "white lightning." Few people who grew up in the county and went hiking, sweet-shrub and honeysuckle hunting, or blackberry picking cannot recall the first time they stumbled upon the rusty remains of an abandoned still—or upon an active one. When the pungent odor sweeping through the trees announced that "a run" was being made, the innocent observer knew he was in the wrong place at the wrong time! But not all moonshine

Twentieth-Century Promises

operations were rural. Stills were operated deep in abandoned mines, in warehouses, and in miners' company houses, where family incomes were supplemented by producing white lightning in two-gallon-capacity rigs on wood stoves. Black miners in the 1930s called the illicit brew "Joe Louis" because of its hard punch.

Between 1890 and 1910 the most bitter political dispute in the county was over annexation. The Commercial Club, the Birmingham Board of Trade, city officials, and merchants realized the city needed a greater tax base to pay for and improve city services, and a larger population to attract more industry. E.J. Smyer, Frank Nelson, T.H. Molton, F.M. Jackson, and Sterling A. Wood, along with others, signed newspaper advertisements supporting annexation. In 1903 Mayor David Fox succeeded in increasing the city's boundaries, but only at the price of excluding the Birmingham Rolling Mill. The mill had actually closed its doors to avoid taxation. In 1908 the "Greater Birmingham" movement began. This drive to secure suburban annexation was supported by the Birmingham Realty Company, successor to the old Elyton Land Company, and a majority of the people in the suburbs. Opposition to annexation came from industries who objected to higher taxation. The 1900 census, which gave Birmingham a population of only 38,351, led to increased support of the Greater Birmingham movement.

In the state legislature, Jefferson County representative Jere C. King led the fight for annexation while county senator Nathan L. Miller opposed King's bill because it included so much industrial property. It was unprecedented for Birmingham to be so well represented in Montgomery. The city's own Braxton Bragg Comer was governor, while the lieutenant governor was Birmingham banker Henry B. Gray. Comer, an industrialist and owner of Avondale cotton mills, would have favored the corporation view, except that he had just won the governorship by uniting the rural sections behind a progressive fight against railroad corporation monopolies. His friend and trusted political advisor, Frank S. White of Birmingham, urged him to support the people's interest against the "selfish corporate interests." Comer agreed, and the Greater Birmingham boundaries he approved included Ensley, the TCI coke ovens at Pratt City, and all the Sloss-Sheffield and Republic iron furnaces, property valued at over $2 million. But TCI's main plants with a value of $3,778,239 were excluded. When City Commissioner Arlie K. Barber later suggested that TCI plants be annexed and taxed, Commission President George B. Ward quickly

Facing page, top: *Birmingham had a parade for its returning World War I heroes. As the soldiers marched through Birmingham they were showered with flowers. From the Department of Archives and Manuscripts, Birmingham Public Library.*

Facing page, bottom: *To welcome home its World War I heroes Birmingham erected an Arc de Triomphe at the head of Twentieth Street in old Capitol Park. The Donahoo Horse and Mule Company took the opportunity of advertising their company by posing in front of the Arc. Courtesy, James F. Sulzby, Jr.*

Above: *On June 5, 1919, the political, social, and business elite of Birmingham gathered outside the Merriman School. As a group, these men were economically and politically powerful and responsible for the leadership of Birmingham in the early years of the twentieth century. Courtesy, Mary Williams Harris.*

Left: *The Tony Rumore family came to Bessemer in 1904, only four years after arriving in the United States from Sicily. Mr. Rumore opened a grocery store and became a valued member of the community. Today the Virciglio, Bruno, Stignani, and Simonetti families own most of the city's supermarkets. Courtesy, Sam Rumore, Jr.*

Twentieth-Century Promises

The people of Birmingham overflowed with joy and pride as the Fourth Infantry Division of the Alabama National Guard, part of the Rainbow Division, marched down Twentieth Street on May 10, 1919. Mrs. N.M. Lamkin of Fountain Avenue was inspired to write:

Welcome! Welcome! Boys in Kahki
To this greeting planned for you;
Welcome from dear Alabama
From the Magic City, too!

Courtesy, James F. Sulzby, Jr.

On the morning of November 11, 1918, Jefferson County awoke to mill whistles blowing, horns blaring, and church bells ringing. The armistice had ended the war, but it also ended government contracts and high wage scales. President J.W. McQueen of Sloss-Sheffield Steel and Iron Company considered these wages excessive—in some cases more than 100 percent increases—and beyond Birmingham industry's capacity to pay when war demands ceased. But World War I also benefited Jefferson County. New plants had been erected and capital investments increased. Congressional appropriations to improve the Warrior-Tombigbee river system, opening the coal fields to tugboats, were accelerated by the war. Lock No. 17's dam at Squaw Shoals provided a 72-foot lift in two locks and a six-foot channel to Atwood's Ferry by June 1915, almost a year after the war began in Europe but before the United States became involved. Although steel and iron made their way to Mobile by river during the war, it was another five years before docking, rail, and storage facilities at Birmingport were completed. Now the district had water transportation to the sea, an alternative to excessively high railroad freight rates that were deliberately designed to favor Northern-manufactured products.

Top: *Docking, rail, and storage facilities were completed at Birmingport by 1920. A railroad connected the city with the port facility and water transportation became very important to the city's economy, especially during World War I and II when steel and iron were shipped down to Mobile to shipbuilding plants. Courtesy, Gary Dobbs.*

Left: *Captain Mortimer H. Jordan, Jr. wrote from France that the arrival of the Alabama troops in the middle of the night became a gala event. The troops were led to their quarters by a French marching band playing "Marching through Georgia," the only American tune the French musicians knew. Captain Jordan was amused that the British kept calling them Yankees. "Think of it," he wrote, "Southern troops being called Yankees! And not minding it in the least either. Surely times change." Courtesy, Mortimer H. Jordan and Virginia Murray.*

Above: *Lock 17 is seen here undergoing construction. The lock, completed in 1915, raised the water level of the Warrior River and provided a six-foot channel all the way to Atwood's Ferry above Birmingport. From the Roland Harper Collection in the William S. Hoole Special Collections, University of Alabama Library.*

Twentieth-Century Promises

Early in the twentieth century, men's service clubs developed in the city as they did throughout the nation. The Rotary Club was founded in 1913. The history of the Civitan and Kiwanis clubs are particularly linked with Birmingham. The Civitan Club was actually founded in the city in March of 1917 by Dr. Courtney W. Shropshire. Three years later Dr. Shropshire founded Civitan International and their international headquarters is still located in the city. A Kiwanis Club was organized in Birmingham in 1917 and the national convention of 1919 was held at the Tutwiler Hotel. During this convention the membership succeeded in purchasing the copyright name "Kiwanis" from the founder, Allen S. Browne. Probably thinking it would be impossible for the group to raise the money since it was a Sunday, Browne demanded payment in cash. But several Birmingham Kiwanians were able to persuade one bank to open and let them have the money. The club grew nationally and internationally on the motto, "We Build." These early service clubs were followed later by the Lions (1922), Junior Chamber of Commerce (1920), Exchange Club (1921), and the Optimist Club (1928). All added greatly to the civic spirit of Birmingham. Soon these clubs spread to the smaller towns of Jefferson County.

In 1903 James A. McKnight proposed that Birmingham send a giant iron statue to the 1904 St. Louis World's Fair. Vulcan, the Roman god of fire and metal working, was selected. The Commercial Club, under the direction of president Fred M. Jackson, Jr., raised the money for the project. Italian sculptor Guiseppe Moretti created the plaster cast in his New Jersey studio, a huge warehouse in Menlo Park. He then cut the cast apart and shipped it to Birmingham in sections. Moretti came to Birmingham to assist in casting Vulcan. James R. McWane, president of the Birmingham Steel and Iron Company, directed the iron casting himself and the statue was shipped in pieces to St. Louis. Although McWane cast the figure, the anvil-block and hammer were cast by the Williamson Foundry across the street. The Vulcan statue was exhibited inside a large building and was the most sensational show at St. Louis. Later when Vulcan was returned to the city, it was erected at the State Fairgrounds where it remained until the Birmingham Kiwanis Club began a drive to place Vulcan atop Red Mountain in 1936.

In October of 1921 Birmingham celebrated its semi-centennial with a gala celebration that lasted five days. The Pageant of Birmingham, a grand epic with more than a hundred people singing and dancing, was presented on an outdoor stage at Avondale Park. The play opened with DeSoto's visit to Alabama.

President Warren G. Harding visited the city during the celebration, arriving at the Terminal Station and driving between cheering children to the Tutwiler Hotel where he was greeted by Governor Thomas E. Kilby and Senator Oscar W. Underwood. In the afternoon President Harding received an honorary doctorate from Birmingham-Southern College, but he left town before the nightly pageant.

Birmingham had come a long way in the 50 years since John T. Milner's dream of a city at the railroad crossing. Many of the people who acted out the Pageant of Birmingham on the Avondale stage had really participated in the growth of the city. Birmingham had grown from a cornfield to the 14th-ranked Southern city by 1900, and to the third most populous Southern city by 1920. Ranking only behind New Orleans and Atlanta, the Birmingham goal of the Jazz Age was to be the largest city of the New South.

Facing page, top: The Birmingham Steel and Iron Company cast in iron this statue of Vulcan which was exhibited at the 1904 St. Louis World's Fair. Courtesy, James F. Sulzby, Jr.

Facing page, bottom: This American soldier monument tops the grave of Willie Cymro Johns who died "fighting for his country in the Philippine Islands" in 1903. The monument stands in Forest Hill Cemetery. Photo by Charles J. McFarlin. Courtesy, Betsy Barber Bancroft.

Below: This view of Third Avenue and Eighteenth Street looking east shows the hustle and bustle of Birmingham in the 1920s. Courtesy, James F. Sulzby, Jr.

Chapter IX

OF SPRINGS AND FARMS AND SUMMER PLACES

The old Tannehill blast furnaces in Bibb County just across the Jefferson County line were a favorite place for afternoon and all-day outings. From the Harper Collection, Special Collections, Samford University Library.

By the 1920s Birmingham had become an urban center and had acquired all the problems that went with urbanization. Carl Carmer, in Stars Fell on Alabama, described the city as: "the nouveau riche of Alabama cities. With an arrogant gesture she builds her most luxurious homes on a mountain of ore yet unmined. Hardly a half-century ago she was the little crossroads town of Jones Valley. Now she numbers her population in hundreds of thousands. She has no traditions. She is the New South. On one side of her rises a mountain of iron. On another a mountain of coal. She lies in the valley between, breathing flame." On the surface city residents seemed oblivious to the problems of industrial pollution, accepting it as the price of progress and jobs. In Birmingham barefoot children, regardless of skin color, had black feet. Washed clothes hanging outside often were ashen before they were dry. If the mines and mills were working, no one complained.

Of Springs and Farms and Summer Places

Whether to escape the smoke and noise or the fast-paced responsibilities of city life, many citizens of Birmingham made a habit of visiting nearby farms, driving into the hills, or staying at hotels near springs or "watering places." But Birmingham was a blue-collar city and the workingman had no funds for traveling; the immigrant had no relatives in the countryside. For them escape and relaxation had to be close and free.

Birmingham city parks were served by trolley cars and, in the early days, the dance and picnic pavilion at Red Mountain Park was usually crowded on weekends. Lakeview Park, built by the Elyton Land Company in 1885, was used for ball games and summer operas even after the noted Lakeview Hotel burned in 1893. Eleven years later the Country Club of Birmingham moved to Lakeview. After 1927, when the country club moved to Shades Valley, the golf course was known as Highland Park. Today it is named the Charlie Boswell Golf Course. Avondale Park was the scene of free band concerts, dances, special pageants, and, for a time, the Birmingham Zoo.

East Lake was the city's favorite site for picnics and Sunday afternoon drives. The resort hotel was destroyed by fire in 1891, but the lake was used for

Below: *An East Lake dummy railroad engine pushes a Red Mountain car up the north face of the mountain. The Red Mountain line was opened in 1889 and connected with the South Highlands line on Fourteenth Street South, continued up the mountain, across the crest, and down the south side of the mountain into Shades Valley to Rosedale. The Red Mountain Casino, which provided weekend entertainment, helped give the line more business. Courtesy of the William H. Brantley, Jr. Collection, Samford University Library.*

Facing page: *Residents of Birmingham, Bessemer, and other small communities would gather up the family and go camping in the woods either to escape the smoke and noise of the city, or simply for a change of pace. The Warrior River and Shades Mountain were favorite camping spots. Courtesy, the Bessemer Hall of History.*

fishing and boating and the park for outings and special events. East Lake was frequently the scene of political rallies and family reunions. Extra streetcars had to be added to the East Lake and Tidewater lines in 1923 to accommodate the crowds of curious spectators who came to watch the public initiation ceremony of the Nathan Bedford Forrest Klan No. 60 of the Ku Klux Klan. About 50,000 people, many of whom had come from outside the county, gathered for a barbecue, car raffle, and fireworks display held during the Klan ceremony. The hooded order also used Edgewood Lake, nestled at the foot of Shades Mountain, for initiations. This lake, somewhat more isolated than East Lake, could also be reached by streetcar. For years it was a popular place for fishing, sailing, and Sunday afternoon recreation, and was the site of the Birmingham Motor and Country Club. On September 11, 1923, some 25,000 people watched the initiation ceremony here of Robert E. Lee Klan No. 1. During the day's festivities, there was swimming, dancing, a barbecue, and a display of daring courage by Birmingham aviator Glenn Messer, who balanced himself on the wing of his plane and then parachuted. The Klan initiated 1,750 men, including then Birmingham attorney, and later United States Senator and Supreme Court Justice, Hugo Black.

Before 1900 city parks were open to everyone, but "Jim Crow" legislation at the turn of the century forced Birmingham to develop a dual system of segregated parks. In Negro neighborhoods Brown's Park was opened in 1895 and Liberty Park three years later. By 1910 all city parks were completely segregated. Traction Park became the elite park for blacks, the site of Sunday afternoon ball games, Sunday School picnics, Labor Day rallies, Fourth of July watermelon cuttings, and family barbecues. The activities of the Masons were always an important part of black social life. P.D. Davis was very active in Masonic work and often directed their social functions. Blacks frequently would swim at Dozier Park along the Pratt Car line near Enon Ridge, particularly on Sunday afternoons. The *Birmingham News* called the June 12, 1919 Colored Picnic at the Fairgrounds, "the greatest celebration ever put on in the state," and the American Cast Iron Pipe Company's annual black agricultural fair was another important event. In the mining villages black recreational halls, game fields, and picnic pavilions were crowded on weekends and holidays. Hosea Hudson remembered that "ball games and singing, that was the social life"; but for some blacks, like Angelo Herndon who lived at Docena, the week was so long and the work so hard, that he "prayerfully looked forward to Sunday" to sleep and rest.

Of Springs and Farms and Summer Places

Some Birmingham residents had rural property with rustic cabins and farmhouses where families could go for the summer months. Fulton Springs to the north of the city and Shades Mountain to the south were popular areas. Mrs. H.O. Williams would take in summer sojourners at Hale Springs (Bluff Park) for $15 a month—room and board. After a new road was cut up the mountain in 1892, tallyhos (horse-drawn coaches) brought weekend guests from the city. In 1907 the Bluff Park Hotel was completed by J.A. Yates. Patrons danced to orchestra music, hiked to Sunset Rock or Lover's Leap to view the Oxmoor blast furnace and see the sun go down, or at night, to watch the Louisville & Nashville train pass through the valley below. In April 1907 Edith Ward London described in her diary an outing to Shades Mountain:

> John drove the big bay horses and a flat dray from the stable to Mountain Avenue where it was loaded with ice and picnic baskets, a folding cot, balls and bats and five hilarious boys, Anna Gage and myself. We drove to our old camping ground, the spring on Shades Mountain, where we

spent a peaceful blessed day. The boys were like wild Indians, and John regretted we had not taken the entire seventeen— the two block neighborhood supply.

The Bluff Park Hotel operated until 1923, then closed, but had just been redecorated for reopening when fire destroyed the building in 1925.

The numerous creeks and rivers in the county that once had furnished food for Indians and power to mill grain for pioneers, gave recreation and sport to modern man. As late as the 1930s there were still creeks close to residential areas where one might catch a bream, and city people who liked to fish seemed happy to throw their lines in any stream. On weekends the banks of Shades Creek, the Cahaba River, and Lake Purdy would be dotted with whites and blacks quietly cane-pole fishing. In the western part of the county there was good creek fishing at Rock Creek and Raccoon Branch, and to the north, Crooked and Ward Mill creeks were favorites. Phillip W. Holland, local black historian and ardent fisherman, rarely returned home without a long string of bass, bream, and crappie.

In her diary Olga Acton described a Birmingham Sunday in 1927 filled with Sunday school, church, and "getting back to the river for a good swim" in the Cahaba where a long rope swing would fly the young people over the river to drop into cool water. Down on the Warrior River, the high dam at Lock No. 17 had backed up Bankhead Lake, deep and clear for good fishing. The Redstone Club, Bell's Showboat,

and the Drennen home were fun places for house parties. Men who went off stag stayed in cabins at Yeargin's on Valley Creek or Smith's camp at Coal Bend Slough and they fished Walker County Shoals, or Prescott or White Oak creeks. Many families spent all summer in cottages at Manley Vines, Warrior River Estates, or Howton's. For years the highlight of July was the barbecue of the Alabama Fishermen and Hunters Association at Camp Oliver with Rainey Warren overseeing the cooking. It was an event that brought people from all over the state.

Everyone had a favorite swimming hole in a lake, creek, river, or rock quarry. There was a deep hole on Shades Creek between Oxmoor and Edgewood lakes where the Blankenship boys and the Edgewood crowd would swim. Four miles up the creek near Bearden's there was another swimming hole cherished by the McElwain group. To the north, Turkey Creek, a long meandering stream, was famous for its deep Blue Hole where the Pinson Baptist Church baptized its new members and the Akin and Thompson families swam. It was here, at Bull Frog Bend, that DuPont and Maude Massey Thompson camped in summers and later built a house. For decades the pine trees echoed the laughter of young and old enjoying life at Bull Frog Bend. Each year the Jefferson County Bar Association held their summer cookout and "Captain" Jack Phillips would stir up a wash pot full of Brunswick stew. "Steer roasters" like Richard Hail Brown, C.E. Rice, and Andrew Thomas would stay up all night, turning the pork on grates over the deep dug-out pit while sopping sauce over the meat.

Facing page: Nestled at the foot of Shades Mountain, Edgewood Lake was connected to Birmingham by streetcar. For years the lake was a popular place for fishing, sailing, and Sunday afternoon recreation. The Birmingham Motor and Country Club maintained a clubhouse here and held barbecues and dances on the lakeshore. During World War II the lake was drained and now part of the lakebed is the site of Homewood High School. Courtesy, Jackie Dobbs, Old Birmingham Photographs.

Above: The big spring at Avondale Park, once known as King's Spring, was a source of fresh, clean water for the farms and later the houses around it. During the 1880s and 1890s, there were free band concerts and plays at the park, and it was the scene of the elaborate semi-centennial celebration in October 1921. From the Department of Archives and Manuscripts, Birmingham Public Library.

Below: Members of the Catanzano family gathered at Turkey Creek on July 4, 1933, to celebrate Independence Day. The Catanzanos, one of Birmingham's old Italian families, operated a large grocery store and fish market on Fourth Avenue for many years and were influential leaders in Birmingham's large Italian community. Courtesy, Project Birmingfind.

CATANZANO BROS PICNIC
B'HAM JULY 4 1933 - TURKEY CREEK

Of Springs and Farms and Summer Places

There was good swimming at Robinwood, Tate's Spring (Cascade Plunge), and at the old Massey place (Tapawingo) where the Jefferson County militia drilled in the 1850s. Silver Lake, near Pinson, cast its spell, for legend told "It had no bottom" and only the brave would challenge its forbidding depths. Roebuck Spring produced the coldest swimming water in the county while West Lake, near Bessemer, had warmer water and a better beach. Mountain Lake beyond Shades Mountain was popular until it disappeared when a flood washed away the dam. Hallie Reed Riddle's diary has many references to picnics at "The Narrows" south of Birmingham during the summer of 1887. Riding by horse, buggy, or later Model-T across the Cahaba River and up Oak Mountain provided excitement, as did wading among the rocks and boulders. Hayrides to Robert Jemison's Spring Lake Farm near Roebuck on the old Clay Road or to the Pizitz farm on Shades Mountain were always looked forward to and remembered fondly. The Birmingham Horseback Club frequently rode out to Vinewood, the home of Dr. James E. Kent in Shades Valley, and only a suggestion was needed for them to ride on to Shades Mountain to sample W.C. White's famous scuppernong (muscadine) wine. Bicycle riding was a favorite recreation. Edith Ward London wrote about a ride to Woodlawn that "it was the most glorious day for riding a wheel." In her diary she told of cards, billiards, tennis, horseback riding, and fox

Below: *The relatives and neighbors of Lat V. Vines gathered at the Little Warrior River at Double Branch Ford in 1912 to witness his baptism. Lat Vines was a picturesque old riverman who owned hundreds of acres along the Warrior River. When he decided to be baptized, he refused to join the church. Finally, he found a Baptist preacher, Reverend Judd Waldrop of Concord Baptist Church, to baptize him. Courtesy, Jackie Dobbs, Old Birmingham Photographs.*

Facing page: *The Reverend and Mrs. Keener Mathews of Wesley Chapel took this group of young people on a bike ride to Fulton Springs in 1908. There they camped on the farm of Asa Hoyt. Fulton Springs was a favorite place for swimming, camping, and picnicking. Bike riding was always popular. Edith Ward London wrote about a ride to Woodland: "It was the most glorious day for riding a wheel." Courtesy, Flora Jones Beavers.*

hunting as popular recreations. In the Pratt City area, those of Welsh and Scottish background played soccer as a favorite pastime.

For decades the great event in the Mount Pinson area was the August 12 barbecue and picnic commemorating that day in 1861 when the men had marched off from Mount Pinson to fight in the Civil War. Stands were erected on the grounds of the Baptist Church and the crowds stretched all the way across the railroad tracks to the old Masonic Hall.

Dinner on the grounds and all-day singings, perhaps Christian harmony or Sacred Harp (fasola), would bring more folks than usual to church on Sunday. Families would arrive with baskets of food. The entire congregation of city churches would travel to the woods, perhaps to Caldwell's Mill on the Cahaba or Woodruff's Mill on Village Creek. Italian feast days, Greek religious holidays, and Russian festivals were also important social and recreational events for these immigrant communities. Decoration Days, like the one at McCalla, brought families together each May to visit while they cleaned up the local cemetery.

The Boy Scout program was organized in December 1910, and proved popular among the young men of the county. Judge N.B. Feagin called for volunteers and Donald Comer, Lee Brent, G.I. McDonald, and E.G. Burchfiel were early Scout Masters. The first campout was held in June 1913 at Mountain Lake beyond Shades Mountain. The following year 150 boys camped at Pole Cat Ridge above Queenstown Lake. In December 1915, Dr. Elwyn Ballard and N.H. Porter, with the help of the *Birmingham News*, began a drive to raise money for a permanent camp for Boy Scouts and young people. Dr. Ballard located a campsite on Kelly's Creek and his wife named the spot Winnataska. Boy Scouts camped there in 1915 and the next year a regular camp was opened.

Winifred Collins organized the first Girl Scout troop in 1919 as part of the Tennessee Coal, Iron and Railroad Company's Social Science Department activities. The girls held camp at Winnataska in 1923, and two years later purchased their own camp, which they named Camp Gertrude Coleman in honor of the first Jefferson County Girl Scout Commissioner. Early Negro Boy Scouts camped under the leadership of E.R. Johnson and P.D. Jackson. Later black Boy Scouts camped at Camp Nawaka, while girls went to Blossom Hill, named in honor of early Birmingham Girl Scout leader Mrs. Blossom Marmion.

In 1884 the Young Men's Christian Association was founded in Birmingham by Robert S. Munger, James Bowron, Robert Jemison, William Francis Tyler, and Edward Harmon Cabaniss. The YMCA purchased property on the old Gadsden Road near Keeler Mountain in 1922 and began Camp Cosby, which became a retreat and camping spot for three generations of boys and young men. For those children mired in industrial poverty who could not afford to attend a camp, Independent Presbyterian Church established a Fresh Air Farm on Shades Mountain in 1923. Robert R. Meyer's gift of $2,000 and 30 acres, coupled with donations and dozens of fund-raising projects and volunteer counselors, allowed hundreds of children to leave the smoke and smog of the city. Each summer they journeyed to the mountaintop to live with the beauties of nature, eat balanced meals, and learn good habits of health and cleanliness in a Christian and loving atmosphere. The church provided medical examinations and dental care by volunteer doctors and dentists. Each child was given his own small flower garden to tend, and music was an important part of each day.

Outside of Jefferson County there were favorite areas used for recreation, and in the early days, if an outing was planned to a distant place, a train would be

117

Of Springs and Farms and Summer Places

engaged to transport the group. In 1885 conductor G.R. Rutherford had charge of the excursion train that took 508 Methodists to Blount Springs for an all-day picnic. Blount Springs remained popular until 1915 when fire destroyed the resort hotel complex. Some people continued to come to the springs, camping out or renting rooms from farmers and residents in the area. Visiting children repeated tales of Duffee Mountain where Mary Gordon Duffee lived as a recluse. The Badham family had a home there, and Julia and Jack Cole built their summer retreat upon the old T.B. Maddox place, atop Robinson Mountain overlooking Blount Springs. The Coles' house was especially noted for its steep rail car tramway that ran down a cliff to a freezing spring-water swimming pool where hundreds of Jefferson Countians have been entertained for almost four decades.

Cook's Spring, another celebrated place, was in St. Clair County. In the summer 200 people at a time might arrive by train and be greeted by the hotel band. Mentone, perched upon Lookout Mountain, and Noccalula Falls near Gadsden, beckoned many city residents. Sunday afternoon train rides to Talladega Springs for Chautauqua lectures brought both pleasure and intellectual stimulation for adults who longed for a more advanced education. For those who dared, a trip down to Montgomery by Model-T was thrilling, but exhausting; it took an entire day. No one would think of making such a trip on chert roads without taking repair equipment and extra tires, and three or four punctures were common. On the way they might stop at Shelby Springs where there was a good hotel with excellent food.

While city residents sought the countryside for relaxation, county farmers came to town for excitement. Trips to Birmingham were fondly awaited. More prosperous visitors found quality merchandise at large department stores and might attend O'Brien's Opera House, the Jefferson Theatre, and later the Bijou or Orpheum theaters. Farmers would buy farm supplies on Second Avenue or staple groceries on Morris Avenue. If they brought produce to market, they would sell it to wholesalers or set up at the Farmer's Market. Some county farmers had regular door-to-door customers.

In the early days of the century, a trip to Birmingham might take two days by wagon, because roads were poor, unpaved, and not always passable. The *Warrior Index* constantly reported the bad condition of county roads, and complained that in wet weather there was no way for farmers to get to town. Wagons routinely crossed creeks at shallow rock shoals and deep rivers at ferries, such as the one run for years by

Above: *The Young Men's Hebrew Association was organized in Birmingham as a religious, social, and fraternal group, but later became the center of sports activity for Jewish young people. This was a YMHA championship basketball team from the 1920s. Courtesy, Jackie Dobbs, Old Birmingham Photographs.*

Facing page, top: *In 1923 the Independent Presbyterian Church established a Children's Fresh Air Farm on Shades Mountain as part of its mission work for economically deprived children. Volunteer counselors and workers, numerous fund-raising affairs and donations, and volunteer work by doctors and dentists enabled hundreds of children who could not otherwise have afforded to go to camp to spend time on the mountain living with nature. From the Department of Archives and Manuscripts, Birmingham Public Library.*

Facing page, bottom: *The Bluff Park Hotel was located on top of Shades Mountain. Completed in 1907 by J.A. Yates, the hotel quickly became a popular recreational spot. Patrons danced to orchestra music and hiked to Sunset Rock or Lover's Leap to view the Oxmoor furnaces, watch the sun set, or at night, look at the L&N train pass through the valley below. From the William H. Brantley, Jr. Collection, Samford University Library.*

119

Of Springs and Farms and Summer Places

Lane Vines on the Warrior River at Taylor's Ferry. Farmers coming from Blount County to Birmingham camped overnight at the spring across from Dolcito Quarry, sometimes stopping at G.W. Thompson's store. Farmers from Walker County coming down the Old Jasper Road or Warrior River Road and those coming from Shelby County by Columbiana Road or Montevallo Road had special camping places. Friends and neighbors often traveled together and the trip itself became a social affair.

Rural free mail delivery began in January 1901 and brought the county and the hills closer to the valley and Birmingham. A.J. Brown was an early postman who knew Route No. 4 so well he could locate the old wooden bridge over Shades Creek even when it was covered with flood waters. But one dark night during a storm he missed the bridge. Horse, carriage, postman, and mail swirled off down the creek. Brown climbed a tree and was later rescued. The mailbag was pulled from the creek, dried, and delivered. Charley Bailey, a postman on route No. 1, was the first in Jefferson County to initiate motorized mail delivery. In May 1908, with *Age-Herald* reporter Walter Harper riding shotgun, Bailey left the old post office on an experimental run. He completed the mail route in two hours and 35 minutes; by horse and buggy it was an eight-hour task.

As the city of Birmingham grew and its ethnic and Northern population increased, the city became more alien to the sleepy villages tucked into the hollows and dales of the county. But a number of special events helped to pull the city and the county together; the most important one was the Alabama State Fair. Beginning in 1889 the Alabama State Fair moved from Montgomery to Birmingham. A new road—Lomb Avenue—and a new bridge over Village Creek were constructed to improve travel to the old fairgrounds where a new grandstand seating 7,000 had been completed. Farmers came to exhibit and to inspect prize cows, horses, and hogs. Pickles, cakes, breads, jellies, and quilts were on display. Spectators enjoyed horse racing, band concerts, shooting matches, and Wild West shows. The Women's Christian Temperance Union served free ice water and tent saloons sold beer. Merchants and manufacturers put up elaborate exhibitions, and the Fair Committee staged special events to catch the imagination of the public. The sensation of the 1890 fair was the "balloon wedding" of Thomas J. Mims and Gertrude Pittman performed by the Reverend S.M. Adams high over Red Mountain. The ride ended abruptly, however, in a tree near Helena. The next year at the fair, the Reverend E. Nicholson performed a ceremony for H.S. Hutchinson and Minnie Cousson in a soaring balloon which came down on J.E. Goods'

Top: *The Birmingham YMCA's board of managers and representatives of the press and community break ground for the new YMCA building in 1911. Chartered in Birmingham in 1889, the YMCA first purchased the Webb home and then after a massive fund raising campaign it built the $200,000 facility that stands today on Twentieth Street. Courtesy, Mrs. A.C. Montgomery.*

Above: *Located on Eighth Avenue North, the Elks Club House was the scene of many parties and receptions. Courtesy, Jackie Dobbs, Old Birmingham Photographs.*

Facing page: *Company C of the Nineteenth Alabama Regiment, Confederate States of America, held its annual reunions during the Mount Pinson August Twelfth Picnics. At far left is Captain W.F. Hanby and eighth from the left is John M. Hudson. Courtesy, Tutt Thomason.*

farm between Coalburg and Brookside.

Another event that brought Jefferson County and Birmingham together was the Confederate Veterans Reunion. Four times—in 1894, 1908, 1916, and 1926—the veterans met in Birmingham and the city decked itself in red, white, and blue bunting for the occasion. The Birmingham chapter of the UCV, organized by Thomas Seay in 1889, sponsored the celebration, but the entire area joined hands. The leading Confederate veteran of Birmingham, General Edmund W. Rucker, hosted the special reunion of Forrest's Cavalry, a group he rode with and one particularly beloved in the city. The 1894 reunion was held at the Winnie David Wigwam, a mammoth temporary structure erected for convention headquarters on First Avenue between Twenty-second and Twenty-third streets. The highlights of the reunion were laying the cornerstone for the Confederate Monument at Capitol Park and the performance of the girls' chorus at the Wigwam. Maud Mims recalled that she was "so determined to be in the chorus" she had to almost defy her parents in order to stay in town after school to rehearse. Fifty years later she remembered the pageantry, the excitement of the parades, the visit of an ex-Confederate cousin she had never met, and what she wore to sing in—a "spring red dress with beautiful trimmings."

In 1910 the Census Jubilee, celebrating Birmingham's growth through annexation, was held at the Fairgrounds. Aviators Eugene Ely and J.J. Ward entertained with daring stunts. Mrs. William P. Sullivan shocked the crowd when she volunteered to be a passenger on a three minute flight, thus becoming the "first Southern woman to fly in an airplane."

But one of the most interesting festivals of early Birmingham occurred on April 24-25, 1913, when the city celebrated the famous "Potlatch," or "burying the hatchet." Politics had torn the city apart for several years. Politically the city was divided into two groups that called themselves the "Moral Elements," and the "Liberal Elements." They fought over prohibition, prostitution, and Sunday blue laws. Reformers attacked politicians; suburbs opposed the city government; newspapers were critical of the operation of utilities and monopolies and bitterly attacked the police department; citizens made charges and countercharges, and suits and countersuits were filed. The debate became bitter after 1911 when the state legislature instituted a commission form of government for Birmingham. Factionalism ran rampant and so threatened the life of the city that the chamber of commerce planned a festival. They publicly invited the hostile men to overlook their differences and promise to practice "peace on earth, good will to men." Invited were City Commissioner A.O. Lane and pastor of the First Baptist Church Dr. A.J. Dickinson; City Commissioner James Weatherly and president of the Birmingham Water Works A.M. Lynn; City Commissioner Culpepper Exum and Mr. Kelley of the Kelley street car interests; Fire Chief A.V. Bennett and president of the Trades Council E.S. Ingram; Park Commission Chairman John Kaul and attorney Frank W. Smith; president of the Birmingham Railway, Light and Power Company A.H. Ford and James Smith of the *Birmingham Ledger*; Police Chief G.H. Bodeker and *Birmingham News* editor Frank P. Glass. The people probably came more to watch these "well-known Birmingham antagonists" face each other than to see the peaceful parade that followed.

Of Springs and
Farms and
Summer Places

Below: *These men gathered in the Tutwiler Hotel lobby for the Confederate Reunion. In 1916, the city had 60,000 veterans, many of them housed in camps established at the Fairgrounds. Churches provided hot and inexpensive meals; the Red Cross established nurse stations with cots throughout the city; and the Boy Scouts helped escort the elderly veterans around Birmingham. Courtesy, Jackie Dobbs, Old Birmingham Photographs.*

Facing page, left: *General Edmund Winchester Rucker, who usually hosted the Confederate Veterans Reunions, came to Birmingham in the late 1880s from his home in Tennessee. Although he was involved with railroad development, iron manufacture, banking and investment firms, he is most well known as the highest ranking Confederate officer in the Birmingham area. General Rucker fought with General Nathan Bedford Forrest's cavalry and at the battle of Nashville in 1864 his left arm was so severely wounded that his Northern captors had to amputate it. Taken to Johnson's Island, General Rucker was soon released when General Forrest secured a special parole for him. Courtesy, Elizabeth Agee.*

Facing page, right: *Many Jefferson County men enjoyed the pastime of dove hunting and several companies operated hunting camps in South Alabama. Here a guest of the Woodward Iron Company, Mr. Wallingford from Cincinnati, is shown the woods by Adiel Wood and served an elegant lunch in the field by employees of the company. From the Woodward Iron Collection, University of Alabama Library.*

Big Chief Potlatch (R.A. Brown) and Princess Potlatch (Mrs. William Rogers, nee Lydia Eustis) arrived by car from Red Mountain amid much fanfare. At Capitol Park Chief Potlatch gave a speech on his mission "to preach the doctrine of get together" and the "boosting and upbuilding of Birmingham." Then, with great ceremony, he buried the hatchet "deep, deep down in the dark soil of Jones Valley." President of the Birmingham Chamber of Commerce, W.P.G. Harding, gave a speech about "too many tomahawks in Birmingham" and how the city was going to "put aside all troubles, no more callin' each other bad Indian. No more hurt each other's scalp. No more swipe each other's heads." The antagonists smoked the peace pipe, and 21 floats obtained from the New Orleans Mardi Gras paraded down Twentieth Street. The city rejoiced for two days. At East Lake there was a potlatch powwow and Indian ball, a great Potlatch fire, and a snake dance. Before many months the divisions were just as deep, but other issued were involved.

The International Balloon Race was another exciting event for the county and city. Selecting Birmingham because of the excellent gas-from-coal by-products plants, balloonists from all over the world met in the city. On October 23, 1920, with 50,000 citizens watching, dozens of balloons left the Sloss-Sheffield by-products plant in North Birmingham. A loud cheer went up when the city's entry, "The Birmingham,"

was cut loose, but the large group of Italians cheered loudest and the Birmingham Italian Band played most vigorously when Italy's two entries left the ground. Farmers in Jefferson County stopped plowing to watch the colorful balloons float over the treetops as they caught winds to the north. But "The Birmingham" came down in an Illinois cornfield and lost the race.

Schools held May Day exercises, which were big events. May Day was the most important day of the year for the TCI schools. Miss Collins, the director of the Social Science Department, planned the pageants. The costumes were made by the home economics department, and the children practiced at their own schools for separate black and white pageants. Special TCI trains picked up the children and their parents, usually on the first Saturday in May, and brought them to Arden Stadium for the festival. Each pageant had a special theme: a salute to King Cotton, folk dances to honor Iron and Steel, or a "Quest for Health" when the "Truths of the Ages" were called to assist in seeking "Health" which had been captured by "Disease." The music and dancing of the black pageants were of such high quality that whites frequently attended. Probably the most elaborate pageant ever presented in Jones Valley was the one that changed the name of the TCI village of Fossil to Wenonah.

For blue-collar workers who could not travel to the springs, and for farmers and rural folk who could not always afford to come to the city, the popular pastime, and Jefferson County's favorite game, was baseball. Whether played in a cow pasture, schoolyard, sandlot, or industrial league, baseball was major league in the hearts of Birmingham and Jefferson County. Schools, churches, companies, and

communities all had teams. The old Volunteer Baseball League composed of Pinson, Chalkville, Center Point, Clay, Bradford, Majestic, and in some years other teams, would play doubleheaders at the Twelfth of August Picnics at Pinson. Every crossroads had its ball field and team.

But it was in the industrial league of the Birmingham Amateur Baseball Federation that championships were most hotly contested. The men played for the companies where they worked and in industrial baseball's heyday, personnel officers were more concerned about a man's batting average and pitching ability than his job skills. Although 35 companies participated in the 1920s and 1930s, the teams from American Cast Iron Pipe (ACIPCO) and Stockham Pipe and Valve dominated league play and produced the greatest rivalry. Five thousand people would turn out when the ACIPCO "Pipers" played the Stockham "Valvers." Both teams won national championships three times, and the Birmingham Paper Company won once. Birmingham baseball produced many major league players, such as Ben Chapman, Dixie and Harry Walker, Virgie "Spud" Davis, and the Bragan boys.

Hosea Hudson, a black molder for Stockham, loved the ball games and recalled one weekday when he was laid off and he went to Ensley to see Stockham play: "Everybody was talking about Stockham and Ensley going to play ball. . . . Stockham had a guy pitching named Jesse Jeeters. He was the ace pitcher for Stockham. . . . He was among the best in Birmingham." There were no blacks on major-league ball clubs until after World War II, but many Birmingham blacks played on all-black teams. James West, the first baseman at Stockham in 1925, played with Cleveland for several years. One of ACIPCO's

Of Springs and
Farms and
Summer Places

Below: *As the number of automobiles in Birmingham increased, demands for better roads followed. In 1910 the* Birmingham Ledger *sponsored a Good Roads Tour. Here a group is headed over Red Mountain at Twentieth Street toward Montgomery. A trip to Montgomery was exhausting because it took the entire day. No one would think of making such a trip on churt roads without taking repair equipment and extra tires. From the William H. Brantley Jr. Collection, Samford University Library.*

Facing page, top: *The Birmingham City Fire Department decorated their horses and wagons for the Fireman's Parade. The parade was part of the 1908 Confederate Reunion in Birmingham. Samuel Thomas Merrit owned the decorated fire wagon on the left. Courtesy, Becky and Billy Strickland.*

Facing page, bottom: *Elaborate May Day pageants such as this 1930 one were put on by the TCI schools. Special TCI trains picked up the children and their parents and took them to Arden Stadium. There were colorful costumes and dancing, and the pageants were excellent. From the Harper Collection, Special Collections, Samford University Library.*

first black teams was so good that the players quit the company en masse and organized the Birmingham Black Barons professional baseball team. "Piper" Davis and Willie Howard Mays were two famous baseball products from Dr. E.J. Oliver's Fairfield Industrial High School.

Birmingham professional baseball had its beginnings at the old "Slag Pile" park on First Avenue near Fourteenth Street, close to the Southern Railroad tracks. One of the most famous games was on May 29, 1885, when C.J. Parsons pitched a no-hitter. By 1901 the old Southern Association was organized and 2,000 fans came to see Birmingham play Atlanta. Professional baseball in Birmingham entered its greatest period after 1909 when Allen Harvey Woodward purchased the minor league club. "Rick" Woodward, the son of an iron and steel family, had a flamboyant personality and a love for baseball. He grew up working in his father's plant and developed a passion for driving trains. As a boy he once drove the old streetcar "dummy engine" through downtown at a fast pace. When his father forbade such escapades he ran away from home to work on a locomotive in the West.

Woodward, who built a new ball park for his Birmingham Barons and named it Rickwood Field, always sought quality players for his team. On August 8, 1910, a crowd of 10,000 saw Birmingham defeat Montgomery 3-2. Baseball may only have been Rick Woodward's hobby, but it dominated the rest of his life and enriched the lives of city and county residents and the history of Birmingham and Jefferson County. Woodward brought night baseball and radio coverage to the city. Baron fans who could not come to the ball park could follow their favorite players by listening to WBRC with Eugene "Bull" Connor, a salesman for Hood-McPherson Furniture and Clark-Jones Pianos giving the play-by-play. Connor, who had been born in Dallas County, received his nickname in early life because of his booming voice, and later parlayed his popularity into a political career that had tremendous impact upon the history of Birmingham.

Favorite players who wore Baron uniforms included Harry "Buttermilk" Smith, "Stuffy" Stewart, "Yam" Yaryan, Walt Dropo, and Jimmy Piersall. The most exciting game ever played at Rickwood was in the opening game of the Dixie Series of 1931 when Ray Caldwell, a 43-year-old pitcher, outdueled Houston's 21-year-old sensation Dizzy Dean. The play Birmingham remembers best was when the game was scoreless and the city's own Billy Bancroft doubled to left field bringing Zach Taylor home and winning the

game by a single run. The *Birmingham News* sports reporter wrote that "The people almost tore the joint down." Although Dizzy Dean came back and Houston sent the series to seven games, Birmingham won the final game and their second Dixie Series.

During the Depression and World War II years, professional baseball suffered, but was revived by Eddie Glennon after 1947. Five years later Rufus M. Lackey, Albert Belcher, and Al DeMent purchased the club and in 1958 the Barons won another pennant. Baron attendance records consistently led the minor leagues. Although Charlie Finley's fiery personality and his fireworks behind the scoreboard increased interest in the Barons in the 1960s, by 1979 Harry Walker's University of Alabama in Birmingham team was playing baseball at Rickwood, and there were no Barons. But in the fall of 1980 the Barons were reorganized and the grand old tradition of Birmingham baseball resumed at Rickwood.

If baseball was first in the hearts of people, football was a very close second. Probably the first organized football game played in Birmingham was on November 11, 1892, when a team from the University of Alabama won over a group of players from Birmingham High School 56-0. Alabama players included future congressman William Bankhead who fondly recalled this famous football game played on the old cow-pasture baseball field near Lakeview. In a later game Alabama was defeated 5-4 by the Birmingham Athletic Club team when J.P. Ross's miracle dropkick of 65 yards scored a five-point field goal. Alabama came back the next month and beat the BAC team 14-0. But the *Birmingham News* was doubtful of the value of football. On November 2, 1897, in a blistering editorial, the *News* condemned the game as unhealthy, too violent, and dangerous.

Two major state universities, Alabama and Auburn, usually scheduled games in Birmingham during the season. In 1901 Alabama played Tennessee to a 6-6 tie and the next year was defeated by Auburn 23-0 at West End Park. The Alabama-Auburn games were the most popular, but were temporarily discontinued, and the great rivalry for the city then became the annual contest between two local colleges, Birmingham-Southern and Howard. The Panthers played the Bulldogs in the 1927 opening game when the new city football stadium, Legion Field, was dedicated to Alabama World War I heroes. Billy Bancroft, later a star player for the Birmingham Barons, scored all nine points for a Howard College victory. The stadium had been promoted by the

Of Springs and Farms and Summer Places

Junior Chamber of Commerce with the support of the American Legion and numerous citizens who purchased certificates. These certificates entitled the owner to purchase 50-yard-line seats to all games or activities held at Legion Field. Today those certificates still in circulation would, if sold, bring many times their face value.

From this beginning Legion Field and Birmingham football expanded together. The Crippled Chidren's Clinic games initiated in 1941 were played annually on Thanksgiving afternoon with the proceeds going to establish a facility for crippled children. The game brought together the top two "Big Five" high-school football teams in a city championship battle. Spirit was always high and the receipts from the full stadium eventually paid for the building of a hospital for afflicted young people. The outlying county high-school teams also played in a charity championship with proceeds going to fund mobile dental units for rural schools. Black high schools vied in the TB Bowl that supported the Birmingham Health and Negro Tuberculosis Association.

Two organizations, the Monday Morning Quarterback Club and the Touchdown Club, enthusiastically supported football. The "Big Game Day," since play resumed in 1948, has been the Auburn-Alabama game. The city dons red and white, orange and blue; hotels, motels, and family guest rooms all over town are full; restaurants hire extra hands to ring up the cash registers; and mothers of mixed households declare the family dinner table neutral territory. Wagering is rampant. There are flagrantly illegal bookie bets, the office football pools, and crazy personal wagers that make Monday-mornings-after special days of pain or pleasure for the bettors and days of hilarity for onlookers. One year a Birmingham man who supported Alabama rode a cow from Legion Field to Twentieth Street after his team lost to the "Cow College," and once a vocal Auburn supporter wore red slacks for a month. But the ultimate dream of Birmingham football promoters remains unfulfilled. Although the Americans and the Vulcans of the defunct World Football League tried, no National Football League team calls Legion Field home; however, the Hall of Fame Bowl each December has absorbed much of Birmingham's football pride and energy.

Springs and farms and summer places; fairs, festivals, parades, and celebrations; fishing, soccer, baseball, and football made life tolerable in an industrial city. Special places helped white-collar executives relax; special events introduced excitement into the lives of blue-collar laborers. And all of these activities tended to bring the people of Jefferson County, living in the lovely hills and hollows, closer to the people living in Jones Valley's Birmingham.

Clockwise from top:

This Bessemer baseball team, circa 1913, included Smith Edge, Chie Wallace, Cleve Earnest, and Bob Bumgardner. Baseball was one of the favorite pastimes of Jefferson Countians. Every crossroads community had its own ball field and team. Courtesy, the Bessemer Hall of History

Everyone could play in the Birmingham Amateur Baseball Federation. The city did not have a Little League for the young boys and being old enough and good enough to make the local team was a big accomplishment in any young man's life. Here, the Woodward Iron Company team's catcher instructs his pitcher. From the Woodward Iron Collection University of Alabama Library.

Baseball was, whether cow pasture, schoolyard, sandlot, or industrial league, number one with the residents of Birmingham and Jefferson County. Schools, churches, companies, and communities all had teams. In the industrial league, the most hotly contested games were between teams from the American Cast Iron Pipe Company and Stockham Pipe and Valve. There were black teams and white teams. This is one of the championship black teams from the late 1930s. Courtesy, Stockham Pipe and Valve Company.

Billy Bancroft was one of Birmingham's most celebrated athletic heroes. In 1927, as a Howard College football player, he led the Bulldogs to a 9-0 victory (scoring all nine points) over Birmingham-Southern College in the Legion Field dedication game. As a professional baseball player for the Birmingham Barons in 1931 in the Dixie Series opening game, he doubled to left field, allowing Zach Taylor to score and Birmingham to win the game 1-0. The game is considered the greatest baseball game every played in Birmingham. Courtesy, Betsy Bancroft.

Chapter X

FROM DEPRESSION TO THREE SHIFTS A DAY

Birmingham at night, looking west toward the Alabama Power Company Building. The statue of Electra can barely be seen in the blaze of light atop the building. Beyond the Temple Theatre the First Methodist Church steeple can be seen. Photograph by Charles F. McFarlin. Courtesy, Betsy Bancroft.

The 1920s opened with Birmingham's anticipation of surpassing New Orleans and Atlanta to become the South's most populous city. Birmingham had 178,806 residents in 1920 with 310,054 in the metropolitan area. The Chamber of Commerce even spoke of the Magic City challenging Chicago within two decades, but the next 25 years did not unfold as Birmingham hoped. The Roaring Twenties, the so called Jazz Age, is frequently portrayed as a period of flappers, elegant entertaining, jazz music, the Charleston, Prohibition, the airplane, and the Ford automobile. And they were indeed all part of the 1920s in Birmingham.

From Depression to Three Shifts a Day

During this decade the residential areas of the city spread from Highland Avenue to Mountain Terrace and Redmont, over Red Mountain into Shades Valley. Edgewood was advertised as the subdivision "without a railroad crossing" and "free of smoke and dust." Hollywood real-estate salesmen suggested buyers move "out of the smoke, come into the ozone." The company of Robert Jemison, Jr., developed the Redmont area on the Shades Valley side of Red Mountain, then established Mountain Brook Estates on 400 acres of land along Watkins Creek. The village was centered around a shopping area of English Tudor design and roads curved with the land around estate-sized lots. Jemison organized the Mountain Brook Land Company to develop additional property along Shades Creek. Although John Perryman's antebellum mill had long since disappeared, Jemison built another on this spot and it became the symbol of the new town. One resident recalled that "real-estate fortunes were made overnight" and men rushed to their offices to make "rich deals." Homewood and Edgewood were served by streetcar transportation, but only the automobile made it possible for men to commute from Hollywood and Mountain Brook, a suburb frequently called the "bedroom of Birmingham" since so many of the city's business and industrial leaders lived there and worked in Birmingham.

In 1927 the Country Club of Birmingham moved into Shades Valley, occupying a new 300-acre golf course and a new clubhouse of English Tudor design located between Redmont and Mountain Brook. Two years later Jemison added the Mountain Brook Club to his Mountain Brook Land Company development. As many of the residents of older neighborhoods — Highland Avenue and South Highlands, Bush Hills and Norwood — moved into Shades Valley, Mountain Brook became the focus of Birmingham society and the elite residential section of the city. Its two country clubs were the scene of debutante balls, black-tie dinners, and the activities of the golf and tennis crowd. The 1920s pictured in F. Scott Fitzgerald's *The Great Gatsby* were to be found here in the elegant salons of mansions and country clubs.

For the middle class the 1920s were also prosperous; but for the many farmers in the hill country of Jefferson County, for the laboring men of the mines and mills, and for those unemployed in the city, the general prosperity the nation enjoyed was not shared. For that matter the entire South did not experience the boom that affected much of the rest of the country in the 1920s, and Birmingham business was somewhat depressed after 1926. This was partly due to reverberations from the collapse of the Florida eal-estate market and from the frenzied speculation weeping the nation. The farm-to-city migrations that ad begun during World War I brought farmers and harecroppers to Birmingham and Jefferson County eeking employment and the good life. This increased he pool of unskilled labor, did nothing to help lready depressed wage scales, and placed additional urdens of relief and welfare on city government and rivate organizations such as the Red Cross and Community Chest. Furthermore rural people thrust nto an urban industrial setting had numerous djustments to make. The Jefferson County Red Cross report of 1927 blamed "overpopulation" of the ity as one reason for the "quiet" industrial onditions in Birmingham, noting a "gradual upward rend in unemployment after 1925." Social problems plagued the area and financial stringency gripped city government as demands for services continued to ncrease more rapidly than tax revenues. Inadequate ducation for both white and black children, and the osts of maintaining separate school systems ncreased the burden. There were conflicts over law nforcement and crime within the city. The decade nded with the stock market crash of 1929, the greatest economic crisis the United States had ever aced. And Birmingham was labeled the "hardest hit ity" in the nation.

Facing page, right: *Robert Jemison, Jr. was a man of vision, dreams, and enthusiasm. He worked with TCI in the development of its model industrial city Corey (Fairfield) and guided his company in the promotion of "over-the-mountain" residential areas like Redmont and Mountain Brook. He usually formed separate land companies to develop the properties. His Spring Lake Farm on the Old Clay Road was a popular place for hayrides and outings until it was subdivided after World War II. From the Department of Archives and Manuscripts, Birmingham Public Library.*

Facing page, left: *Margaret Gage Bush, shown here in 1931, was the grand dame of Birmingham society for four decades. Born in Charleston, South Carolina, she married Morris Bush, a wealthy industrialist of Birmingham who was many years her senior. They had one child—Gage. Mrs. Bush was left a young widow and in the years that followed, she became the unofficial hostess of the city, entertaining all the official visitors to Birmingham including opera stars, politicians, artists, and writers. From the Auburn University Archives.*

Below: *The 1920s opened with Birmingham's anticipation of surpassing New Orleans and Atlanta as the South's most populous city. The chamber of commerce even spoke of the Magic City vying with Chicago within two decades. This view of Twentieth Street in the 1920s shows the L&N Railroad Station, Metropolitan Hotel, Woodward Building, and Empire Building on the left side of the street and the First National Bank Building, the Brown Marx Building, Frank Nelson Building, Watts Building, and Tutwiler Hotel on the right. Courtesy, Jackie Dobbs, Old Birmingham Photographs.*

From Depression to Three Shifts a Day

Above: *After the Birmingham Public Library moved into its new building in 1927, the Jefferson County Free Library operated out of this truck offering books and library service to rural Jefferson County. In this photo, circa 1930, the book truck calls on the commissary at Sayre, a mining community in western Jefferson County. The arrival of the book truck was an important event for the bright young children and adults of the isolated communities of the county; books brought the world to their doorsteps. From the Birmingham Public Library.*

Facing page, top: *When President Warren G. Harding visited Birmingham on October 26, 1921, he attended the inaugural exercises of Guy E. Snavely as president of Birmingham Southern College and received an honorary doctorate degree in law from Birmingham Southern College. He later spoke at Woodrow Wilson Park to a large audience and surprised Birmingham by selecting "the negro" as his topic. He advocated more educational, economic, and political advantages for black people. Turning to the white portion of the audience and leaving his prepared text, the President said: "Whether you like it or not, our democracy is a lie unless you stand for that equality." The black section of the audience applauded, but the whites remained silent. Courtesy, James F. Sulzby, Jr.*

Facing page, right: *St. Paul's Catholic Church, constructed in 1893, was the target of threats during the height of anti-Catholic sentiment in the early twentieth century. At one time, the church was under armed guard at night. Father James E. Coyle was shot by Reverend E.R. Stephenson while the former sat on the porch of the rectory. Courtesy of Jackie Dobbs, Old Birmingham Photographs.*

Facing page, bottom: *The social problems and tension of the 1920s were reflected in the rise of the Ku Klux Klan. Birmingham's Robert E. Lee Klan was Alabama's first klavern and for many years was the most powerful. By 1924 it boasted 18,000 members. The klan spread as a patriotic organization with a secret and elaborate ritual controlling many government officials. As the decade of the twenties progressed, the klan was associated with more and more violence, until it was discredited and lost both power and respect. But during the mid-Twenties, no one could be elected to any office in Alabama without klan connections, membership, and approval. This is why Hugo Black joined the klan. Courtesy, Birmingham News.*

Perhaps the events of 1920-21 should have forewarned of trouble. Although the semi-centennial celebration of October 1921 was the highlight of these years, there was also a bitter coal strike, a sensational murder, a large Ku Klux Klan rally at the Fairgrounds, a furor over charges of police-protected prostitution, and a mild economic recession. Since the area was so dependent upon heavy industry, labor strikes unsettled the economy and polarized the population. Margaret Mitchell Bigalow, a historian of early Birmingham, observed the "interesting phenomenon that the rural people who came into the city to labor in mines and furnaces quickly became unionists while the other rural folk in the town retained a traditional opposition." Merchants and industrialists were anti-union. During the coal strike Birmingham businessmen issued a statement in 1920 supporting Governor Thomas E. Kilby's use of the National Guard. They favored his pro-operator arbitration settlement and condemned the United Mine Workers' representatives in the city. At the same time 2,000 delegates attending the Birmingham Trades Union Council denounced Kilby's anti-union stand. The main issue in this strike, union representation, was not won; UMW membership fell to 2 percent, and many strikers were forced to leave the district since blacklists prevented them from getting jobs.

The social problems and tensions of the decade were reflected in a ceremony on a cold, wet January night in 1921. Cars with covered license tags converged on the Alabama Fairgrounds. Armed horsemen guarded the site. In the center of the racetrack, white-robed men holding lights formed a living cross that seemed to rise from a throne where a purple-gowned man was sitting. Five hundred white-clad candidates marched four abreast toward the platform. They were being initiated into the Robert E. Lee Klan, No. 1, Knights of the Invisible Empire, Ku Klux Klan. This group was founded in 1915 in Atlanta by William Joseph Simmons (who claimed to be a Birmingham native but actually was from Harpersville, Alabama). The organization, with its secret and elaborate ritual, soon spread. Birmingham's Lee Klan, organized by Simmons himself in 1916, was the first klavern in Alabama and for many years, the most powerful, boasting 18,000 members by 1924.

The first evidence of Klan activity in Jefferson County occurred when a strike leader visited a defense plant and the "Invisible Empire intervened." The newspapers reported the man has not been "heard of since." The Klan pictured itself as the protector of Americanism, the Caucasian race, and the moral and religious tenets of Protestantism. It also opposed strikes and unions, dancing and

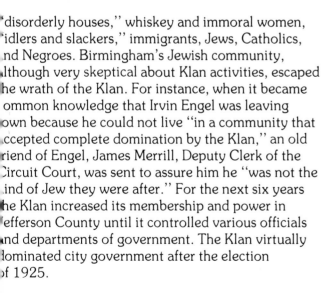

"disorderly houses," whiskey and immoral women, "idlers and slackers," immigrants, Jews, Catholics, and Negroes. Birmingham's Jewish community, although very skeptical about Klan activities, escaped the wrath of the Klan. For instance, when it became common knowledge that Irvin Engel was leaving town because he could not live "in a community that accepted complete domination by the Klan," an old friend of Engel, James Merrill, Deputy Clerk of the Circuit Court, was sent to assure him he "was not the kind of Jew they were after." For the next six years the Klan increased its membership and power in Jefferson County until it controlled various officials and departments of government. The Klan virtually dominated city government after the election of 1925.

Differences on moral and political issues in Birmingham between Catholics and Protestants at the turn of the century, and the activities of a secret anti-Catholic group called the "True Americans," provided a fertile foundation for the Klan's anti-Catholicism. Many Birmingham Catholics were intimidated and lost jobs. Gone was the spirit of tolerance evident in the early city when some of Birmingham's pioneer and most beloved families— the O'Briens, O'Connors, Cahalans, and Whelans— were Catholics. Night riders burned a convent and Catholic school at Pratt City and armed guards were stationed during the night at St. Paul's in downtown Birmingham when federal authorities warned of a plot to burn the church.

The most sensational incident of violence however, was the murder of Father James E. Coyle, rector of St. Paul's. The priest was shot by a Methodist minister, the Reverend E.R. Stephenson, who had no church, but was known as the "courthouse minister" because he married so many couples there. Stephenson, who was enraged because Father Coyle had married his only daughter, Ruth, to a middle-aged Catholic Puerto Rican paperhanger, Pedro Gussman, attacked the priest as he sat on the front porch of the rectory. Father Coyle had long been the object of attacks of anti-Catholics, but the city was stunned by Coyle's murder. Although most citizens were aware of the city's problems, they bitterly resented the coverage of the *Nation*'s reporter,

133

From Depression to Three Shifts a Day

Above: *The murder of Father James E. Coyle, rector of St. Paul's Catholic Church, was the most sensational violent incident to occur during the 1920s when the Ku Klux Klan was vehemently anti-Catholic. Coyle was shot by Methodist minister E.R. Stephenson who was extremely angry at Father Coyle for marrying his daughter Ruth to Pedro Gussman, a Catholic. From St. Paul's Catholic Church Archives.*

Facing page, top: *Driven by Kathleen Franklin, this was one of Jefferson County's first school buses. It served the Alliance School in the western area of the county near Toadvine. Eula Richardson, Liladel Vance, and Madge Salter are seen boarding the bus. Transportation has been a continuing problem in Jefferson County and the county's schools were faced with transporting students over very poor roads to consolidated high schools. Courtesy, Jackie Dobbs, Old Birmingham Photographs.*

Facing page, middle: *In an area of poor roads with people too poor to own cars, streetcar transportation was important. Here, the row houses on Thirty Seventh Street and Fifth Avenue North face a dirt road and streetcar tracks. Grass yards were unheard of; one simply swept the yard clean with a broom. Courtesy, Sam Rumore.*

Facing page, bottom: *Since motor vehicles gave the Klan mobility, secrecy, and speed, it is not surprising that the rise of the Ku Klux Klan paralleled the rise of the automobile. Birmingham streets had been designed for the horse and buggy and the increased number of cars in the city caused many problems. Though streets in downtown Birmingham were wide, there was no electric traffic light system downtown until 1923. Courtesy, James F. Sulzby, Jr.*

Charles Sweeney, who called Birmingham "the American hotbed of anti-Catholic fanaticism." This was not the first time that Birmingham was indignant over news coverage, nor would it be the last. Stephenson was indicted on a charge of second-degree murder, but former county prosecutor Hugo L. Black headed a team of lawyers whose defense resulted in a unanimous verdict of not guilty by reason of temporary insanity.

Indeed Stephenson was considered insane by the vast majority of citizens, yet the violence of the Klan increased. As floggings and harassments occurred with regularity in the county and city, officials who earlier had denied Klan involvement in these crimes stood to rebuke the Klan. The *Post* and *Age-Herald* pointed a finger at the Klan in many editorials and condemned mob violence. Even Sheriff Thomas J. Shirley, whose Klan connections were well known, finally voiced a strong appeal for the apprehension of persons guilty of violent acts. The Reverend Jack Johnston, pastor of the Eleventh Street Baptist Church, said he had always "had a very high regard for the Klan, but if this is their method of doing business, then I am ready to change my opinion of them. Let us stop the floggings at any cost."

By 1925 Klan strength peaked in the rest of the country, but the height of Klan power in Jefferson County was not reached until 1927 when a 19-year-old orphan boy from Blount County, Jeff Calloway, was seized during a Sunday night service at the Antioch Baptist Church. Calloway was abducted and beaten severely because he had been drinking. Dr. Henry M. Edmonds of Independent Presbyterian Church challenged his congregation to fight for righteousness in the open as Jesus did, saying: "Every Alabamian ought to be fighting at this minute over the Oneonta whipping of a defenseless boy by a group of men." Dr. E.R. Hendrix, minister at Highlands Methodist Church, denounced the Klan and preached that the cross which symbolized the "hope of a sinful soul" should not become "a terror at the front gate . . ." and that the American flag was "out of place at a mask and lash party."

Those responsible for Calloway's flogging were caught, tried, and found guilty. This first conviction against the Klan was the beginning of the end and the Klan finally began to crumble. In December 1927 the Klan announced plans for a statewide parade with 25,000 to 50,000 klansmen participating. Birmingham Mayor Jimmy Jones reminded the Grand Dragon, as he issued him the parade permit, of the city's new ordinance against covered car licenses. The Klan leader replied that they would walk. The ight of the parade, it rained and turned cold. A *Birmingham News* reporter counted only 828 men, ~02 women, 4 children, and 2 vehicles with muddied ~gs. More significantly the marchers were jeered and ~eckled by a few spectators and by drivers upset ~ver blocked traffic. One man, hanging from a third-~oor fire escape, shouted the password for Barney ~oogle's secret organization, the Billy Goats, a ~artoon mockery of the Klan. Although the Klan was ~ctive in the presidential election of 1928, and never ~ompletely disappeared from Jefferson County, it was ~uiet during the 1930s and almost vanished in the ~940s. In the 1950s the Klan revived, but its days of ~olitical power and widespread following ~anished forever.

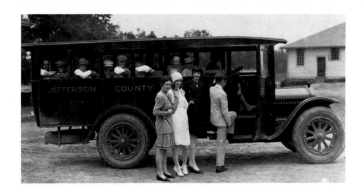

~hat the rise of the KKK paralleled the rise of the ~utomobile was no coincidence. Motor vehicles gave ~he Klan mobility, secrecy, and speed by allowing ~ansportation where public trolleys did not go. The ~creased number of cars in the city caused many ~roblems since streets and roads had been designed ~or horse and buggy. Jefferson County had ~pproximately 16,000 motor vehicles by 1920. ~ithin ten years this increased to 70,000, which ~epresented 25.3 percent of all the registered vehicles ~ the state of Alabama. In the city, policemen were ~ationed at downtown intersections to direct traffic, ~ometimes an impossible task. Complicating traffic ~ms were "jitneys," large old touring cars or trucks ~hat had been refitted with several crude bench seats ~ carry 12 to 20 people. They frequently carried ~ommuters from small towns in the county to the ~ity, and often competed with taxicabs and street ~ailway transportation on downtown streets. The City ~ommission banned jitneys from the central business ~istrict in 1923 and regulated their dangerous ~perations. A modern system of traffic lights was ~nstalled that year and the traffic code greatly ~xpanded, but congestion continued to be a problem.

~he 1920s was also the decade of the airplane and ~irmingham was a leader in aviation. As early as ~909 E.F. Odum built a plane. The Birmingham ~lying Club was organized in 1919 by Major James ~. Meissner, a World War I flying ace. Meissner's ~'Early Birds," reorganized as the 106th Observation ~quadron of the Alabama Air National Guard, were ~sing a 90-acre "air patch" donated by Republic ~teel. Built in 1922 the airfield was named Roberts ~ield in memory of Lieutenant Arthur M. Roberts, a ~irmingham flyer killed in 1918 in France. There ~ere no paved runways and no lights on the field. ~hen the pilots had to land after dark, they found the ~irstrip by the glow of the Republic furnace pouring ~teel and the slag heap reflecting red against the sky. ~ioneer Birmingham pilots were John B. Thomas,

From Depression to Three Shifts a Day

John M. Donaldson, and Donald Croom Beatty, who later became internationally renowned as an explorer for his Latin American Expedition of 1931-1932, as an inventor for his electronic communication systems, and as a pilot and executive for Pan-American Grace Airways.

Aviation activity increased after Glenn E. Messer, nationally famous stunt pilot, decided to stay in the city in 1920 and lease an airfield with Eddie Stinson. The two built the Dixie Flying Field with the help of Virgil Evans and began to train pilots. Messer met Charles A. Lindbergh in the early 1920s when he went to Georgia to pick up a plane. Lindbergh was there to do the same, but had never flown that style plane. Messer gave him a test flight in the "Jenny" airplane and Lindbergh flew off on his very first solo flight toward home and fame. When Lindbergh was on his way to Paris in 1926, the *Age-Herald* called him "the flying fool" and warned "the time is not at hand for transatlantic aviation." After Lindbergh reached Paris, the *Age-Herald* "jettisoned its skepticism" and prophesied that "crossing the ocean in aeroplanes will soon be no more perilous than going down to the sea in ships." Four days after Lindbergh reached France, Major Sumter Smith of Birmingham flew a Jefferson County state legislator to Washington, D.C., to prove the feasibility of airmail, and in July 1927 the Post Office initiated round-trip airmail service between New Orleans, Mobile, Birmingham, and Atlanta.

To encourage aviation and convince the American people that air travel was safe and dependable, Lindbergh embarked on a nationwide tour and arrived in Birmingham, his only stop in Alabama, on October 5, 1927. The day was designated "Lindbergh Day" in the city, and schools closed early for the festivities. The *Spirit of St. Louis* touched down at Roberts Field at exactly 1:57 p.m. and Lindbergh was greeted by cheering crowds. He motorcaded to the fairgrounds, gave a brief speech, later had a press conference in the Louis XIV Suite of the Tutwiler Hotel, and attended a banquet at the Municipal Auditorium. Master of ceremonies Hugh Morrow and Governor Bibb Graves toasted the hero. In his speech Lindbergh asked the city of Birmingham to construct a municipal airport and to support commercial aviation and airmail. His visit, planned by the Junior Chamber of Commerce and directed by Thad Holt, Mark Hodo, and Major Sumter Smith, was a resounding success. Plans were made immediately for a new landing facility for Birmingham.

In the 1920s the city embarked upon a school building program. The burned-out Central High School was replaced by the John Herbert Phillips

Facing page, top: *John Herbert Phillips High School was considered the best academic preparatory school in Birmingham. Young people would ride trolley cars or buses to attend school. The school's namesake, Dr. John Herbert Phillips, came to Birmingham in 1883 and six years later became superintendent of the city's schools, a position he held until his death in 1921. Courtesy, Jackie Dobbs, Old Birmingham Photographs.*

Facing page, bottom: *In the spring of 1921, the people of the community of Pinson (then called Mount Pinson and before the Civil War, Hagoods Cross Roads) met at the Baptist Church to discuss the school situation. The children needed a better school, but Jefferson County lacked the funds to help build one, so the people collected donations to buy the land, and then built the school themselves. This six-room schoolhouse was constructed during 1921 and 1922 and was occupied by the children in September 1922. Courtesy, James Price.*

Top left: *This replica of an old Curtis Pusher with a newly designed motor, was brought to Birmingham for a 1937 air show. These air shows attracted large crowds to the Birmingham airport. Courtesy, Jackie Dobbs, Old Birmingham Photographs.*

Above left: *Glenn Messer, early Birmingham aviation pioneer and genius, stands beside this original experimental Air Bass model that he built in 1926 to demonstrate his theory of balance. This two-seated plane with its extremely short fuselage was manufactured in Birmingham for several years. Other airplane manufacturers soon used Messer's design. Courtesy, Glenn E. Messer.*

Above: *Early Birmingham aviator Donald Croom Beatty poses by his airplane at Roberts Field in the 1920s. Later, Beatty became famous for a Latin American expedition in 1931-32 and was a pioneer in South American aviation for Pan-American Grace Airways. Courtesy, Mary Alice Beatty Carmichael.*

From Depression to Three Shifts a Day

High School and Dr. A.H. Parker's dream for a new black high school materialized in the "New Industrial High School," later named for its first principal, Dr. Parker. Fairfield Industrial High School was organized in 1924 and for 43 years its principal was Dr. E.J. Oliver, a beloved black educator. Fairfield produced a remarkable number of graduates who achieved honor and success in life, including "Piper" Davis and Willie Mays in baseball, Jim Tolbert in football, General Oliver W. Dillard of the U.S. Army, and Birmingham Mayor Richard Arrington. Although these schools stressed job-related training and industrial skills, they provided a good academic foundation and the best educational opportunities for blacks in Jefferson County. Those students bound for college, perhaps Miles College or Daniel Payne College in Jefferson County, received their educational foundations here. Although numerous school programs were instituted to help blacks, they were still insulted by Jim Crow laws, such as streetcar segregation, and were hampered by lack of skills and education. The abolition of the convict-lease system in 1928 opened up more mining jobs for free black labor. Coming just before the Depression, however, these jobs proved only temporary.

One of the best opportunities for Birmingham Negroes was through music. Singing had always been an integral part of black religious services and in the 1920s there was an explosion of musical talent. Julia Wilkerson, wife of Malachi Wilkerson, a much-beloved teacher himself, was teaching music at Industrial High School where she encouraged and trained many young people. Gospel and quartet groups like the Dolomite Jubilee Singers, the Rolling Mill Four, and the Heavenly Gospel Singers, began singing over radio stations WAPI, WBRC, and Bessemer's WJLD, as well as entertaining at churches and parties. Charles Bridges, known for his magnificent baritone and harmony techniques, formed the area's most famous quartet—the Birmingham Jubilee Singers. With Lot Key, Dave Ausbrooks, and Ed Sherrill, it became Alabama's first professional quartet to land a recording contract. The Jubilee Singers performed outside the state, and by 1929 were the top black quartet on Columbia records. They toured with Ethel Waters and cut such hit records as "Sweet Mama, Tree Top Tall," "Southbound Train," and the "Birmingham Boys."

Southern harmony was not the only type of music made famous by Birmingham blacks. William C. Handy organized his first brass band when he was working at the U.S. Pipe foundry in Bessemer before he left for Memphis and "blues" fame. Birmingham blacks were quick to experiment with the new sounds wafting up from New Orleans and down from New

York. This new music, exciting the young, shocking the old, became known as jazz. Calvin Ivory, one of Birmingham's first jazz musicians, began playing the cornet for medicine shows around Birmingham. In 1919, when Fess Whatley started teaching at the high school, he switched Ivory to the clarinet and he became the first jazz reed player at Industrial High School. Whatley organized a band called the Jazz Demons which played at dances, in hotels and clubs all over the county and introduced Birmingham to the sound of the 1920s. Ivory soon headed for New York where he worked with Bill Robinson and Fats Waller, but returned in the late 1930s to teach music at Industrial (now Parker) High School. Seven of his students eventually played with Birmingham musician Erskine Hawkins's band. During the Big Band era Glenn Miller selected one of Hawkins's songs about an Ensley streetcar stop as the flip side of a single. This number by Hawkins became Miller's greatest hit as people all over the world danced to "Tuxedo Junction."

The reality of life in a segregated Southern city amid poverty not only produced a distinctive and enriching black subculture, it also produced white stereotypes. Birmingham's black community of the 1920s and 1930s became known to whites across America through the Octavus Roy Cohen stories published in the *Saturday Evening Post*. Cohen, a writer for the *Birmingham Ledger*, wrote 168 stories for the *Saturday Evening Post*, describing a group of urban blacks such as Florian Slappey, Lawyer Evans Chew, and Julius Caesar Clump and their comic antics in the area of Eighteenth Street and Fourth Avenue North. Although the stories were humorous, there was little similarity to real blacks of the area and no understanding of dialect. Birmingham black attitudes toward Cohen's tales varied. Dr. A.H. Parker thought Lawyer Chew a "monstrosity" and an insult to the

Facing page, top: *The Birmingham Municipal Airport opened the summer of 1931 with an exciting air show. Though the terminal was a busy place during World War II when people waited for loved ones to return, most people traveled by train and the train station was the busier place—during the war and directly after. With the great expansion of air traffic in the 1950s, Birmingham was hurt by a high state tax on aviation fuel. Courtesy, Jackie Dobbs, Old Birmingham Photographs.*

Facing page, bottom: *Black architects Taylor E. Persley and Walter T. Woods designed the Black Masonic Temple in 1922. In the early years the Booker T. Washington Insurance Company and the state headquarters of the black Masonic organizations were housed here. This building was the scene of black social activities during the years of segregation. Today, the building is used less as a social center, but it still provides office space for black doctors, dentists, accountants, and lawyers. Courtesy, Jackie Dobbs, Old Birmingham Photographs.*

Top: *Former Industrial High School printing teacher Fess Whatley performs with his band in the 1920s. For four decades Whatley's various bands were in great demand, playing at high school proms, civic club dances, and debutante balls. Whatley's band was originally called the Jazz Demons and it introduced Birmingham to the sound of the 1920s. From the Department of Archives and Manuscripts, Birmingham Public Library.*

Above: *One of the city's popular black singing ensembles was the Louisville and Nashville Railroad Company's Old Reliable Choral group. Benjamin F. Adams and Maurice W. Ryles directed the group. Courtesy, Jackie Dobbs, Old Birmingham Photographs.*

From Depression to Three Shifts a Day

state bar, while Mrs. August Zuber, secretary of the black YWCA, called Cohen's characters "buffoons" and not real people. Although neither believed that race relations were affected by the stories, attitudes of both whites and blacks were affected. One white writer observed that Birmingham's Eighteenth Street blacks bore little resemblance to Cohen's Negroes until they read the stories and began to imitate the characters.

Cohen organized the Loafers Club, a group of Birmingham writers who met and discussed writing as an art and a profession. Among this group at various times were Jack Bethea, James Saxon Childers, Eric Levison, Henry Vance, Jack Caldwell, and James E. Chappell. The membership changed over the years with the interest in fiction writing among Birminghamians with literary ambitions. Other writers associated with the Loafers Club were David Solomon, Edgar Valentine Smith, Perkins J. Prewitt, Artemus Calloway, Garrard Harris, and Petterson Marzoni.

There were, however, a number of real black characters in the community who were famous to Birmingham whites but never made the pages of national magazines. One was a young Negro woman known throughout Birmingham as "Walking Chaney" because she walked everywhere with a long stride and a fast gait. Once when a child asked her why she never rode the streetcars, she said: "Because I don't have time." Stories about her abound. She had a reputation as an excellent cook and her large, high-rise biscuits were legendary. The amount of work she could accomplish in a short time has increased with the telling. One story relates that she was "slightly tipsy," was put in the Birmingham Jail, was horrified at the dirt, asked for soap and water, and cleaned up the entire "Big Rock" before daybreak! Then there was "Whistling Jim" who

Below: *In the 1930s the Adamsville Cafe had the typical separate entrances for white and colored patrons. Adamsville was a small town that grew up along the Jasper Highway on the farmland belonging to William Adams when the coke ovens and mines began to open up in this area in the late 1880s. The town was not incorporated until 1901 and had no charter until 1950. At the turn of the century it was known as a rough, hard-drinking frontier town with many saloons and wooden side-walks. During the 1920s, the Ku Klux Klan made many visits to Adamsville and once closed a dance hall there. Courtesy, Jackie Dobbs, Old Birmingham Photographs.*

Below right: *This 1926 photo shows the East End Cafe which was located at 111 North Twenty-fourth Street. During the segregation years, eating establishments, if they elected to serve both white and colored patrons, were required to have separate entrances for blacks and to provide a partition between the areas so neither side could see the other. For a white to eat at a table with a black was considered taboo. That is why Southerners were so shocked when President Theodore Roosevelt invited Booker T. Washington to lunch with him at the White House. Courtesy, Jackie Dobbs, Old Birmingham Photographs.*

Facing page: *In this Arthur H. Parker High School social science class young women are learning about hand and hair care. Originally called the New Industrial High School, the school stressed industrial skills and trade education. Courtesy, Jackie Dobbs, Old Birmingham Photographs.*

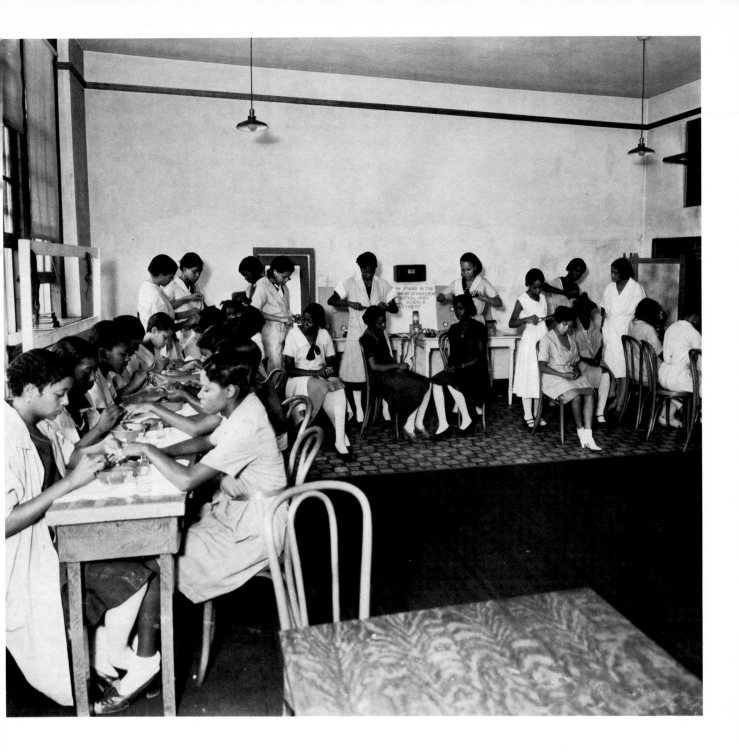

played the banjo and delivered for Gorman Gamill Seed Store; "Kid Wonder" who never missed in his fortune telling; and "Blue John" who greeted everyone at the Terminal Station when they arrived or left Birmingham.

Since 1900 Birmingham city government had been volatile. George Ward, a colorful and flamboyant mayor, dominated politics. In 1907, when he left the country for six weeks, he came home to find that a new city government had ousted him. What followed reminded some of a courtroom scene in a Wild West movie, as Ward brought a pistol and a squad of loyal policemen into the council meeting. This was not to be the last time that Birmingham had two contesting

city governments. Ward, with Culpepper Exum, Arlie Barber, James Hornady, J.D. Truss, and James Weatherly led the city into the 1920s. Birmingham suffered two catastrophes in the early 1920s: city hall with the public library on the fourth floor burned, and the city treasury "lost" funds totaling $50,000 that were never recovered. In 1925 J.M. Jones, Jr., was elected to the city commission and until 1940 he was the city's guiding spirit. Jimmy Jones was a "battler first and last," who "bulldoggled" and dragged the city through the Depression without default. He was one of the first to suspect the economic downturn would be long-lasting and he stopped city appropriations and instituted strict economic measures.

From Depression to Three Shifts a Day

Above: *On the afternoon of April 23, 1925, Birmingham City Hall burned. The fourth floor of the city hall building had housed the Birmingham Public Library and most of the books were destroyed. Earlier the citizens had rejected the idea of building a new library, but after the fire, the city constructed the new library building in Woodrow Wilson Park. In 1944, the city hall burned again and a new building was constructed across from the Jefferson County Courthouse. Courtesy, Mary Alice Beatty Carmichael.*

Facing page, top: *Oscar W. Underwood, who represented Jefferson County and Birmingham in the United States Congress and later represented Alabama in the United State Senate, was a major floor leader in both houses for the Democratic Party. Underwood was considered for the Presidency, but his vocal and uncompromising opposition to the Ku Klux Klan lost him much support. Once, when he accused the Klan of trying to intimidate him, he said, "I am not afraid either in a political or a personal sense of the Ku Klux Klan. I maintain that the organization is a national menace . . . It is either the Ku Klux Klan or the United States of America. Both cannot survive. Between the two, I choose my country." From the Department of Archives and Manuscripts, Birmingham Public Library.*

Facing page, bottom: *The Ridgely Apartments, Birmingham Public Library, and Jefferson County Courthouse stand out prominently against Enon Ridge and the North Highlands in this photo taken in the early 1930s. The Ridgely Apartments were constructed in 1914 by the Robert Jemison Company and financed by Major E.M. Tutwiler. These luxury apartments were once considered the fashionable place to live. The Birmingham Public Library was built after fire destroyed the library on the fourth floor of the city hall in 1925. In 1927 the neo-classical building opened and today houses over five million books, including the excellent Tutwiler Collection in Southern History and the Rucker Agee Map Collection, the finest collection of maps of the southeastern United States in the world. The Jefferson County Courthouse opened on December 4, 1931. Courtesy, Jackie Dobbs, Old Birmingham Photographs.*

As the critical years of the Great Depression neared, Birmingham and Jefferson County not only had firm leadership at home but also a foundation of three decades of quality political representation in Washington, D.C. For 32 years Birmingham's voice in Congress, first in the House of Representatives (1893-1914) and later in the Senate, was Oscar W. Underwood, one of Alabama's most noted statesmen. As floor leader for Woodrow Wilson, Underwood steered much of the president's Progressive legislation through the House. He was a serious contender for the Democratic presidential nomination in 1912 and again in 1924, but his strong and vocal opposition to the Ku Klux Klan at this time lost him much support and probably cost him the nomination. Many Alabamians recall listening to the Democratic Convention of 1924 over that new invention "radio" and hearing Alabama Governor William W. Brandon announcing on each ballot: "Alabama casts twenty-four votes for Oscar W. Underwood." When Underwood went to the Senate, George Huddleston, another able politician, took his congressional seat. In 1927 Birmingham lawyer Hugo Black was elected to Underwood's Senate seat and served for 10 years until he was appointed to the United States Supreme Court. Thus, at the crucial time when federal programs multiplied and New Deal policies increased federal government spending, Birmingham and Jefferson County were well represented by men of ability with political experience in the nation's capital.

Jefferson County and Birmingham were optimistic when Herbert Hoover became president in March of 1929. The election of the Republican had pleased Protestants and conservatives who were bothered by Al Smith's religion (Catholic), his stand on Prohibition (wet), and his residence and brogue (Brooklyn). People noted "a thrill in the air." Surely the steadying hand of Hoover would improve the quiet condition of industry in the county. On October 8, 1929, Leo K. Steiner returned to Birmingham after one month in New York, and said that "better times are here," the "period of dullness" merely normal. On October 26 the *Birmingham News* reported the "Mart Slumps in Orderly Manner." Three days later stock prices suddenly collapsed as frantic sellers dumped millions of inflated shares on the market. The bottom fell out of the "Roaring Twenties" and the Great Depression had begun. Spending by consumers was curtailed and capital investments by Birmingham industry ceased. Pig iron and steel piled up; mills and mines were closed; furnaces went out of blast. In Jefferson County 123,000 people lost their jobs. The old Birmingham adage that "hard times come here first and stay longest" was at work again.

In Howell Raines's novel, *Whiskey Man*, an old
moonshiner nears Birmingham during the Depression
with his load of illegal white lightning. He comments
that the land still has "a rural character, but it was a
land ruined for farming by the opening of the mines
and ruined for living by their closing." Employee
programs of industries were cut back as plants shut
down, but credit cards, dubbed "Pity Slips" by
employees, allowed them to purchase food at the
commissary. Credit for rent was extended. The Red
Cross planned a spring planting program with free
seed and land for gardens. People became unhappy
with city government, and circulated a petition
calling for Jimmy Jones's resignation because he had
"no effective plan for relief of the dire distress in the
community" and had been guilty of "positive
misrepresentation to the Federal Government"
respecting conditions in the city. When Alabama
Senator Hugo Black wired Jones asking if
Birmingham needed federal aid for charity, the
Birmingham leader had answered no, but the city
could use help with its roads.

Businessmen were warned to find some way to feed
the population or face riots. Communist organizers
passed out leaflets in Negro communities and party
workers organized black committees. The violence
surrounding the Sharecroppers Union in South
Alabama and the Scottsboro case in the northern part
of the state increased racial tensions within the city,
and were used by the Communist Party to recruit
members. The *Southern Daily Worker* was published
in the city and it attracted some local support among
desperately poor, angry people. In the 1930s
Birmingham began a program of public work relief

From Depression to Three Shifts a Day

which was the first such program in the state. City and county governments cooperated in funding as the unemployed were given jobs on worthwhile social projects. The full resources of the community were organized. The staffs of libraries, schools, home demonstration departments, parks, and other recreational facilities were mobilized to provide education and entertainment for the idle times of the unemployed. Community Chest director Harry Early assumed a leadership role in relief work, and the Community Chest Appeal of October 1931 under Mervyn H. Sterne, who "worked night and day raising money," resulted in an "outpouring of funds."

Birmingham and Jefferson County voted overwhelmingly for Franklin D. Roosevelt and saw hope in the Democratic victory of a presidential candidate who had promised a "New Deal for the American people and the forgotten man." But the city was unsure whether to be insulted or pleased when the new President referred to Birmingham as "the worst hit town in the country." The Depression deepened between Roosevelt's November 1932 election and his March 1933 inauguration. The bank crisis grew more alarming in Birmingham and there were mild runs. Hill Ferguson recorded in his diary the day of FDR's inauguration that "Everybody [was] looking forward to Roosevelt as the Messiah." After becoming president Roosevelt closed all banks. Charles Fell, believing there "would be excitement adding up to some sort of revolution," walked down to the corner of Second Avenue and Twentieth Street where he "could see the doorways" of the First National Bank and the Birmingham Trust National Bank. He thought there would be "frantic depositers beating on the bank doors," but he found only a few people, sober-faced, some joking about "how much or little they had in the bank." Victor Hanson, publisher of the *Birmingham News,* called grocery stores and utility companies requesting they give his employees "what they need and put it on my bill. We'll settle when the banks open." A & P and Hill grocery stores issued food tickets. Crawford Johnson's Coca-Cola Company paid its men with orders for Coca-Colas and Britling Cafeteria extended credit to downtown office workers. By March 14, five banks in the city had reopened. There were big deposits and few withdrawals, and the banking crisis was over.

Many of Roosevelt's New Deal programs helped Jefferson County. Relief money poured into the county through agencies like the Civilian Conservation Corp, the National Youth Administration, the Civil Works Administration, and the Works Progress Administration. Construction on TVA projects drew many unemployed to North Alabama. Part of the National Industrial Recovery

From Depression to Three Shifts a Day

Act, known as "Section 7a," gave workers the right to organize, and the UMW and the CIO were quick to move into the district. In June of 1933 John L. Lewis appointed William Mitch as the Birmingham UMW organizer, and in the next few years, there were violent strikes in the coal mines. Birmingham had one of the largest Communist Party organizations in the United States in the 1930s. This faction supported the coal strikes. One Communist worker in Birmingham recalled that the Party had hoped for fights among the miners, were "issuing leaflets and talking to miners, and trying to get the members of the Party units in the mines more active in the strike." City government continued to need funds, but in 1933, Oscar Wells and the First National Bank came to the rescue, lending the city $1 million. Within four years the federal government had spent or lent $361 million in Jefferson County.

By 1934 the hard times were easing. In March of that year the Frisco, St. Louis, & San Francisco Railroad ordered 20,000 tons of steel rails from TCI, the largest single order placed in the Birmingham district for the past three years. Before the month was over Southern Railroad placed an order of 10,000 tons of rails, and Seaboard Air Line Railroad ordered 11,200 tons. Demands continued to come in from railroads all across the country for new rails for repairs and new roads. London Bridges recalls leaving from the Terminal Station for New York with her grandparents. The city was depressed and so were the people on the train as they slowly passed the Sloss furnaces, standing cold and empty. Their trip lasted several weeks. On their return to Birmingham the people sitting by the train window grew excited as they approached the Sloss furnaces. News spread in the car that the Sloss furnaces were "fired up and pouring!" People crowded to the train windows to glimpse the glowing furnaces and slag piles that meant jobs and a return to prosperity for the district. The Depression must be over! Of course, they were wrong, but at least the despair had abated.

Roberta Morgan, who as Red Cross worker and later as director of the Jefferson County Department of Public Welfare, led relief efforts in the county, believed the Depression was "an interlude, a period of waiting, and a nightmare." Men lost businesses and were too old or too beaten down to begin anew. But it was a time when she believed that Birmingham produced "the best leaders" she ever knew, when the people "rose to the great challenge in a truly remarkable way."

The people of Birmingham and Jefferson County were so preoccupied with local economic conditions during the 1930s that they had little time to be concerned with international events. But with Hitler's rise to power and the beginning of the European war in 1939, attention was drawn to Germany and to the Far East where Japan had taken military action against China and Southeast Asia. The first Birmingham responses were isolationist—the distance too far, the issues of no concern to entangle the United States. Gradually, however, opinion changed to more of an internationalist view with Birmingham residents favoring preparedness and defense spending. Of course, most people realized that such military hardware would be constructed of iron and steel, ideally much of it from the Birmingham district. Jefferson County plants were operating on a busy schedule well before the bombing of Pearl Harbor in December of 1941 as orders from Great Britain added to Roosevelt's defense spending. By the fall most of the Birmingham press realized that America would be drawn into war. The *Birmingham News* indicated in early December that war with Japan was imminent, but when news of the Pearl Harbor attack came across the radio stations in the city, citizens were shocked and furious.

The war caused a rapid expansion of Birmingham industry as military orders flooded the city. Factories went on three shifts a day and living habits altered. Men began working swing shifts, women took jobs on

Facing page, top: *The old First National Bank Building clock, located at Second Avenue and Twentieth Street, provided a well known location where Birmingham shoppers would often arrange to meet one another. The clock is no longer there and Twentieth Street has been turned into Birmingham Green. Photo by Charles F. McFarlin. Courtesy, Betsy Barber Bancroft.*

Facing page, bottom: *In the 1920s Mansion Joe, Loo Choy, Loo Bing, and George Sai opened a Chinese Restaurant called "King Joy" in Birmingham. In 1925 the restaurant moved to Twentieth Street. Three generations have operated the restaurant: Mansion Joe, his son Joe Wing Soo, and grandson Henry Joe. The restaurant's location, directly across the street from the Tutwiler Hotel made it a favorite dining spot for out-of-towners, but it was also popular with Birmingham residents. The restaurant was usually packed on Sunday after church services and weekdays at noon with businessmen and downtown shoppers. Once, in the 1920s, the Ku Klux Klan visited the restaurant to show some opposition to "immigrants and foreigners," but this seemed to make the cafe even more popular. In October 1980, the restaurant was moved from the downtown area to a shopping center. Courtesy, Jackie Dobbs, Old Birmingham Photographs.*

Below: *Jefferson County farmers sold their products from roadside stands during the Depression. This stand was photographed by Walker Evans in 1936. This fish market purchased fish from fishermen trying to supplement their income, and then sold the fish to the public. Courtesy, Library of Congress.*

From Depression to Three Shifts a Day

Top: *The Avondale Mills band poses in front of the Jefferson County Courthouse before joining a parade. Parades in downtown Birmingham brought spectators from all over the county. They would ride the street-cars into town and line Twentieth Street or First Avenue to view the bands and floats. Courtesy, Jackie Dobbs, Old Birmingham Photographs.*

Above: *Birmingham high school students attend a lecture on airplane identification and flight basics at the Birmingham airport in July of 1945 as part of the war preparedness and civil defense programs. This Waco Custom airplane was similar to one flown in Birmingham for many years by Bernard A. Schrader. Courtesy, Jackie Dobbs, Old Birmingham Photographs.*

Facing page, top: *Birmingham celebrated the end of World War II with a giant victory parade downtown. Here the parade is on Nineteenth Street moving south. Courtesy, Jackie Dobbs, Old Birmingham Photographs.*

Facing page, bottom: *Birmingham miners take a break from work in November of 1946. World War II stimulated the economy of the Birmingham district and created new jobs. Demands for coal, iron, and steel had never been higher and the population of Jefferson County increased 17 percent as men and women came from across the South to work in war industries. Courtesy, Jackie Dobbs, Old Birmingham Photographs.*

assembly lines, and traffic jams occurred on shift changes. Birmingham was called the "great arsenal of the South," and felt pride in being told the enemy had marked the city its number two bombing target behind Pittsburgh. Steel and iron rolled from the mills to Birmingport (now the Birmingham Port), down the Warrior River to Mobile and Mississippi shipyards. Robert I. Ingalls, Birmingham steel fabricator, converted a World War I shipyard in Pascagoula, Mississippi into a manufacturing center for cargo ships. The largest ordnance plant in the South making smokeless powder and explosives was the DuPont Alabama Ordnance Works located at Childersburg, and many Jefferson County men commuted down Highway 280 to work there. The Bechtel-McCone Aircraft Modification Plant located at the Birmingham Airport modified and equipped half of all the B-29's used in the war. The O'Neal Steel Works, founded by Kirkman O'Neal, made steel fabrications for thousands of bombs and expanded to become one of the largest independent companies in the Birmingham district.

Jefferson County boys were quick to respond to the call for troops, and the area produced its military heroes. Captain John A. Williamson, United States Navy, designed the still famous "Williamson Turn," which allowed a ship at sea to rescue sailors overboard. Birmingham's General J.C. Persons, one of the most decorated soldiers, was commander of the Thirty-first Division, and Brigadier General John E. Copeland commanded one of General George Patton Third Army divisions in the sweep through France and Germany in 1944-1945. Birmingham and Jefferson County boys participated in all the major campaigns. One of the immediate results of having so many native sons fighting around the world was an instant interest in geography and the mastering of strange names and places. V-E and V-J days were jubilant. The war had stimulated the economy of the Birmingham district and created new jobs. County population had increased 17 percent as men and women came to work in war industries. The war ended the Depression, which the New Deal had been unable to do. But the war also took the lives of many brilliant young men and women who never had the opportunity to come home and contribute their talents to making Jefferson County a better place to live.

As the war ended the Depression was still in the minds of many citizens. Would hard times come back again? Would recession follow this war? The future was unknown, but in September of 1945 peace was the important accomplishment. Jefferson County and Birmingham would think about postwar adjustment and the problems this would bring—tomorrow.

149

Chapter XI

TIMES OF TROUBLE AND TRIUMPHS

Birmingham feared the elimination of government contracts plus competition for jobs by returning soldiers would cause widespread unemployment and the Depression might return. But this did not occur. War savings, pent-up demands for consumer goods and housing, and continued orders for iron and steel combined to keep the district's economy humming.

To many Americans, Eugene "Bull" Connor came to epitomize Southern white intransigence on racial issues. Known for his predeliction to use force against protesters, he provided Dr. Martin Luther King, Jr., with the confrontation King needed in May of 1963 to bring the Civil Rights Movement in Birmingham to a head. Courtesy, the Birmingham News.

Times of Trouble and Triumphs

The GI Bill sent veterans to college and delayed their entrance into the job market. As a result, students enrolled at a much faster rate at Birmingham-Southern, Howard, Miles, and the Birmingham extension branch of the University of Alabama than facilities could be built to accommodate them. Classes met temporarily in churches, secondary schools, and vacant buildings. Extension courses of the University at Tuscaloosa had been offered in Birmingham since 1936, but there was no degree program. In 1943 the Alabama legislature created the Medical College in Birmingham as a branch of the University of Alabama. The consolidation of the Jefferson-Hillman hospital complex with support from the city and county governments, plus population density and the medical needs of a growing urban area, convinced the university to move its health services department to Birmingham. By 1955 the University of Alabama in Birmingham was established and became a degree-granting unit 11 years later.

Dr. Joseph F. Volker, first president of UAB and later chancellor of the University of Alabama System, said in the early 1960s that "we would do a great disservice to Birmingham if we dreamed too little dreams." UAB dreamed big. In 1969 it became an independent campus of the University of Alabama System, occupying 15 square blocks around the University Hospital. Six years later the state legislature appropriated money to purchase 45 additional blocks for campus growth. The Medical Center is one of the finest hospital-teaching complexes in the nation, with its Spain Rehabilitation Center and the Spain Heart Tower, the first public diabetes hospital in the nation, the Lister Hill Medical Library, and cancer research programs. Dr. John Kirklin has made the center world renowned for its heart surgery. The University brought more white-collar professionals into the city, helping to balance the "heavy steel based blue-collar working force." In fact health care and related occupations have surpassed iron and steel as the dominant economic forces in the city and UAB has become Birmingham's largest single employer. The presence of the Medical College no doubt encouraged the development of other fine medical centers: the Baptist Medical Centers at Princeton and Montclair, the Carraway Methodist Hospital and Clinic, and the more recent Brookwood Medical Center. But UAB also developed its College of General Studies, which added to the educational opportunities within the city.

Howard College, established by Alabama Baptists, outgrew its East Lake campus in the postwar period; under the leadership of President Harwell G. Davis, it moved to a new Georgian-style campus in Shades

Below: *The College Theatre and the Doris W. Kennedy Art Center of Birmingham Southern College make the campus the scene of frequent community cultural events. The art center was named for a famous Birmingham artist. Courtesy, Birmingham Southern College.*

Facing page: *Samford University President Leslie S. Wright and members of the board of trustees, Ben B. Brown, Richard J. Stockham, and Frank P. Samford, examine plans for the university's Ralph W. Beeson Student Center. Howard College changed its name to Samford University to honor trustee and long-time benefactor Frank P. Samford. Courtesy, Samford University.*

Valley in 1957. The pharmacy degree program at Howard College remains one of only two in the state, and its Cumberland School of Law is one of the largest law schools in the South. In 1965 Howard changed its name to Samford University, honoring trustee and benefactor Frank Parke Samford and recognizing the development of a diversity of degree programs including master's degree.

Birmingham-Southern College, a Methodist liberal arts college located on Flint Ridge, one of the highest points in Jones Valley, has long provided a resource for community leadership. The college's planetarium, music hall, theater, and amphitheater house various cultural events. Miles College has provided quality education for blacks and achieved remarkable growth in the decades following World War II. For many years the college was led by Dr. Lucius Pitts. The faculties of Samford, Birmingham-Southern, Miles, and UAB provide cultural and intellectual leadership for the area. Faculty members are active in church and religious organizations and civic clubs, and serve on government committees and community boards. The faculties of two junior colleges, Lawson State and Jefferson State, are also significant leaders in community affairs, and their colleges provide a general two-year educational program.

A number of federal housing complexes—Elyton Village, Southtown Central City, and Smithfield—had been completed during the New Deal era, but returning GIs found that the legislature had banned federal low-income housing from the city, a mistake later rectified. Building trades experienced heavy growth because of new housing demands and federal financing programs. New subdivisions and federal "608" projects sprang up in West End and Powderly, Hueytown and Bessemer, Center Point and Woodlawn, Pleasant Grove and Gardendale, and 150 "garden-type" apartments were approved for Lane Park in Mountain Brook. The development of these suburbs and continued building in Shades Valley caused the city of Birmingham to lose some of its leadership and resources.

In 1946 Mangel's advertised mink coats for $89, Pizitz had a $10 fall and winter dress sale, and Birmingham celebrated its Diamond Jubilee. For three days in November the city rejoiced in 75th Anniversary festivities. A children's Tab section, created by the *Birmingham News*, told about the founding of the city, a tale likened to the story of "Jack and the Bean Stalk" for its miraculous growth from 4,000 acres to 53 square miles. It was fitting that Irving Olds, chairman of the board of directors of

Times of Trouble and Triumphs

including a new civic center, civic symphony, civic ballet, art museum, botanical gardens, and even a zoo. Tom Martin, president of the Alabama Power Company, had been instrumental in founding the Southern Research Institute and in 1950 he organized a Committee of 100 to encourage new industry to locate in the county. By the mid-fifties even United States Steel, under the leadership of Ben Fairless, joined in the push for diversification of the economy of the Birmingham district.

Birmingham unexpectedly found itself in the summer of 1948, hosting a presidential nomination convention that made the city a symbol of revolt against the Democratic Party. Alabama, disgruntled by President Harry S. Truman's support of a fair-employment code, replayed the event of 1860 when Alabama led a walkout at the Democratic Convention. At Philadelphia in 1948, after the party adopted a strong civil-rights plank, Alabama led a "states' righters" walkout with the seceders convening in Birmingham on July 17. Most of the Southern states were represented, but with no officially elected delegates. Temporary headquarters were established in Birmingham's leading hotel, the Tutwiler. The Municipal Auditorium, where the meeting was held, was festooned with the Stars and Stripes, but the Confederate flag usually seen waving over Southern political meetings was conspicuously absent.

the United States Steel Corporation, came from Pittsburgh to address the opening banquet at the Municipal Auditorium. Olds praised Birmingham people for their "patriotic and effective contributions" to war productivity of the Birmingham Ordnance District. Jefferson County produced 75 percent of all the war materials of the entire district, which comprised five states. Olds called Birmingham "a City of Destiny" with "unlimited growth" ahead. But he also reminded the audience that the recent coal and steel strikes had been harmful to the district.

Part of the celebration included the Crippled Children's Clinic game on Thanksgiving Day in which Ensley played Ramsay before a sellout crowd. Donations to the hospital reached a record $85,000. Birmingham, England, even sent a goodwill ambassador to the celebration. The Diamond Jubilee parade down Twentieth Street featured floats and the area's high-school bands. Bill Stern of NBC joined WBRC president Eloise Smith Hanna in broadcasting the event. Glenn Miller's orchestra played at the Carnival Dance; Margaret Gresham, as Queen Joy XII, and John Foster, as King Cheer XII, reigned over all the festivities.

Soon after this 75th birthday celebration, the city was challenged by Irving Beiman's trenchant and critical appraisal. The *Birmingham News* reporter accused the city of suffering from "civic anemia" and of failing to "develop a real community spirit." He criticized absentee industrial ownership, the failure of polluting industries to abide by the city's 1946 smoke-abating ordinance, and Big Steel's iron-fisted negative attitude toward attracting new industry to the district. Beiman said the city had no civic symphony orchestra and not even a zoo. He called the city a "steel giant with a glass jaw" for putting all its economic eggs in the one-industry basket of iron and steel. Some citizens bitterly disagreed with Beiman. Others rolled up their sleeves and accepted the challenge. They went to work to attract more industry, create a more diversified economy, and lay the foundation for a more sophisticated urban culture

154

President L.H. Pitts. When the club sent Governor George Wallace a resolution, the governor responded that he had placed it "in a special file" he kept for "communists, integrationists, and outside agitators."

Another organization that worked for civil rights was the Birmingham Council on Human Relations, which some claimed gave Salisbury information for his article. In 1962 the Young Men's Business Club agreed to allow a CBS film crew to film their meeting for a program on Birmingham addressing the question of whether the Salisbury article represented accurate reporting. The producer, David Lowe, assured the club and the city of Birmingham that the program entitled "Who Speaks for Birmingham," would be a fair evaluation. However, when the program aired, citizens reacted with fury for there was little good said about the city. In the 90 minutes filmed at the YMBC meeting, only the bad comments were aired, the rest was cut from the program, radically distorting the image of the city.

By this time a number of civic leaders became convinced that the way to effect a change of political leadership was to change the form of city government. New and moderate leadership could alter the city's direction. They began a campaign to shift from the mayor-commission form to a mayor-council form. This would give more representation to neighborhoods and communities within the city, and perhaps eliminate one of the reasons Homewood and Mountain Brook had opposed annexation to Birmingham. Petitions were circulated and on September 25, 1962, Probate Judge J. Paul Meeks handed Mayor Art Hanes a document certifying that enough voters had approved the change in government to call for an election. When Hanes refused, Meeks informed him as Probate Judge that it was his duty to call the election and he did. Everywhere citizens debated the two forms of government. When the election was held in November 1962, voters approved the mayor-council form, and Judge Meeks set March 5, 1963, as Election Day for new officials. Although the incumbent commissioners challenged the constitutional legality of the legislation allowing a change in government, the courts upheld the law and a number of the old commissioners, including Connor, filed for the election. Moderates were hopeful the election would be a turning point for the city and it was. Albert Boutwell, former Lieutenant Governor, with the support of newspapers and moderates, defeated "Bull" Connor. Boutwell was known as a moderate segregationist. Unfortunately the incumbents refused to relinquish their offices and the newly elected mayor-council was forced to return to court to evict the old commissioners. It was in this

scenario, with no one in unquestioned authority at City Hall and a rudderless ship of state, that Birmingham was to play out the "Crisis of 1963."

Nationwide, the civil rights movement had "hit a slump," according to Ed Gardner, Southern Christian Leadership worker in Birmingham. Martin Luther King, Jr.'s, SCLC had been frustrated in a long campaign in Albany, Georgia. Gardner said they "needed a shot in the arm." The Reverend Fred Shuttlesworth convinced Dr. King to come to Birmingham. King realized that Birmingham presented the "best testing ground" for segregation across the nation since "Bull" Connor's intransigence and predilection to use force would provide King the confrontation he needed to gain nationwide support. As early as September of 1962, white leaders learned of the invitation to King and had A.G. Gaston arrange a meeting between white businessmen and Shuttlesworth. Compromises were made and demonstrations were delayed until after the scheduled city elections in the spring of 1963. Some of the desegregation agreements could not be achieved because they violated the segregation code of the city and Connor was determined to enforce the laws. Therefore demonstrations began after the election on April 2. When Martin Luther King defied an injunction prohibiting further marches, he was arrested and placed in jail.

For decades the Birmingham Jail had been familiar across the South because of a popular mountain ballad with the refrain: "Down in the valley, valley so low, Hang your head over, hear the wind blow, . . . Write me a letter, send it by mail, And back it in care of the Birmingham Jail." King must have been familiar with this song when he wrote the famous "Letter from the Birmingham Jail," his answer to seven Birmingham clergymen who called his demonstrations "unwise and untimely." This letter became well known as a defense of King's nonviolent tactics and his justification for violating unjust laws.

In the weeks ahead, downtown stores were boycotted; teenagers and children left school and joined the marches around Kelly Ingram Park on May 2-7, spilling out from headquarters at the Sixteenth Street Baptist Church and the A.G. Gaston Motel; Connor promised to "fill the jails," which he did, then housed hundreds of those arrested at temporary quarters at the Fairgrounds; and President John F. Kennedy sent special representatives from the Justice Department to try and mediate the crisis. Demonstrations went on for some 45 days. But the most regrettable occurrence, and the one Birmingham citizens of both races have worked hard

Times of Trouble and Triumphs

since 1963 to insure would never happen again, was the dog-and-firehose scene at Kelly Ingram Park. Police dogs were used by most cities for crowd control, and Birmingham had used the K-9 dogs to break up Klan activities around the bus terminal in 1961. Birmingham firehoses had been turned on unruly strikers at least once before. Now full-force water knocked marchers down, many of them teenagers, and national news media coverage was there to key in on the most violent incidents. Birmingham businessmen working downtown were not aware of any disturbances until the evening network newscast showed films of the demonstrations at the park. The white community reacted to this brutal violence by anger and shocked incredulity which stiffened their determination to restore racial harmony. An editor of the *Birmingham News* was so disgusted when misting water was turned on a line of very young black children all "dressed in their Sunday best" that he left the park convinced "Connor and what he stood for must go." The fireman's union informed the city that they "were hired on to fight fires, not people" and the union would never again respond to such a call.

When President Kennedy offered to send federal troops, Sid Smyer went to Washington and promised the President that Birmingham would work out its own problems. When Smyer returned he called a meeting of the leading businessmen and told them "if we're going to have good business in Birmingham, we better change our way of living." He said: "I'm a segregationist from bottom to top, but gentlemen, you can see what's happening. I'm not a damn fool. ... We can't win. We are going to have to stop and talk to these folks." And talk they did. A Senior Citizens Committee reached an agreement. Downtown stores agreed to hire blacks in sales and clerical positions and desegregate lunch counters and restrooms; jailed demonstrators were released; a permanent biracial committee was formed to handle problems; and Dr. Martin Luther King prepared to leave town. That night the Gaston Motel where King was staying and his brother's home were bombed. Street riots flared around the motel and the park, and the city tried desperately to prevent the crisis from

escalating, which would bring back state troopers. Strong action by both whites and blacks reinforced the agreement and the compromise stood. With the lines of communication now open between the white and black communities, the gap began to close. It was now possible to ameliorate grievances.

Throughout this crisis the question of who controlled the reins of Birmingham's city government was being debated in state courts. Jesters described Birmingham as "the only city in the world with a King, two mayors, and a parade every day." Albert Boutwell was not able to take over the government until May 23rd when the Supreme Court of Alabama upheld the new government. Boutwell, along with a City Council composed of M.E. Wiggins, Dr. John E. Bryan, Allan T. Drennen, John Golden, Don A. Hawkins, Dr. E.C. Overton, George Seibels, Jr., and Miss Nina Miglionico assumed the power vested in them by the electorate months before.

But the event which jolted the city more than anything that had ever happened occurred on a hot, muggy Sunday (September 15, 1963). An explosion tore open the side of the Sixteenth Street Baptist Church and killed four young black girls. Their deaths became the catalyst assuring that social change would come to the city. Duard LeGrand, editor of the *Birmingham Post-Herald,* pondered "the healing effect of human sacrifice." This tragedy "like an explosion of lightning" had "seemed to clear the air and show the city and its people, black and white, that the time had come to make a new start." For Birmingham 1963 was a year of troubles; years of triumphs were to follow. A new leadership emerged, determined to "change the image" of the city. In 1963 Operation New Birmingham was founded as an outgrowth of the old Downtown Improvement Association. Together with the Downtown Action Committee, the biracial Community Affairs Committee, and the Women's Committee of 100, Operation New Birmingham stressed progress, the development of the inner city, racial accord, and a new image for Birmingham. In 1965 Republican George Seibels, Jr., won an upset victory over Boutwell in the mayoral race, and continued the progressive development of the city, which included the approval of the largest bond issue ever—$50 million for civic improvements. New projects for the city included Twentieth Street's Birmingham Green, the Birmingham-Jefferson Civic Center Complex, Morris Avenue restoration as a downtown entertainment center, the Red Mountain Expressway, Municipal Airport expansion, and improvements and more seating at Legion Field.

Less success was achieved in the Greater Birmingham move. Annexation drives of the late 1940s and 1950s had failed, particularly the Homewood and Mountain Brook annexation attempt. In 1964 Mountain Brook opposed annexation and Homewood voted for annexation by seven votes, but the election was thrown out on a technicality in a subsequent appeal. In a revote, Homewood's merger with Birmingham failed by 1,700 votes. In 1971 a number of civic organizations supported the "One Great City" concept, which would have increased Birmingham's population to 100,000 more than Atlanta's. But the plan failed because the surrounding communities feared loss of school control through consolidation, higher taxation, and racial integration. Pressure was applied from both sides, but the Alabama Legislature refused to act on annexation legislation.

When a vacancy occurred on the city council in October 1968, the council voted to appoint black Birmingham attorney Arthur Shores to the position. Nothing up to this point had so well illustrated Birmingham's changed racial attitudes. Shores—a Talladega College graduate, former teacher and principal in the Bessemer schools, and University of Kansas law graduate—was for 20 years the only black practicing attorney in Alabama. His home had twice been bombed. When asked why he stayed in Birmingham through those times of trouble, he seemed surprised: "This was my home. I was born here." He said he always believed that Birmingham would "be one of the garden spots of the country" when the race question was settled, and he feels his "predictions are being vindicated."

In the 1960s and 1970s, downtown Birmingham took on new life. Construction began everywhere and new skyscrapers dotted the horizon: Central Bank, Daniel Building, Bank for Savings, Liberty National expansion, First National Bank-Southern Natural Gas, South Central Bell, the 2121 Building, and the First Alabama Bank Building. In 1970 Richard Pizitz, the president of the Birmingham Area Chamber of Commerce, aggressively went after the National Municipal League and *Look* magazine's All-America City award. A biracial committee was appointed to prepare Birmingham's entry, which focused on three areas of accomplishment: the biracial Community Affairs Committee; the Birmingham Festival of Arts, which was the oldest continuing arts festival in the United States; and the Youth Forum Activities. On the eve of Birmingham's Centennial Celebration, Mayor George Seibels, Jr., accepted the All-America City award at a luncheon at the new Civic Center. Vincent Townsend, Sr., of the *Birmingham News,* commented that the award was a sober reminder of new and deeper obligations for the city, and Mack

Gambell of Carraway Hospital advocated the goal of making Birmingham an "All-International City."

In October 1975 Republican Seibels was defeated in the mayor's race by Democrat David Vann, and the city's march forward continued. Cooperation with the Jefferson County Commissioners increased and the Birmingham-Jefferson Civic Center was completed. The Birmingham Bulls moved into the Coliseum, bringing the city its first professional hockey team.

The Birmingham Museum of Art, which had begun in one room of the City Hall, moved into the Oscar Wells Memorial Building in 1959 and completed the addition of the William M. Spencer Galleries in 1975. The museum not only houses the Kress Collection but the Beeson Wedgwood Collection, a fine collection of Remington bronzes, the Frances Oliver Collection of eighteenth-century porcelain and silver, and representative paintings and artifacts from around the world. The Birmingham Symphony Orchestra moved into the Concert Hall of the Civic Center in 1974. The Birmingham Music Club held regular performances there until 1981, when they moved to the Leslie S. Wright Fine Arts Center on the campus of Samford University. The Birmingham Children's Theatre gives performances at the Civic Center Theatre as well as traveling to schools in the area.

Birmingham industry is now diversified. Iron and steel jobs comprise only 10 percent of total employment in the county. The 1950 discovery in Venezuela of Cerro Bolivar and La Frontiera, mountains of iron ore of "almost theoretical maximum purity" sealed the fate of Jefferson County's low-grade Red Mountain iron ore. It was cheaper to freight Venezuelan ore to Mobile and up the Warrior River to Birmingham Port. The South American ore was at first mixed with Birmingham district ore, but TCI stopped mining ore in 1958 and the Woodward Company ceased mining ore in 1970. Because of the energy crisis, however, the district's coal reserves will remain significant natural resources. Birmingham's location on the fringe of the Sun Belt, its progressive business outlook, its willingness to tackle problems and to solve them, and the community support for its first black mayor, Richard Arrington, elected in 1979, have moved the metropolitan Birmingham-Jefferson County area into the second most favorable spot for new business locations in the United States, according to a study by Dun and Bradstreet.

The 1970s saw the development of a greater appreciation and awareness for Birmingham and

Times of Trouble
and Triumphs

Jefferson County history. The Jefferson County Historical Commission was established by the state legislature in 1971 and Dr. John E. Bryan was named chairman. Under his direction, historically significant buildings in the city and county were marked with a commission placard that included the original names of the buildings and the date of construction. The commission was also responsible for the Thomas Jefferson statue by Georges Bridges, which was unveiled in Woodrow Wilson Park before the courthouse that bears his name, and for assisting in the publication of a number of local history manuscripts. Interest in historical preservation saved

On January 20, 1980, Justice of the Alabama Supreme Court and Cumberland School of Law professor Janie Shores administered the oath of office to Mayor-elect Dr. Richard Arrington, former Miles College professor and city councilman. Holding the Bible is Mrs. Arrington, while former Birmingham mayors George Seibels and David Vann watch. It was a momentous occasion for the city of Birmingham and symbolized a remarkable change from the days when the city was charged with being America's most segregated city. Courtesy, Birmingham News.

many older homes along Highland Avenue and in Forest Park, but regrettably this concern did not materialize before Birmingham and Jefferson County lost some of their most elegant architectural gems from the past: the George Ward home "Vestavia," the Terminal Station, the Morris Hotel, the Tutwiler Hotel, and the Temple Theatre.

The West Jefferson County Historical Society restored the Sadler, McAdory, and Owen homes, began an annual Christmas Open House, and created the Hall of History in the basement of the Bessemer Library. This museum contains the largest collection of Jefferson County historical artifacts and memorabilia in the area. Community history collection projects were begun in Adamsville through the efforts of the *West Jeff-Zonian*. In Warrior, Pinson, Leeds, Trussville, and Tarrant City, local history programs were started, many of them resulting in published histories. The Birmingham Historical Society was revitalized after many years of inactivity. The Birmingham-Jefferson Historical Society was organized to stress city and county history. This organization of more than 500 members supports research and stimulates interest in the area's local history. The Birmingham Branch of the Association for the Study of Afro American Life and History was established by Dr. Charles A. Brown to preserve the black heritage of the community.

The Birmingham Public Library, under the direction of George Stewart, created a Department of Archives and Manuscripts headed by Dr. Marvin Y. Whiting to collect, preserve, and catalog materials relating to the history of Birmingham and Jefferson County. Birmingfind, a program of the Birmingham Alliance for the Humanities funded by a grant from the National Endowment for the Humanities in 1980, began a search to discover Birmingham's ethnic and community history. Their packet begins with a quotation from the 1887 Birmingham Public School report:

> Our people are too busy in the intensely practical channels of industry and trade to think of our city's history—they are too busy carving out her future to think of the past. Why should it be otherwise? The city has no relics, no legends, and but little history. But the time will come when the traditions of early Birmingham, her garnered relics, silent reminders of her former struggles and victories and her wonderful history, will be eagerly sought and cherished.

It has been almost 100 years since this was written; surely that time has now come.

Top: *Architect William E. Benns designed this Bessemer house for H.W. Sweet in 1906. The house has two identical porticos supported by Corinthian columns and a large octagonal turret on the corner. Courtesy, Mickie H. Blackwell.*

Above left: *John Turner Milner was commissioned by Governor A.B. Moore in 1858 to survey the South and North Alabama Railroad route through the mineral district of Jefferson County. With the financial backing of Josiah Morris of Montgomery, Milner purchased the land for the city and founded the Elyton Land Company. It was his dream of a city in Jones Valley, built upon the mineral resources of coal and iron ore with a railroad to transport its products to the world, that materialized in the city of Birmingham. Courtesy, State of Alabama Department of Archives and History. Photo by John Scott.*

Above middle: *Joseph F. Johnston moved to Birmingham in 1884, served as president of the Alabama State Bank in the city, was the first president of the Sloss Iron and Steel Company, was elected governor of Alabama in 1896 and 1898, and went on to become a United States senator in 1907. Courtesy, State of Alabama Department of Archives and History. Photo by John Scott.*

Above right: *From a planter, merchant, and banking family in Barbour County, Braxton Bragg Comer became president of the City National Bank and later established the Avondale Cotton Mill. Elected governor of Alabama in 1906, Comer was a colorful and exciting political figure known as a progressive for his fights for railroad reform and regulation by the state. Courtesy, State of Alabama Department of Archives and History. Photo by John Scott.*

COLOR PLATES

Wholesale Section of Morris Ave.
on a busy day.
Birmingham, Ala.

Facing page, top: *Morris Avenue, named for Josiah Morris, became the wholesale district of Birmingham at the turn of the century. The street was always filled with drays loaded with groceries, lumber, or machines. Courtesy, James F. Sulzby, Jr. Photo by Dicki Arn.*

Facing page, bottom left: *This United Daughters of the Confederacy medal appeared on a memorial card sold at one of the four United Confederate Veteran's reunions held in Birmingham in the late 1800s and early 1900s. Courtesy, James F. Sulzby, Jr. Photo by Dicki Arn.*

Facing page, bottom right: *Carry Lewis Montgomery painted this watercolor of Arlington, Birmingham's antebellum mansion. The house was located only a few blocks from the center of Elyton, the county seat for Jefferson County. In 1953 the city of Birmingham acquired the house and the Arlington Historical Association restored the mansion and decorated it with authentic antebellum furniture. Courtesy, Mrs. Ruby Munger Montgomery. Photo by Dicki Arn.*

Right: *The Blossburg coke ovens were built by Edward Magruder Tutwiler in 1889 of brick, rock, and sand. They are located near the Number Four Mine in Couglar Hollow. Few of the old ovens remain. Tutwiler, the owner of the Tutwiler Coal, Coke and Iron Company, built the Tutwiler Hotel and the Ridgely Apartments, and was a much beloved Birmingham industrialist. The Tutwiler Collection of Southern Literature was established in November 1926 by his widow and her sons at the Birmingham Public Library. Photo by Eddie Smith.*

Below: *The increased use of the automobile in the early 1900s caused traffic problems for the city. Here on Second Avenue and Nineteenth Street, a policeman holds up stop and go traffic signs. Courtesy, James F. Sulzby, Jr. Photo by Dicki Arn.*

Top: *Charging molten iron into a Q-BOP (basic oxygen process) steel-making vessel at U.S. Steel's Fairfield, Alabama, works. The Q-BOP represents the latest in steel making. Courtesy, United States Steel.*

Left: *Red iron ore mines are located behind the United States Steel, Tennessee Coal Iron and Railroad Division Wenonah Ore Processing Plant on Red Mountain. Photo by Dicki Arn.*

Above: *Once the center of Birmingham's iron and steel industry, the Sloss Furnace was shut down in 1970. In 1881 Colonel James Withers Sloss organized the Sloss Furnace Company and built two blast furnaces on First Avenue. Later, the company name was changed to the Sloss-Sheffield Steel and Iron company and in the 1940s the company became part of U.P. Pipe and Foundry Company. In 1970 the owners—now the Jim Walter Corporation—donated the site to the city of Birmingham for an iron and steel museum. Photo by Dicki Arn.*

Top left: This statue of a World War I soldier stands in Woodrow Wilson Park (originally known as Capitol Park). It is dedicated to the men from the Birmingham area who fought in World War I. Photo by Dicki Arn.

Top middle: The First Presbyterian Church, built in 1888, is the oldest church building in downtown Birmingham. The First Alabama Bank Building is in the background. Photo by Dicki Arn.

Top right: One of the more interesting monuments in Oak Hill Cemetery is the Holt Cradle, the resting place of "Baby" Mary, who was the child of T.H. and M.E. Holt. Laid out in 1871, the city cemetery contains the graves of many cholera victims who perished in the 1873 epidemic. Courtesy, Oak Hill Memorial Association. Photo by Dicki Arn.

Above: The Red Hill Cemetery, once the site of the Pinson Presbyterian Church, is one of the oldest cemeteries in Jefferson County. The older graves are marked with hand-carved stones or piles of rock. Members of the Anderson, Hurst, Sanders, and Swafford families are buried here. Photo by Leah R. Atkins.

Top: *Arlington, Birmingham's antebellum house, is filled with numerous antiques. This is one of its many displays typifying nineteenth-century life. Photo by Dicki Arn.*

Above left: *This hand-made pine door on iron hinges is part of the Mervyn H. Sterne house on Tyler Road. The house has an interesting history. Mrs. Ed Beaumont saw the house boarded up and abandoned on the Huntsville Road. Peeking through the crevices, she saw the wide pine floors, hand-hewn log walls, and handmade doors. She purchased the house and moved it across Jefferson County to Shades Mountain. In the*

1950s the Sternes bought the house from the Beaumonts. Courtesy, Mrs. Mervyn Hayden Sterne. Photo by Dicki Arn.

Above right: *The Sterne house dining room contains a wide hearth and pine floor. Courtesy, Mrs. Mervyn Hayden Sterne. Photo by Dicki Arn.*

Top: *The Beaumont house is one of the oldest in Shades Valley. Portions of the house were used as a commissary for the Cahaba Furnace of Wallace McElwain, but one section is much older. The original part of the house is of hand-hewn oak with squared logs and dovetailed ends. Courtesy, Mrs. Edward P. Beaumont. Photo by Dicki Arn.*

Above left: *These plates shown against a background of hand-hewn square logs can be found in the Beaumont house. Courtesy, Mrs. Edward P. Beaumont. Photo by Dicki Arn.*

Above right: *The oldest part of the Beaumont house indicated antebellum origins. Courtesy, Mrs. Edward P. Beaumont. Photo by Dicki Arn.*

Right: *The largest water oak tree in Alabama stands twenty feet nine inches tall and is located on the property of Mrs. Edward P. Beaumont. Courtesy, Mrs. Edward P. Beaumont. Photo by Dicki Arn.*

Above: *Dr. A.G. Gaston, one of Birmingham's most respected and admired men. The founder of the Booker T. Washington Burial Insurance Company, Dr. Gaston became Birmingham's first black millionaire. He has been awarded numerous honorary doctoral degrees in recognition of his humanitarian activities which have included establishing a senior citizen's home and the A.G. Gaston Boy's Club. In 1969 the Sertoma Club bestowed their "Service to Mankind" award on him. Dr. Gaston and his wife are considered the cultural, social, and economic leaders of Birmingham's black community. Courtesy, Dr. A.G. Gaston.*

Above right: *Rufus N. Rhodes came to Birmingham from his native Tennessee after a brief law practice in Chicago and founded the* Birmingham News *on March 14, 1884. Rhodes immediately began to use the* News *to push for the progress of the city. At a dinner for the directors of the Associated Press (Rhodes was a vice president of AP) at Delmonico's Restaurant in New York, Birmingham News cartoonist Charles Koops pictured his boss as a jockey pushing the city of Birmingham on to greatness. Courtesy, James F. Sulzby, Jr. Photo by Dicki Arn.*

Right: *Governor Frank M. Dixon was born in California and educated at the University of Virginia and Columbia. A popular lawyer in Birmingham, he was elected governor of Alabama in 1939. During the 1948 Dixiecrat convention in Birmingham, he gave a rousing pro-Southern speech. Courtesy, State of Alabama Department of Archives and History. Photo by John Scott.*

Top: *The Sadler House, built by Isaac Wellington Sadler in 1838, is a two-story "dog-trot" of unusual design. The Sadlers were early Jones Valley pioneers. The house is listed on the* National Register of Historic Places. *Photo by Dicki Arn.*

Above: *The swinging bridge over Turkey Creek at Bull Frog Bend led to the summer retreat of DuPont Thompson. In his log book of November 3, 1934, Thompson wrote: "Thanks to the gods that be for some place where I can come and forgive mine enemies and forget what I owe. And when at last Time, for me, no longer marches on, I'd like to leave my forwarding address with St. Peter and come on back to Bull Frog Bend." Photo by Leah R. Atkins.*

Above right: *Robert Jemison, Jr. built the Old Mill on the foundation of the antebellum Perryman Mill on Shades Creek as a promotion for his new subdivision Mountain Brook. Photo by Leah R. Atkins.*

Above: *George Ward's lovely home, Vestavia, was a copy of the Roman temple of Vesta. When the round home was razed to make way for the Vestavia Hills Baptist Church, all that remained was this Temple of Sibyl that stood on the crest of the mountain in front of the larger Vestavia, Ward's home. Today the structure stands on the crest of Shades Mountain about a mile from its original spot. Photo by Leah R. Atkins.*

Facing page: *This view of Shades Creek in Shades Valley makes it difficult to believe that Indians moving through the hill country found the valley so dark and dangerous that is was originally named the Shades of Death Valley. Photo by Leah R. Atkins.*

Facing page, top left: *The South Central Bell building dwarfs the First Methodist Church, showing the contrast between new and old in Birmingham. Photo by Dicki Arn.*

Facing page, top right: *The Reverend James A. Bryan, a Presbyterian minister, was the official chaplain of the city of Birmingham. Georges Bridges sculpted this statue of him in 1934. It is now located at Prayer Point overlooking the city. Photo by Leah R. Atkins.*

Facing page, bottom left: *Birmingham has always been a football town and Legion Field, opened in 1927, is annually the scene of many football battles. The Auburn-Alabama game at the end of the regular season is the "Big Game Day" for the state rivals and the Hall of Fame Bowl each December has absorbed much of Birmingham's football pride and energy. Courtesy, Hall of Fame Bowl.*

Facing page, bottom right: *Birmingham claims to be the "Football Capital of the South" and the major Southeastern Conference game pits the University of Alabama against cross-state rival Auburn University the last regular season game each fall. Legion Field is packed for this game. Courtesy, Leah R. Atkins.*

Above: *A view of the city skyline from Red Mountain. Courtesy, Birmingham Area Chamber of Commerce.*

Left: *New Dart buses travel the inner city. This is Twentieth Street looking north toward downtown. Courtesy, Birmingham Area Chamber of Commerce.*

ham-Jefferson Civic Center
t Hall   Theater

PARTNERS IN PROGRESS

The history of the New South's Magic City—Birmingham—is closely linked with the success of the industries and businesses that breath life into the city that so audaciously rose from a worn-out antebellum corn field in the hill country of Jefferson County. That a city did rise from Jones Valley was amazing. At first tied to railroad construction and real estate booms, the development of Birmingham depended upon the exploitation of the mineral resources of the district. But investment capital was always scarce, much of the ownership was absentee, and corporations were underfinanced. For these reasons, and because the city's lifeblood was concentrated in heavy industry, in the early years Birmingham's economy was not secure and whenever the nation's economy slipped into recession the city's business cycle went into depression.

But this brash newcomer to Alabama was soon the largest city in the state, and for years its "Big Mules"—the term political opponents applied to the industrial giants of Jefferson County— threw their weight in the contests of state politics. The city did not grow concentrically; the physical nature and geography of Birmingham was determined by its industrial birth. Mining and mill villages dotted the hills and hollows of Jefferson County and its population was composed largely of blue-collar labor. Today Birmingham does have its elegant bedroom suburbs, but its industrial suburbs came first. The lack of transportation that isolated Jefferson County and prevented its antebellum development soon was ended by a maze of railroad tracks that honeycombed the county, connecting mines, mills, and towns with each other,

and through main lines joining the Birmingham district with the rest of the nation. In the twentieth century, river transportation was added when the Warrior River's Squaw Shoals were flooded by Lock No. 17 and Birmingham became a port city with a navigable river flowing to the Gulf of Mexico.

For eight decades, the iron, steel, and coal industries dominated the entire metropolitan area. In the late nineteenth century, in the boom periods of the 1920s, and during World War II, the Tennessee, Coal, Iron and Railroad Company was the largest single employer in the county, its business success directly affecting nearly one-fourth of the population. Across the county, smoke belched and darkened the noonday sky and red reflections of molten iron danced against the clouds by night.

Today there are tensions between those who recognize that the very industrial base of the district means strip-mining, pollution, and quarries, and those who appreciate Birmingham's location in the Sun Belt and relish the opportunity of being only fifteen minutes away from a creek fishing hole; tensions between those who wish to preserve the land and those who accept desecration as the price of progress. Southerners are a people by heritage tied to the land. In a scene from Margaret Mitchell's *Gone with the Wind*, Gerald O'Hara tells his daughter Scarlett: "Land is the only thing in the world that lasts. . . ." Despite its New South birth, Birmingham is a southern city still tied to the land in a number of ways—by its antebellum farming past, by its mineral wealth out of which the city grew, and by its traditional appreciation of the

land's natural beauty.

Only after the passing of the raw frontier mineral stage did diversification come to Birmingham and Jefferson County. Concerted efforts after World War II succeeded in forging a more sophisticated economy. Today the skyline of the city has changed. Modern skyscrapers tower over the city's golden gems from the past—the Steiner Building, the YMCA Building, and others. The old wholesale warehouses of Morris Avenue, once the trade center of the city, are now part of a restored business and entertainment district. The intersection of First Avenue and Twentieth Street, once billed as the "heaviest corner on earth," is downtown to the new uptown skyscrapers on Fifth and Sixth avenues. Fittingly, the largest employer in the city is a university with its medical complex located on the south side, where elegant homes once stood linking Twentieth Street to Highland Avenue. But Birmingham cannot escape its industrial heritage. Peeking between those mirrored skyscrapers that house booming insurance companies, banks, and hospitals are rusting blast furnaces; and over on Red Mountain silent tramways stained iron ore red still stand beyond the trees, pointing to the minerals below. Tourists driving through the city on the interstate system pass foundries and steel mills that stretch for blocks, their smoke, now filtered white puffs, curling heavenward. The history of Birmingham and Jefferson County cannot be understood without studying the industry and the business of the district. They are more than "Partners in Progress." They are the real reason for the city's being.

ALABAMA POWER COMPANY

In 1906, a newly formed company began with an idea to make living and working in Alabama homes and factories easier by making electricity readily available. That idea, by a young Alabama Power Company, drastically changed the economics of the state of Alabama.

In its early years, however, there was a different Alabama Power Company than we know today. The first practical use of electricity in Alabama was in 1882 by the Woodstock Iron Company, which used steam from its operations to light the streets and furnaces in Anniston, a small mill community. In 1884, one of the first generating and distributing systems in the South was built in Mobile by a draftsman who worked on Edison's original electrical system, Colonel H.M. Byllesby. In 1886, the Elyton Land Company in Birmingham began operating the first public utility electric plant in Alabama. When it proposed to use electricity for street railways, public opposition surfaced in this statement from the Birmingham *Evening News,* on November 5, 1888: "Overhead electrically charged wires to propel dummy trains are deemed more deadly . . . than yellow jack (malaria) . . ."

In spite of opposition and skepticism, those pioneering electric companies, along with several groups with plans for hydroelectric development, paved the way for progress through electricity in Alabama. A number of those early companies eventually became part of today's Alabama Power.

At the turn of the century, Alabama's agriculturally based economy was struggling, while the rich natural resources needed for hydroelectric generation to attract industry remained virtually untouched. To few areas of the country could electric power offer more.

The name Alabama Power Company was first used in 1906 by Captain William Patrick Lay. He headed one of several farsighted groups that envisioned the potential for development of the rivers for power production and navigation and acquired dam sites and land on the Coosa, Tallapoosa, and Tennessee rivers to use for electric power generation and economic development.

Although their intentions were good, it was financially difficult for the individual companies to obtain the sizable amounts of capital required to build the hydroelectric projects to provide dependable and low cost electricity. The answer to this problem came in 1912, when Captain Lay turned his company over to Canadian-born James Mitchell.

Mitchell, along with Tom Martin, a young, enterprising Montgomery lawyer, provided the leadership for Alabama Power's growth in the early years. Mitchell formed a holding company to combine the independent electric groups, resolve their conflicting interests, and formulate comprehensive plans for development. This led to the incorporation in 1912 of the Alabama Traction Light and Power Company, Ltd., created for the specific purpose of acquiring the common stocks of the isolated electric companies in Alabama. To secure the necessary funds to acquire those companies, Alabama Traction in the beginning sold its own securities to English and Canadian investors.

Those early days of the company saw dreams become realities as Lock 12, now Lay Dam, was developed and the first steam plant at Gadsden was completed. Transmission lines were put into service between those generating plants and a number of cities and towns, including Birmingham. The economics of the state began to show improvements as the availability of electricity hastened industrial development and helped agriculture.

In 1912, Alabama Power Company moved its general offices from Montgomery to Birmingham, the industrial capital of the state. In 1925, the general office building was constructed on the corner of Eighteenth Street and Sixth Avenue North in downtown Birmingham. This structure was considered to be one of the three most beautiful public utility buildings in the world, according to a 1926 edition of the London *Daily Express.* This same facility is still the headquarters building for Alabama Power Company operations.

Then, the outbreak of World War I brought all but total ruin to the company. England entered the war in August 1914, and the result was the immediate cut-off of funds from English investors in Alabama Traction Light and Power Company, Ltd. Alabama Traction had to stop all construction and faced bankruptcy when it could not meet its obligation to its creditors or pay interest on bonds due in September.

In a meeting in London on October 21, 1914, the English bondholders of Alabama Traction agreed to waive interest on their bonds for three years and to allow its subsidiary, Alabama Power, to issue and sell bonds and preferred stock to the public. This action placed the company in a position

Above: *Tom Martin, a pioneer in the production of electricity for Alabama, saw dreams become realities as dam sites along Alabama rivers were developed to generate electricity. In the background is Martin Dam, one of the early hydroelectric projects on the Tallapoosa River.*

Below: *This load dispatcher in the Alabama Control and Dispatch Center, located in Birmingham, monitors the entire Alabama Power electrical system, from generating plant production to the flow of electricity on transmission lines.*

Opposite: *One of the early uses of electricity was in streetcar transportation, as this vintage Birmingham Electric Company display explains. Until their merger in 1952, both Alabama Power Company and Birmingham Electric served electrical customers in Jefferson County.*

to execute a new first mortgage on its properties, thus enabling it to sell bonds in America and to continue its ambitious plans for the electrification of Alabama. Under Martin's leadership a holding company, Southeastern Power & Light Company, was formed in the early 1920s. The firm, headquartered in Birmingham, was very similar to The Southern Company of today, with common stock ownership of Georgia, Gulf, Mississippi, Alabama, and South Carolina power companies.

In 1916, the federal government proposed to build a nitrate plant for World War I munitions, and the power plant to supply its electricity, on a site owned by Alabama Power Company in Muscle Shoals. To expedite construction, the company transferred this site along with studies and plans for a power dam to the government for the nominal sum of $1. In 1933, Congress turned those facilities into the Tennessee Valley Authority.

Officials of the power company had the leading part in the development of the Southern Research Institute. This organization has gained international acclaim for its scientific and technological research.

Alabama Power Company is one of the operating affiliates of The Southern Company, along with Georgia Power Company, Mississippi Power Company, and Gulf Power Company. Also a part of The Southern Company is Southern Company Services, Inc., providing

engineering support and other services to the four operating companies. The Southern Company is a public utility holding company organized in 1947 to provide substantial savings in operating costs and fixed charges for the four operating companies. All of Alabama Power's common stock is held by The Southern Company.

In 1914, Alabama Power Company contracted to supply power to large Birmingham industrial customers, and also to Birmingham Railway, Light and Power Company, predecessor of the Birmingham Electric Company. This led to numerous requests from industrial, commercial, residential, and rural customers in areas adjacent to Birmingham for direct service from Alabama Power Company. In many cases, the transmission lines of the two power companies paralleled each other. In 1925, an agreement was made to define the operating territories of both companies.

In that agreement, Birmingham Electric Company provided light, transportation, and steam heat service to metropolitan Birmingham, and the municipalities of Bessemer, Fairfield, Tarrant City, and certain unincorporated areas of Brighton, Homewood, Irondale, Lipscomb, and Mountain Brook. Alabama Power provided electric service in the other areas of Jefferson County.

Since Alabama Power Company supplied Birmingham Electric Company its electricity, transmission lines connected at various points and duplication of service was inevitable. It was obvious that a union of the two companies would be most advantageous for Birmingham customers. In 1950, this long-awaited agreement was reached and stockholders of Birmingham Electric were offered an exchange of their stock for common shares of The Southern Company. The merger was completed on December 1, 1952.

Today, Alabama Power Company serves approximately one million residential, commercial, and industrial customers in over 860 Alabama cities, towns, and rural communities.

AVONDALE MILLS

Avondale Mills, one of the great textile manufacturers of the South, has been moving lockstep with Birmingham for the past eighty-three years. And although its original Birmingham mill was phased out in the 1970s, Avondale retains sales and promotional offices in the city and continues to play a key role in Birmingham's economic and cultural blue-chip future.

The company was launched in Birmingham in 1897 by Braxton Bragg Comer, Alabama planter, banker, and businessman who was later to become governor of the state and then senator. A delicate balance of northern investors, machinery manufacturers, and local interests formed the nucleus of Avondale's first mill. Times in the South were hard for the farmer and for industry, with unfinished fabrics selling for less than two cents per yard.

The hard-driving Comer, with the support of a few friends in finance, bought $10,000 worth of stock in the community-founded mill and took over operations. A company history notes that in the beginning he was his own secretary, his own buyer, and his own, and only, salesman.

Comer was elected governor of Alabama in 1907 and accomplished great improvements in education and economic growth. Today his great-grandson, Donald Comer III, is president, treasurer, and chief executive officer, representing the fourth generation of family leadership.

Steady, well-planned expansion has

been a part of Avondale Mills' business policy through the decades. Today the company operates sixteen plants in three southern states. Avondale Mills, with almost 6,000 employees, is among the textile industry's leaders, and it is generally conceded that Avondale's personnel policies and its ongoing concern for the people who are Avondale are vital to the company's success.

Avondale is the largest producer of sales yarns for the apparel trade. It is also one of the leading producers of apparel fabrics and carpet yarns for the tufting industry. The firm manufactures a variety of cotton and synthetic yarns for automobile upholstery, drapery, furniture, hosiery, coated fabrics,

sportswear, outerwear, and underwear. In its fabrics division, the company manufactures sports denims, yarn-dyed flannel shirtings, home furnishing fabrics, and greige goods for the jeans markets.

Whatever the firm produces, and whatever its sales figures are, Avondale employees, from the president on down are quick to attribute the company's success to one thing: its people. Avondale Mills' concern with employee safety and health has attracted national attention in the trade. Long before OSHA, long before Ralph Nader, Avondale was launching and enforcing its own careful employee protection program on a continuous and strictly enforced basis.

Above left: *Braxton Bragg Comer, Alabama planter, banker, and businessman who later became governor and senator, founded Avondale Mills in 1897.*

Above right: *Donald Comer III, representing the fourth generation involved in the business, is the current president, treasurer, and chief executive officer of Avondale Mills.*

Below: *This artist's rendering depicts Avondale Mills' original plant in Birmingham.*

BAGGETT TRANSPORTATION COMPANY

Trucking is a singular industry, a fraternity of the self-reliant and the enterprising. But even within that unique fraternity, Baggett Transportation Company of Birmingham is exceptional. For the unusual feature about Baggett Transportation is that, while it is a trucking company in the usual sense, it specializes in—and restricts its cargo to—explosives.

The firm, founded in Birmingham by brothers Jess and John Baggett, began as a small, three-unit freight carrier on July 13, 1931. With American business paralyzed by the depression, that was not a promising year to start a new enterprise. But the company has successfully weathered decades of challenge and today offers direct single-line service to forty-eight states, with sales and service offices located throughout the country.

The firm, of course, was not always a specialist in explosives. It began as a general commodity contract carrier and continued to operate in general commodities for many years. But it carried its first load of high explosives early in 1928 and quickly gained expertise and an excellent reputation in this field. Baggett's first contracts were with Du Pont and with the equally well-known Atlas and Hercules companies—all of them foremost producers of explosives. The firm now restricts itself to hauling explosives.

Explosives—a broad word—actually includes Class A, B, and C explosives; ammunition; ingredients and component parts for ammunition; blasting materials; blasting supplies; blasting agents; and empty explosive containers. Baggett also hauls other items declared "sensitive" by the federal government.

Although the name "Baggett" was retained for business reasons, the firm actually was taken over altogether in 1941 by William Sellers and he has remained at the helm ever since. It was under Sellers' leadership that Baggett developed from a general commodity carrier to an explosives specialist,

William D. Sellers, Jr., is chairman of the board and chief executive officer of Baggett Transportation Company.

enjoying its period of greatest expansion. The company first branched out into the Southeast, then slowly expanded into all corners of the country. Baggett finally discontinued the general commodity phase of the business altogether in 1977 upon the sale to Consolidated Freightways.

Baggett is the first in the nation in its field. It was the first carrier to file with the federal government for government freight transportation, and it was the first carrier licensed by the Interstate Commerce Commission to haul explosives and ammunition in all forty-eight states. Baggett Transportation is one of the largest common carriers for the U.S. Department of Defense and commercial explosives manufacturers, and its trucks are a familiar sight on the nation's highways, from the Atlantic to the Pacific and from Maine to the Gulf.

Although Baggett Transportation's cargo specialty is a highly sensitive one, the firm has an excellent safety record and maintains a string of safety inspection stations in key areas. Baggett's success in its safety efforts is evident—the company's insurance premiums continue to decrease.

Officials of Baggett Transportation include William Sellers, chairman; Howard Durden, president; Lucille Thomas, vice-president and assistant secretary; Horace Grant, senior vice-president sales and traffic; Tom Sinclair, senior vice-president operations and safety; Marlin Brown, vice-president traffic; Robert Nunnally, treasurer; John Randall, vice-president maintenance; Michael Cleveland, assistant treasurer; and Ormond Somerville, secretary.

THE BAPTIST MEDICAL CENTERS

The Baptist Medical Centers trace their genesis to January 20, 1922, when the Birmingham Infirmary, a 90-bed hospital, was purchased by the Birmingham Baptist Association. A nurses' training school (now the Ida V. Moffett School of Nursing) was acquired with the hospital.

The first years were filled with adversities, but even so, improvements were effected. A nurses' residence was built in 1925, and a crippled children's ward was established three years later. A second hospital, Gorgas Hospital-Hotel, later Highland Avenue Baptist Hospital, was acquired in 1930. A new nursing school was built at this location in 1945, one of the most modern of its kind. A pathology department was organized in 1942, followed by a school of medical technology and a pathology residency program.

Because both hospitals were so extensively used, planning began in the 1940s and 1950s to expand services. Birmingham Baptist established the first electroencephalogram lab in a private Birmingham hospital, organized the city's first bone bank, and became the first private hospital in Alabama to do clinical research with cortisone.

After a successful fund-raising campaign, a major expansion took place at the west end site during 1953-56, with a four-story east wing being added. A community-wide fund-raising campaign was then launched to replace the old Highland Avenue Baptist Hospital. Since the site on Ridge Park Hill was not large enough for a modern hospital, a new site was acquired on Montclair Road.

In 1966, two new hospital buildings graced the Birmingham scene — Birmingham Baptist Hospital (now BMC-Princeton) at West End and Baptist Medical Center-Montclair, which replaced Highland Avenue Baptist Hospital.

There followed a continuous additon of new services. Princeton's new intensive care unit featured the first use of electronic monitoring equipment for patient care in an Alabama community hospital. In 1965, its laboratories, which had pioneered the use of automation, received the first multi-channel autoanalyzer in the Southeast. Open-heart surgery was performed at Montclair, the first in an Alabama community hospital.

During the 1970s, emphasis was placed on improving facilities for diagnostic and treatment services, an ever-continuing building program, and quality health education programs. The Center for Neurological Sciences was established at Princeton in 1972 and a stroke rehabilitation unit was opened at Montclair. That same year, BMC assumed management of the Jefferson Tuberculosis Sanatorium, now Lakeshore Hospital. This was the first of several hospitals for which BMC contracted management responsibility.

Today, The Baptist Medical Centers comprise the largest nonprofit hospital system in Alabama. The BMC system includes ownership of two modern major referral centers in Birmingham, BMC-Princeton and BMC-Montclair; a primary care center, BMC-Leeds Family Health Center, on the outskirts of Birmingham; and The BMC Center for Health Promotion with cardiovascular rehabilitation facilities located at Lakeshore Hospital in Homewood, Alabama. BMC leases two community hospitals, BMC-DeKalb in Fort Payne, Alabama and BMC-Cherokee in Center, Alabama, and provides management services for two other hospitals — Cullman Medical Center in Cullman and Lakeshore Hospital in Homewood, Alabama. BMC also manages Princeton Towers, a 12-story apartment complex for the elderly and handicapped located on the BMC-Princeton campus.

The BMC hospitals have never accepted construction or operating funds from local, state, or federal governments. Facilities have been constructed and operated completely from funds generated by the hospitals through patient revenues and contributions from community citizens. The Baptist Medical Centers' general offices are located at 3201 Fourth Avenue South in Birmingham. BMC president is Emmett R. Johnson.

The Birmingham Baptist Hospital on Tuscaloosa Avenue West, seen in this 1922 photograph, has grown into a regional medical center. Baptist Medical Center-Princeton has developed into a modern 439-bed hospital operation and will add another 55 beds when a multimillion-dollar expansion is complete.

BIRMINGHAM BOLT COMPANY

The present Birmingham Fabricating and Birmingham Bolt companies are successors to an enterprise incorporated in 1925 as Birmingham Fabricating Company, Inc. The firm originally produced ornamental iron, steel plate work, other fabricated steel products, and wooden mill work. During its first twenty years it was managed by Leonard H. White. E.J. Lee Rust, for whom Leonard had worked as an engineer, furnished the majority of the capital to the small company.

The first years of operation were difficult ones. During the Great Depression Leonard White, with the help of Rust, barely managed to keep the company solvent. They managed in part due to orders for fabricated steel from Rust and to Leonard White's patents on designs of road forms and guardrails. In 1934 Erskine White graduated from Auburn at the top of his class in engineering and in 1936 went to work for the company. That same year, Claude Carlos White joined the firm after graduating from Auburn.

E.J. Lee Rust was president of the company from 1927 until his death in 1939. At the time of his death he held a majority of shares of the business as collateral on loans he had made about ten years earlier; these obligations to Mr. Rust had just been discharged when he died. Shortly after his passing the shares were delivered to Leonard White, by his sons, George and Henry.

In 1939, Leonard White, being the only stockholder, dissolved Birmingham Fabricating Company, Inc., and formed a partnership of himself, F.E. White, and C.C. White as owners of Birmingham Fabricating Company. That same year the firm purchased the bankrupt Birmingham Pressed Steel Company plant near Pratt City. This structure has been expanded and is the main facility of the Birmingham Fabricating Company today.

In the early stages of World War II, most of the management was ordered to active duty in the U.S. Army and Navy. Leonard White had five sons in military service. The number of employees in the plant dropped from 150 men in

1941 to 55 men in 1945, due to the draft of soldiers. The plant produced components of war ships and Liberty ships. After the war Leonard H. White, Jr., and Lewis P. White became partners and Leonard H. White, Sr., withdrew from the partnership.

Fortunately for the company, in the early 1950s, the first large-scale trial use of roof bolts to support mine roofs was conducted at Concord Mine of U.S. Steel near Bessemer. The success of this trial prompted Alabama Power Company to try them at Gorgas Mine. Birmingham Fabricating Company furnished these bolts, marking the

beginning of the company's roof bolt business.

Roof bolt usage grew slowly and steel fabricating remained the principal business during the 1950s. However, the roof bolt sideline ultimately far exceeded the fabricating activity. Birmingham Bolt Company was organized as a separate corporation in 1957. In 1959 "big steel" was "on strike" for ninety-five days. Birmingham Bolt and one other roof bolt manufacturer were the only suppliers able to furnish bolts during the strike. This opened up new sales areas and resulted in increased sales volume for years.

In the 1960s Birmingham Bolt built a new plant at Madisonville, Kentucky, for the manufacture of roof bolts. The equipment in this plant was designed by Erskine White and is still the most sophisticated in the world. In the 1970s, four other plants were built with additional improvements. The Kankakee Electric Steel Company, a mini-steel mill with a 100,000-ton-per-year capacity, was purchased and became the main source of steel rods for the companies. Later, the Southern Electric Steel Company in Birmingham was purchased and is currently being modernized to produce reinforcing rods used in bolts as well as other products.

The four White brothers sold all companies in May 1980 to United Coal Company, a Virginia-based corporation. It is a tightly held, very successful producer of quality coals, with mines in Virginia, Kentucky, West Virginia, Ohio, and Oklahoma.

Above: *Leonard H. White, a World War I veteran, managed Birmingham Fabricating Company, predecessor of today's Birmingham Bolt Company, for its first twenty years of operation.*

Below: *Birmingham Bolt's steel mill is located in Kankakee, Illinois.*

BIRMINGHAM-JEFFERSON HISTORICAL SOCIETY

There is always room for one more historical society in any city or community, and so it has been with Birmingham. On October 9, 1975, a group of interested citizens met to establish an organization later to be known as the Birmingham-Jefferson Historical Society. The original thirteen members pledged themselves to the purposes of discovering, collecting, preserving, and publicizing facts and materials that might help to illustrate the history of Birmingham and its surrounding areas. Within a year the organization boasted a membership of over 400.

The Birmingham-Jefferson Historical Society holds regular meetings with addresses, lectures, papers, discussions, and historical site visitations. The Society has cooperated with other historical groups in the county, and has enjoyed ties with the Jefferson County Historical Commission, the Alabama Historical Association, and Tannehill Historical State Park.

J. Morgan Smith was the Society's first president, serving for two years; Dr. Margaret D. Sizemore served in that capacity for two years; Elmer C. Thuston, Jr., was president for one year; and Edward T. Douglass is the current leader. Each of these individuals has supplied excellent guidance, helping to lead the Society to a record of high achievement.

Among the activities sponsored by the Society was an early but comprehensive history presented by J. Morgan Smith at the opening assembly of the Alabama Historical Association at its annual meeting in Birmingham in 1977. The Birmingham-Jefferson Historical Society membership has provided numerous programs for civic and literary clubs and schools throughout the county. Society members have visited Tannehill Historical State Park and sponsored a luncheon at the park for members of the Alabama Historical Association. A trip to Horseshoe Bend National Military Park was enjoyed by the members. The society enjoyed a Saturday at the famous Alabama Theatre in Birmingham, at which time the architectural design of the theater

was thoroughly explained.

During its short existence, the Birmingham-Jefferson Historical Society has been actively involved in many community-oriented activities. One such activity is the sponsorship of this book, which illustrates the Society's dedication to promote the history of the Birmingham area. This publication is the best and most comprehensive history ever published in connection with Birmingham and its surrounding areas.

Below top: *Birmingham was encircled with industrial suburbs, mining and mill villages, and company towns. Ensley was one of the first steel mill villages. It was named for Enoch Ensley, an early leader of the Tennessee Coal, Iron and Railroad Company. This picture of early Ensley shows Nineteenth Street, looking west with the Ensley Bank on the left.*

Below bottom: *Twentieth Street, looking toward the Confederate Monument in Woodrow Wilson Park, shows a busy scene during the 1920s. The Britling Cafeteria on the left was a Birmingham institution for many decades. Women are hurrying across Third Avenue headed downtown to the shops and stores.*

184

BIRMINGHAM SAW WORKS

Birmingham as an incorporated city was just fourteen years old when Joseph M. Thuston saw his chance. The young town survived on coal and iron, and where there was coal and iron there was excavation and construction, activities that required tools. One tool very much in demand was the saw. And Thuston was a saw maker by trade.

So in partnership with Thomas DeVou, he founded the Birmingham Saw Works in 1885 at 2119 Morris Avenue, then a new street of flourishing trade and commerce and now an officially recognized historic district in downtown Birmingham.

Thuston and DeVou's saw repair business, known simply at the beginning as "The Saw Shop," prospered steadily as the city flexed its economic muscles. There was work to be done in this hub of smokestacks and mining pits and there was great demand for an expert in the business of selling and sharpening saws.

DeVou sold his interest in the growing concern to Thuston in 1895, and Thuston soon moved to 2226 Morris Avenue, just a block down the street from the original saw works. At about this time, too, Thuston's son Elmer joined the business. The firm became known around town as both Joseph Thuston & Son and Birmingham Saw Works.

In need of more operating room once

again, Birmingham Saw Works moved for the second time in 1909, this time to 2614 Second Avenue North. The elder Thuston died in 1917, thirty-two years after he had launched his now-thriving saw works, and Elmer C. Thuston took over full management of the company.

The business in 1931 incorporated as Birmingham Saw Works, Inc., with Elmer Thuston as president. The firm,

---

Above: *Joseph Thuston and Thomas DeVou stand at the entrance to the saw repair shop they established in 1885. Originally known as "The Saw Shop," the enterprise was located at 2119 Morris Avenue.*

Below: *Today the Birmingham Saw Works, now located at 910 North Twenty-eighth Street, handles highly sophisticated woodworking and metalworking machinery and supplies.*

---

coping with the Great Depression, managed to survive. Continuing the original Thuston line of management leadership, Elmer C. Thuston, Jr., became active in the company in 1938 and upon the death of his father in 1956 became president of the firm.

For the third time, Birmingham Saw Works moved to a new location, and settled into a plant at 910 North Twenty-eighth Street. With this desperately needed increase in operating space, the firm continued to expand and augment its services to Birmingham's booming industrial complex.

With the advent of the 1970s, three great-grandsons of founder Joseph M. Thuston joined the company. Elmer C. Thuston III came aboard as vice-president and general manager, William L. Thuston as vice-president and legal counsel, and Robert D. Thuston as vice-president and sales manager.

By then, of course, the name "Birmingham Saw Works" was in some ways a misnomer. The greatly enlarged company had long since gone beyond the limits of a saw repair shop in the old-fashioned sense of the phrase, and had adopted much more advanced and sophisticated undertakings, handling highly technical woodworking and metalworking machinery and supplies used in the wood and metal fabricating industries.

BIRMINGHAM-SOUTHERN COLLEGE

Birmingham-Southern College, perhaps more than any other establishment of higher education in Alabama, has been historically associated with academic excellence. An educational institution of the United Methodist Church, the college had its beginnings as Southern University in Greensboro, Alabama, in 1856. The present campus on the west side of the city, known by all as the Hilltop, was first occupied by Birmingham College in 1898. In 1918 the two schools merged and Birmingham-Southern College was established. The picturesque, tree-shaded campus includes over thirty-five buildings, some dating back to the turn of the century, the newest with construction started in 1980.

While Birmingham-Southern stresses the liberal arts, for which it has a national reputation, preprofessional programs are also strong, including medicine, dentistry, law, and business. Equally well regarded are its fine arts programs in music, art, drama, and dance.

Reflecting its national academic status, B-SC sends a higher percentage of its graduates on to professional and graduate schools than any other college in the Deep South. It has long been regarded as among the academic leaders of the nation. Sixty percent of B-SC first-year students were "A" students in high school. The college has one of two Phi Beta Kappa chapters in Alabama.

The faculty is composed of some of the South's outstanding professors and researchers. Dr. Neal R. Berte, described by the American Council on Education as "one of America's 100 emerging leaders in higher education in 1980," became Birmingham-Southern's tenth president in February 1976. He joined a long line of nationally recognized educators who have headed the college.

Not only is campus life intellectually stimulating, it provides students with a variety of experiences and activities. The college has an active Greek system with eleven national fraternities and sororities. Also, the college has produced seventeen talented Miss Alabamas.

Left: *The plaza of the Rush Learning Center attracts students for between-class conversations.*

Right: *A newer segment of the 83-year-old campus is seen from one of the many hilltops.*

Rarely found in such a scholarly environment is the strong athletic program at Birmingham-Southern. The basketball and baseball teams are regularly found among the top ten teams of the nation's small colleges and tennis has developed swiftly to such status.

While many small liberal arts colleges were experiencing enrollment declines and financial troubles in the late 1970s, B-SC was growing. In 1978 the college ended a decade of deficits, moving into a balanced budget. Enrollment increased from 727 students in 1975 to over 1,440 in 1980, with a similar trend of enrollment increases indicated for the 1980s.

The Hilltop's graduates have strong nationwide representation in the "U.S. Who's Who" in business, the professions, the arts, religion, and education, with a number of university presidents among its graduates. And Birmingham-Southern has been a vital factor in the growth and development of Birmingham itself. Many graduates have gone on to become the city's mayors, congressmen, legislators, businessmen, ministers, teachers, and lawyers. Their influence has helped to put the "magic" into Birmingham's development as one of America's great industrial cities.

During the mid-1960s lawyer Charles A. Speir used to lead his young sons on Christmas tree hunts on the slope of a mountain south of downtown Birmingham. At the time, the steep slope looked like anything but the future home of a 474-bed, eight-level hospital with offices for 109 physicians and a medical staff of 500. Yet within ten busy years, not only would Brookwood Medical Center be erected, but nestled adjacent to this sprawling six-acre medical complex would be the corporate headquarters of one of the nation's ten largest hospital management companies, Brookwood Health Services, Inc. And Speir, having played a central role in the founding of both the medical center and the management company, would put aside his law practice to become president of the $105-million operation.

In early 1966, when the idea for the hospital was being formed, Birmingham already had more than a dozen hospitals, but they were all to the north of Red Mountain. To the south, beyond Vulcan's back, was a wide area of rapidly growing residential communities where young professionals were settling their families as they accepted positions in the numerous service industries that were coming into the city. Connecting the newcomers with the city's health care facilities was a single path, Highway 31, which struggled up Red Mountain and veered past Vulcan's feet to the city below.

Speir became an enthusiastic supporter

of the plan to build a hospital for the growing "over-the-mountain" communities, and joining businessmen such as realtor Art Rice, Jr., and physicians such as urologist Van Scott, he helped lay the groundwork for a hospital that would include practicing physicians in all aspects of its management and decision-making. The founders' group, which consisted of an equal mix of businessmen and physicians, also determined that the hospital should be operated as a free-enterprise venture, supporting itself without adding to the tax burden of the community. It took seven years to turn these ideas into a functioning hospital, but in March 1973 Brookwood Medical Center opened with 288 all-private beds, becoming the city's only investor-owned facility.

The year 1976 was a key one for Brookwood Medical Center. In that year, the hospital began the first in a series of expansion projects that have continued without interruption into the 1980s, adding in turn a four-story office building for physicians; an 86-bed hospital addition; a seven-level ambulatory care center; a six-level parking deck for Brookwood Medical Center's more than 1,200 employees; and, in coordination with another health care company, a 112-bed long-term

Brookwood Medical Center of Birmingham is a major medical complex and one of the nation's leading hospital management companies.

care unit and rehabilitation hospital.

The stream of expansions made it possible for Brookwood Medical Center to become the second largest deliverer of babies in Alabama and to provide the community with a number of significant services, including open-heart surgery, a community cancer center, an alcoholism detoxification unit, an executive health center, a hotel for outpatients and relatives of inpatients, a pain management center for victims of chronic pain, and a same-day surgery program that gives patients an opportunity to have numerous surgical procedures performed at a substantial cost savings.

Also in 1976, Brookwood entered the expanding multi-facility hospital management field, acquiring two other hospitals, one in Alabama and another in Florida. Within four years, Brookwood climbed into the ranks of the ten largest such companies in the nation, with sixteen hospitals and three alcoholism recovery centers under ownership, management, or development in seven states.

The major reason for Brookwood's rapid success in the hospital management field was its corporate commitment to close involvement of physicians in the planning and management of its affiliate hospitals. Says Speir, "What we have shown is that a physician-controlled hospital can move forward in the best trends of medicine."

CARRAWAY METHODIST MEDICAL CENTER

Carraway Methodist Medical Center is one of the oldest health care facilities in Jefferson County. Carraway Infirmary, as it was originally known, had its beginnings in a small house in Pratt City in 1902 with a capacity of 16 patients. This facility served its founder, Dr. C.N. Carraway, quite well until 1916.

In that year, Dr. C.N. felt the need to expand his patient care facility, and to move to the rapidly growing city of Birmingham. Thus, he and four other men of vision and foresight formed the holding company through which the hospital was incorporated, with a capacity of 35 beds. The affluent Norwood community was selected as the site for the new hospital, to be located on the corner of Sixteenth Avenue and Twenty-fifth Street North. The Norwood Hospital, as it was named, was remodeled and an additional floor of patient rooms was added in 1928. The main entrance was moved from the corner of the building to open on Sixteenth Avenue North. In 1947, at the annual meeting of the North Alabama Conference of the Methodist Church, the name was changed to Carraway Methodist Hospital.

Dr. Benjamin M. Carraway assumed the mantle of leadership from his father, as chairman of the hospital's board of directors, in 1956. Under his dynamic leadership CMMC has enjoyed unparalleled growth and development. In 1957, the first phase of major hospital expansion was completed.

Known as the South Purcell Wing, this facility was soon filled to capacity and the need was felt for more patient rooms. The second phase of this construction was finished in 1961. The second major expansion was occupied in 1966, when the North Purcell addition was completed. Full occupancy of the entire facility was raised to 419 patients. This expansion also permitted larger facilities for the pharmacy, laboratory, and surgery, as well as new areas for patient care.

Dr. C.N. Carraway (right) founded the Carraway Infirmary in Pratt City (above) in 1902.

Below: *In 1916 Dr. Carraway expanded his patient care facility, moving to the affluent Birmingham community of Norwood.*

Above: *Dr. Benjamin Monroe Carraway, son of Dr. C.N. Carraway, became chairman of the hospital's board of directors in 1956.*

Above right: *Dr. Robert Posey Carraway, son of Dr. Benjamin Monroe Carraway, was instrumental in beginning the Life Saver program.*

Below: *Known as Carraway Methodist Medical Center since 1971, the new hospital facilities were completed in 1974.*

In 1971 the institution's name was changed to Carraway Methodist Medical Center to describe its services more aptly. Construction of the Goodson Wing, begun in 1971, was the largest expansion undertaken by the Medical Center. In addition to increasing the capacity of CMMC to 617 patients,

Goodson brought a large cafeteria, lobby and waiting room, laboratory, vastly expanded radiology, physical therapy, inhalation therapy, pulmonary lab, a new laundry room, a parking deck, and a tremendous expansion of data processing facilities. The special care units—medical-surgical intensive care, neuro-intensive care, and coronary care—were vastly expanded as well.

The Sanders Emergency Department wing was occupied in 1976. This facility, capable of handling any type of emergency or major disaster in the area, represents an innovative approach to emergency care. The second phase of construction to the Sanders Building was completed in 1979. This addition included open-heart surgery, expanded facilities for neurosurgery, orthopedic surgery for replacement of artificial hips

and joints, as well as chest and vascular surgery. A most unusual wing of CMMC was added in January 1981—a helicopter known as Life Saver. Life Saver is a portable emergency department housed in a helicopter, capable of landing on or alongside any Alabama parking lot, street, highway, or interstate, ready to begin treatment immediately in the event of an accident or disaster. A physician, flight nurse, and pilot are assigned to each Life Saver flight. They are prepared to lift off 24 hours per day, 7 days per week.

Today Carraway Methodist Medical Center has a capacity of 617 patient beds, with modern facilities and sophisticated equipment to diagnose and treat nearly any illness or injury. It has been designated as one of the state's Category I Trauma Centers to serve those patients who are critically injured.

The history of the Norwood Clinic, opened in 1924 across from the YMCA in downtown Birmingham, is closely related to that of CMMC. Dr. C.N. Carraway was also one of its founders. The seven physician members of the clinic moved into their newly constructed office building on the corner of Twenty-fifth Street and Sixteenth Avenue North in 1926. Because of continued growth in professional membership and the addition of more medical specialties, a new building was completed in 1975, able to house the more than 85 physicians who are active members of the Norwood Clinic.

CHICAGO BRIDGE & IRON COMPANY

Chicago Bridge & Iron Company's Birmingham plant is virtually tailor-made for a city whose image is historically tied to that of iron and steel. And, like the city itself, CBI's track record since it opened in Birmingham fifty years ago is one of growth and innovation, of challenge and change.

Located at 1500 Fiftieth Street North, CBI's sprawling facility spans more than a half-million square feet, a considerable increase in size over the 140,000-square-foot plant acquired by the company when it began local operations in 1930

The move into Birmingham was dictated by the promising possibilities offered by the southeastern states and, too, by the close proximity afforded to steel supplies. It was a simple matter of economics that customers in the Louisiana and Texas oil fields, for example, could be more easily and efficiently supplied by the Birmingham regional facility, today a highly productive partner in a dynamic, worldwide operation.

The history of the Birmingham plant has been one of steady and logical expansion—a structural shop, several crane runways, a loading yard, bath house, blasting and painting yard, cafeteria and time office, field erection warehouse, shop office, two welding shops, an X-ray building, and a new construction office have been added to the original structure.

CBI's activities, embracing a wide range of heavy metal fabrications, include the construction of nuclear reactors and containment vessels, pressure vessels, hydroelectric penstocks, oil and chemical storage tanks, cryogenic vessels for liquefied gas, offshore structures and systems, water storage tanks, and much more.

CBI was officially incorporated in Illinois in 1889 by Horace E. Horton. The founder of the company, he originally began building bridges soon after the Civil War. The first Chicago plant was equipped to do heavy work for railroads, standpipes, and elevated water tanks. The firm built its first water storage standpipe in 1893, and shortly afterward constructed the first riveted steel tank with a full hemispherical bottom connected directly to the cylindrical shell. This development placed CBI in a position of leadership in the water tank business—a position it retains today.

Plants in Pennsylvania and in Canada were opened in the early 1900s, and during World War I the firm produced elevated tanks and steel plate structures for the military and fabricated structural steel for warships. CBI began its first overseas work in 1916, exporting fabricated materials to Cuba, Venezuela, Mexico, and Japan.

CBI began construction of large oil tanks for the great oil fields of the Southwest and West in the 1920s,

---

Below: *Shown here is the Chicago Bridge & Iron Company plant in 1926.*

Bottom: *Chicago Bridge & Iron Company's sprawling facility at 1500 Fiftieth Street North, Birmingham, spans more than a half-million square feet.*

---

significantly advancing that technology. During World War II CBI built cat crackers, blast furnaces, floating dry docks, and other facilities to aid the war effort, including landing ships for the navy.

Expanding its plants at home and opening subsidiaries abroad, CBI went through a far-reaching period of growth following the end of World War II. The company moved into the new fields of cryogenics, hydroelectric power, nuclear and liquefied natural gas energy fields, and offshore petroleum storage tanks.

CBI has remained in the vanguard of its field through intensive research, resulting in the development of new and innovative techniques, and through continued expansion of its physical facilities. CBI subsidiaries have been established in Australia, Canada, Germany, South Africa, and Brazil.

As the world's leading designer and erector of metal plate structures, CBI is today an international corporation, proud to be a member of Alabama's industrial community.

190

CONNORS STEEL COMPANY

The South's swiftly expanding steel business at the turn of the century created an attraction for the talents of an already established Atlanta sales executive which, within a few years, led to the establishment of what today is a thriving element of Birmingham's industrial complex, the Connors Steel Company.

The son of a South Carolina Civil War cavalry commander, George Washington Connors, and his business partner, Samuel Weyman, joined other Atlantans in 1901 to form the Atlanta Steel Hoop Company. After seven years' experience as secretary-treasurer of the steel company, Connors was ready to take off on his own in the business. In 1908 he and his partner launched Connors-Weyman Steel in Helena, Alabama, near the southern center of the dynamic metals industry, Birmingham. The venture was an immediate success.

In 1916 the fledgling enterprise acquired the facilities of a bankrupt industrial plant in Birmingham and relocated the Connors-Weyman operation in that city. In 1920 Connors-Weyman became Connors Steel Company. Connors was president and general manager, a position he held until 1937, when he became chairman of the board. His son, George W. Connors, Jr., succeeded him as president.

The rapid expansion of Connors Steel testified to the founder's astuteness. The plant moved from the production of cotton ties and cooperage hoops to the manufacture of reinforcing bars from rerolled rail. In 1939, Connors Steel installed its first electric furnace, casting steel into billet-size ingots. The plant was adapted during World War II to accommodate production of fragmentation bombs from wire coils.

In 1950 Connors was acquired by the H.K. Porter Company, Inc., of Pittsburgh, Pennsylvania, and a multimillion-dollar expansion was undertaken to meet the demands of a rapidly growing market. In 1956 Connors constructed the first integrated cold-finished bar mill in the South.

Heat is being tapped from one of the electric furnaces at the Birmingham plant of Connors Steel.

Connors acquired West Virginia Steel and Manufacturing Company of Huntington, West Virginia in 1956. Products of the newly acquired concern included light rail and track work, mine roof bolts, special sections, sub-purlins, and hot-rolled bars. Continual expansions were necessary at both facilities to accommodate the ever-increasing demands for steel.

With the installation in 1964 of 2 two-strand continuous casters, Connors became one of the first American mills ever equipped with a sequence caster. In 1970, with the launching of the largest single equipment expansion in Connor's history, a 14-inch in-line rolling mill and supporting facilities were built. The 1970s also saw the installation of sophisticated air pollution equipment at both plants.

Connors became a wholly owned subsidiary of the H.K. Porter Company, Inc., in 1974. Robert L. Mueller was named chairman of the board and president in 1975. Both the Birmingham and Huntington plants continued to experience large capital expansion programs. By late 1980, the Birmingham facility completed the installation of five new mill break-down stands and a 100-ton reheat furnace, as well as additional changes in the melt shop which increased production capacity.

Today, Connors Steel represents the fulfillment of the aims and ambitions of a turn-of-the-century businessman who decided to make his fortune in the growing metals industry.

191

COWIN AND COMPANY, INC. Cowin Equipment Company, Inc.

Birmingham's mining industry continued to develop rapidly in the 1920s and attracted many specialists from outside the state, among them Percy G. Cowin, a mining engineering graduate of the University of Minnesota. The young Minnesota native came to the Magic City in 1919 after completing military service in World War I. In 1923 he started his own business. The following year, joining with a friend and associate, he formed Salmon & Cowin, Inc., a mining engineering and contracting firm. That same company (in which the Cowin family years later acquired 100 percent interest) is now known as Cowin & Company, Inc., and carries on its same mining engineering and contracting function today.

The original enterprise started in business at 711 Ninth Street North. The early days were difficult. Cowin had a brother in Minnesota who also was in business. Every once in a while they had to borrow money from each other to meet their respective payrolls.

A substantial number of local mines were developed by the company in Alabama. One of the Cowin excavation projects away from home in the late 1920s was the elevator shaft at Ruby Falls, one of Chattanooga's tourist attractions.

While Cowin & Company continued its traditional type of work, it was forced to diversify in the '50s and '60s into other related activities because of declining coal mining development in Alabama during this period, as well as the eventual discontinuance of iron ore mining due to imported ores. Thus, Cowin & Company expanded its operations to the southeastern and mid-Atlantic states and undertook greater

Above: *Percy G. Cowin and an associate founded Salmon & Cowin, Inc., predecessor of today's Cowin & Company, Inc., in 1924.*

Below: *"The Castle," erected in 1937, was the early headquarters of the Cowin companies, located at 930 Second Avenue North.*

varieties of work. Today Cowin & Company maintains its emphasis on mine-related work—such as the construction of shafts and slopes—as well as more diversified projects such as highway, railroad, sewer, and hydro tunnels.

The forebear of Cowin Equipment Company emerged in 1940 as Mine & Contractors Supply Company, a division of Cowin & Company which leased and sold compressors, drills, bits, and associated equipment. It soon began developing as a full-line dealer in construction machinery and equipment and, in 1955, its present-day name was adopted. The equipment dealership established a branch in Mobile in the 1950s and one in Montgomery in 1969. The company now serves Alabama, northwest Florida, and southern Mississippi.

Percy Cowin died in 1963. His two sons, John and Peter, continue management of the Cowin companies. John Cowin is president of Cowin & Company. While still a teenager, he worked summers with his father before entering Stanford University where he received a bachelor of science degree in mining engineering. He holds a master of science degree from the University of Alabama. Except for service during the Korean War as a first lieutenant in the Army Corps of Engineers, he has spent his entire career in mine development and other forms of underground excavation and construction. Peter Cowin is president of Cowin Equipment. He received a bachelor of arts degree in economics from Oberlin College in Ohio. The two brothers have equal interests in both companies but specialize in their management responsibilities.

An architectural feature which identified the Cowin business for many years is "the Castle," a small two-story engineering building at 930 Second Avenue North which was erected in 1937. In the late '40s Cowin & Company moved to its present location on Eighteenth Street Southwest. The main Birmingham office of Cowin Equipment now is located at 2300 Pinson Valley Parkway.

DANIEL ORNAMENTAL IRON COMPANY, INC.

Devising a cutoff valve for municipal water systems ingenious enough to be patentable launched an involvement for a Birmingham family in steel and iron fabrication that four generations later finds the enterprise a recognized leader in its specialty.

Personal interests, changing marketing conditions, and the depression of the 1930s have changed the direction of the family enterprise several times, but involvement with Birmingham's major product and industrial symbol, iron and steel, has been the lone economic interest of the Daniel family, represented by the Daniel Ornamental Iron Co. For over seventy years the Daniel family has contributed strongly to the economic and civic activity of Birmingham.

W. Homer Daniel, a machinist with strong inventive capabilities stimulated by the technological advances distinguishing the early part of the twentieth century, obtained a patent for the cutoff valve and organized the Daniel Manufacturing Co. to produce it in 1913.

Five years later Daniel's inventiveness took another twist, when he conceived and patented a machine for ice cream cone preparation. Having dissolved his previous company he formed a new corporation, The Daniel Machine Co., to manufacture the product. At the same time he involved himself in auto repair and maintenance with the Daniel-Deramus Garage Co.

Selling the process four years later, Daniel tried his hand in the oil business with a successful well in Franklin, Kentucky. He abandoned that venture after two years of fruitless efforts to connect his well by pipeline to a railhead. He returned to Birmingham to involve himself again in metal fabrication.

In 1929 he started specialization in a facet of metal fabrication that today comprises a large share of the product line of the family business. With the

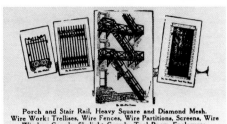

Porch and Stair Rail, Heavy Square and Diamond Mesh. Wire Work: Trellises, Wire Fences, Wire Partitions, Screens, Wire Window Guards, Skylight Guards, Tool Room Enclosures.

Daniels' Ornamental Iron & Wire Corp.
Manufacturers of
RESIDENCE BURGLAR WINDOW GUARDS
A SPECIALTY
Estimates Gladly Furnished
Ornamental and Miscellaneous Iron and Wire Work
PHONE 3-8649   725-31 Third Ave., N., BIRMINGHAM, ALA.

organization of Daniels' Ornamental Iron and Wire Corp., Homer Daniel filled both residential and industrial needs for porch and stair rail, producing fire escapes, heavy square and diamond mesh, trellises, fences, partitions, screens, window guards, and tool room enclosures.

The Great Depression dealt the company a fatal blow and forced the retirement from business of Homer Daniel. But the family's involvement with iron and steel was just beginning. In 1940 Daniel's son, W. Harry Daniel, who had grown up in his father's business, founded his own operation, the Daniel Iron Works. He began an enterprise that today, under the direction of his son, James E. Daniel, is an industry leader in metal fabrication. In 1947 W. Harry Daniel changed the name of his firm to Daniel Ornamental Iron Company, the name it bears today.

Starting at the age of twelve in his father's business, working Saturdays and during school vacations, James Daniel joined the company business on a full-time basis after completing service in the U.S. Marine Corps. James Daniel's son, J. Dashwood Daniel, represents the fourth generation of the family in the business, serving as vice-president.

The firm today, located at 620 Goldwire Way Southwest, within a few blocks of where the family originated its business in 1913, creates a varied line of metal products, including commercial and industrial metalwork, with the emphasis still on miscellaneous and ornamental metals.

Above: *This advertisement for the firm appeared in local publications during the 1920s.*

Below: *Daniels' Ornamental Iron and Wire Corp. was established by W. Homer Daniel, grandfather of the president of today's Daniel Ornamental Iron Company.*

193

DANIEL INTERNATIONAL CORPORATION

It can be said, in the literal sense of the phrase, that Daniel International Corporation has left its mark on Alabama. The physical evidence — skyscrapers, sprawling industrial plants, schools, mills, public buildings — dots the state from one end to the other.

Daniel's construction operation in Birmingham is the regional arm of Daniel International, headquartered in Greenville, South Carolina, and as such is an integral part of one of the greatest construction company success stories in America.

Daniel Construction Company, as it was known in its early years, began in 1934 as a team of two brothers, Charles E. and R. Hugh Daniel, in Anderson, South Carolina, and moved to Greenville, South Carolina, in 1942. In the meantime, Hugh Daniel, having moved to Alabama in 1930, opened an office in Birmingham in 1936. This was the first in a series of expansion moves that was to make the company national, then international, in scope.

The firm's steady expansion in the United States and abroad was directed from Birmingham and Greenville, with Hugh Daniel figuring significantly in the company's growth. During the early years, most of the managers chosen to direct these ambitious new divisions had served their apprenticeship with the Birmingham operation.

The early Alabama projects ranged from schoolhouses to hospitals. Daniel's first million-dollar job was the Jefferson County Hospital, now a part of the University Hospital complex, in 1937.

Today, physical evidence of Daniel's many contributions to the growth of Birmingham and Alabama sprinkle the state from border to border with emphasis in the industrial field, such as chemicals along the Gulf Coast, pulp and paper in the mid-state region, and synthetic fibers and textiles throughout the state.

Included among the projects constructed in Birmingham are John Carroll High School; Shades Valley High; U.S. Steel's office building and many structures for Samford University,

Birmingham Southern College, and the University of Alabama in Birmingham; the Oscar Wells Memorial Museum; the Bank for Savings building; hospitals such as Baptist Montclair, Children's Hospital, and Baptist Princeton; the U.S. Post Office; and, of course, a striking contribution to the local skyline, the sleek, 20-story Daniel office building on Birmingham's south side.

Below: *Daniel International's own office building on Birmingham's south side, is an impressive contribution to the local skyline.*

Opposite: *The Monsanto Textile plant in Decatur, Alabama, was constructed by Daniel International in 1950. Expansion has continued into the 1980s.*

194

With the death of Charlie Daniel in 1964, Hugh Daniel moved from the presidency, a position he had held since 1955, and became chairman of the board, chief executive officer, and treasurer. Buck Mickel, named president at that time, was subsequently elected chairman in 1974, with Hugh Daniel retaining the titles of chief executive officer and treasurer. Charles Cox then became president and chief operating officer.

The firm changed its name to Daniel International Corporation in 1971, a realistic recognition of its enormous expansion during the 1960s and 1970s. In the meantime, the 20-story Daniel building had been completed in Birmingham in 1970 and was taking on new tenants. Among them was Daniel Realty Corporation, which had been established in Birmingham in 1964.

Daniel International had become a full-service construction company, providing all services from site analysis and engineering to construction and post-construction maintenance. This resulted in the announcement by chairman Mickel in 1974 that the corporate structure was being realigned to provide for all operations to be handled by two principal divisions: Daniel Construction Company, then with thirty-seven divisons and subsidiaries in the United States and abroad; and Daniel Industrial Services, composed of the existing twenty-two non-construction related divisions and subsidiaries.

Fluor Corporation, a major engineering and construction company based in Irvine, California, and a world leader in the energy field, made an offer in 1977 to purchase all outstanding shares of Daniel stock, and Daniel subsequently became an independent operation of Fluor.

Hugh Daniel entered full retirement after the acquisition was completed in the spring of 1977. He had spent forty-three active years as an executive in the company, all of them in Birmingham.

There he had established his first office in 1936 in one room on the seventeenth floor of the Webb Crawford building, now the John Hand branch of the First National Bank. He constructed the company's first office building in 1938 at 822 Seventh Avenue South.

During his successful business career, Hugh Daniel also was active in Birmingham's educational and cultural life and served on numerous civic, institutional, and business boards, including major coroporations. He was active in the establishment and growth of the Bank for Savings and Trust, now part of the Birmingham Trust National Bank, and the Central Bank.

Today, Daniel's operations based in Birmingham consist of its South Central regional construction division, the South Central maintenance-mechanical operation, and Daniel Realty Corporation, a subsidiary engaged in real estate development, brokerage, and property management.

DUNN CONSTRUCTION COMPANY, INC.

With its roots in the earliest days of Birmingham, the Dunn Construction Company has for over 100 years played a major role in the economic development of Birmingham, Alabama, and the South.

Evans Johnson Dunn and Thomas Dunn were brothers living in Lynchburg, Virginia, who joined together to form Dunn Brothers Construction Company in 1878. The business was founded to handle railroad construction and the Dunn brothers moved their business to Birmingham in the very early 1900s to carry out a tunneling construction contract for the Georgia-Pacific Railroad (now an element of the Southern Railroad). Evans Dunn assumed guidance of the firm soon after locating in Birmingham when his brother Thomas was robbed and shot while en route to a construction project in Texas.

A growing, dynamic Birmingham invited Dunn's permanent location here and the company is thought to be the oldest construction firm in Alabama. Ownership of the company, as well as its management, has continuously remained with the Dunn family for four generations.

From its start in railroad construction, Dunn moved into water system projects and then into street construction

coincident with the early development of automotive transportation. Further developing its road construction business, Dunn erected one of the country's first asphalt plants in 1915 in Birmingham. Today Dunn carries out contracts for industrial streets, parking lots, subdivisions, municipal streets, and interstate and general highways. The single asphalt plant of 1915 is now four plants, with three located in Birmingham and one in Jackson, Mississippi.

In 1940 Dunn expanded its operations by entering the general building

construction business. During the '40s most projects were for the military. Since then Dunn has built a strong reputation with projects including industrial facilities, warehouses, office buildings, and medical facilities.

A successful experience in general building construction encouraged Dunn to enter the field of industrial construction in 1945. In that category Dunn has earned respect in the cement, coal, metal, and electric utilities industries. Included in its projects have been heavy manufacturing facilities, power plant work, equipment foundations, material handling systems, and slip form work. The latter, one of Dunn's specialties, is concrete construction in which Dunn is unique in that it is one of the few general contractors in the Southeast capable of doing this work.

Emphasizing quality, economy, and speed is the design-and-build phase of Dunn's operation, providing control over every facet of a project from land acquisition to completion.

Providing a continuity-of-business philosophy from 1878 to today is the previously noted uninterruped management of the company by the Dunn family. From Evans J. Dunn, control of the company passed to his son, William Ransom Johnson Dunn, Sr., and from him to his son W.R.J. Dunn, Jr. Today the president and chief executive officer of the contracting firm is J.S.M. French, son-in-law of W.R.J. Dunn, Jr.

Above: *Evans J. Dunn founded Dunn Brothers Construction Company with his brother Thomas in 1878.*

Left: *From Evans J. Dunn, control of the company passed to his son, William Ransom Johnson, Sr. (left), and from him to his son, W.R.J. Dunn, Jr. (right).*

EAST END MEMORIAL HOSPITAL AND HEALTH CENTERS

The word "Memorial" in East End Memorial Hospital is a significant one. The institution, now grown to 282 beds, is a memorial to a specific area within a larger metropolitan zone, a memorial to the civic-minded citizens and physicians who conceived of it, a memorial to the East Lake Lions Club and the Woodlawn Civic Club, and, officially, a memorial to the men and women of the community who served and died in World War II.

East End Memorial Hospital, which opened in a converted dormitory in September 1946, and East End Memorial as it exists today are two different institutions in size and operation—but not in spirit and original concept. The idea began in the minds of certain civic leaders and doctors to fill an obvious need in Birmingham's eastern community. With financial support from area residents, the founders settled on the purchase of the Mamie Mell Smith Hall dormitory on the old Howard College site for $55,000.

Guided by a board of directors and community stockholders, East End opened as a for-profit hospital with 66 beds and the goal of providing short-term, general care, the end result of a true community effort. Success bred its new demands, however, and the addition of 39 beds, emergency room facilities, blood bank, and laboratory was completed in 1956. Similar expansion programs have continued since that time.

And the East End Memorial Hospital of today? Now a not-for-profit corporation, there is the main hospital and an adjoining six-story professional building. The complex includes the latest in technical services manned by highly trained physicians, nurses, therapists, technicians, and aides.

East End Memorial Hospital offers a full range of health services covering family practice, pediatrics, obstetrics, gynecology, and internal medicine, and specialties such as cardiology, orthopedics, urology, hemotology/oncology, gastro-enterology, vascular surgery, and rheumatology. There is a modern, computerized radiology department, along with its special-procedures room for cardiac implants, a nuclear medicine suite, and a special room for emergency X-rays.

A new intensive care wing offers 24-hour computerized monitoring for intensive care patients. Other new techniques and programs include a new computer system, a pharmacy with its highly efficient unit-dose system, a time-saving pre-admission program, and a full-time Patient Relations Program which operates around the clock to solve almost any patient-related problem.

But efforts to restore good health are only part of EEMH's outreach. There is the widespread belief today that medical experts should work to help individuals keep and maintain good health, and EEMH is setting an impressive pace in

East End Memorial Hospital, which opened in a converted dormitory in 1946, and East End Memorial Hospital and Health Centers as it exists today are two different institutions in size and operation—but not in spirit and original concept.

this field. Its Department of Educational Services offers a wide variety of community health education programs, most of them free to the public; more than 2,300 persons took advantage of these services in 1979.

The hospital's concern goes even further. Its annual Spring Community Health Screening, sponsored by the EEMH Auxilians, encourages community residents to visit the hospital for a free basic check-up. The purpose is to provide an overall health evaluation and possibly detect any medical problem in the developmental stage.

The hospital took still another major step to work hand-in-hand with the people it serves when it opened its Center Point Health Center on the campus of Jefferson State Junior College in 1977. The Center offers a family practice unit, a basic emergency medical services department, laboratory, and therapy services, along with medical specialists in various fields.

Since that time, four other health centers have opened—the East Lake, Woodlawn, Trussville, and Odenville family practice clinics—and the hospital's name has been altered to reflect these additions. While not as extensive as the main health center, each offers the highest quality family-oriented health care in convenient community settings. And that, as its staff points out, was exactly what East End Memorial Hospital and Health Centers was designed to do in the first place.

THE FIRST NATIONAL BANK OF BIRMINGHAM

The First National Bank of Birmingham, founded in 1872, is just one year younger than the city itself. Thus, for more than a century, it has shared in both the labors and the achievements as Birmingham earned its place among the great metropolitan centers of the South.

The bank, known as The National Bank of Birmingham when it was organized on October 17, 1872, by Swedish immigrant and former sea captain Charles Linn and six associates, opened its doors for business on January 3, 1873. In 1884, it merged with The City Bank and thereafter was known as The First National Bank of Birmingham. With that merger, the new bank boasted total deposits of $723,944.

Another merger followed, this time with the Berney National Bank of Birmingham in 1902, and that consolidation led to the construction of one of downtown Birmingham's first skyscrapers, the 10-story First National Bank Building, known today as the Frank Nelson Building.

With the bank rounding out its first half century just after World War I, total deposits had grown to some $20 million. When First National merged with American Traders Bank in 1930, the bank's deposits soared to $72 million. Oscar Wells, president of First National, became chairman of the board at that time, and General John C. Persons, president of American Traders, became president of the new and larger First National.

It was in these same eventful years that six neighborhood banks became the first branches within the First National family. First National today, with its thirty-six offices, is the largest bank in the state.

With the onset of World War II, General Persons was called into active service as commanding officer of the 31st Infantry Division. This leave of absence was the only break in his thirty-seven years of service to First National, which ended in 1967 when he retired as chairman of the bank's board of directors.

In 1940, the bank moved its headquarters to a newly renovated

The First National Bank of Birmingham's main office is located in the First National-Southern Natural Building. The 30-story building was completed in 1971.

building at First Avenue and Twentieth Street. This elegant landmark, former headquarters of the merged American Traders Bank and built in 1912, with its great columns of Alabama marble in the lobby, remained the heart of The First National Bank's operations until the bank moved into the 30-story First National/Southern Natural Building in 1971. The former headquarters building was then renamed for John A. Hand, who served First National as president beginning in 1956, chief excecutive officer beginning in 1958, and as chairman of the executive committee beginning in 1969.

By the end of the 1950s, First National had opened six additional branches and the staff had grown to a total of 600. These were dynamic years for the bank under the leadership of John A. Hand and Harvey Terrell. In the early 1970s, with total deposits of $700 million, the bank acquired Engel Mortgage Company. Hand retired in 1972 and Terrell in 1974. Robert H. Woodrow was named chairman and chief executive officer in 1972. John W. Woods, president since 1969, became vice-chairman of the board and M. Eugene Moor, Jr., president.

A significant step in the bank's development occurred in 1972 when The First National Bank of Birmingham became the lead bank and first affiliate

of Alabama Bancorporation (renamed AmSouth Bancorporation in 1981). Later that year, American National Bank and Trust Company of Mobile and the First National Bank of Decatur affiliated with the new corporation. John W. Woods became chairman of the board, president, and chief executive officer of AmSouth Bancorporation. With First National of Birmingham as its lead bank, Alabama Bancorporation was and continues to be the state's largest multi-bank holding company.

AmSouth Bancorporation was the first financial institution in Alabama to record a billion dollars in assets. By 1977, it had achieved $2 billion in assets, and as the decade of the 1970s ended, the corporation was rapidly approaching the $3-billion mark. By the end of 1980, AmSouth Bancorporation consisted of eighteen banks with almost 100 banking offices statewide, and two subsidiaries, Engel Mortgage Company and Alabanc Financial Corporation, with twenty-six offices throughout the Southeast.

One of the people instrumental in the growth of The First National Bank of Birmingham was Newton H. DeBardeleben. He was elected chairman of the board and chief executive officer of the bank in 1976, and at the end of that year, First National became the first bank in Alabama to record $1 billion in deposits.

Dan L. Hendley, who served as president of First National since 1977, was named chief executive officer of the bank following DeBardeleben's death in 1979. Later that year, Hendley was named chairman of the bank's board, and William A. Powell, Jr., was named president of both the bank and AmSouth Bancorporation.

First National entered the 1980s with more than 2,000 employees sharing the bank's 108-year-old legacy of meeting the financial needs of a dynamic city, state, and region. Unlike its early years, however, First National's opportunities for today and in the future extend beyond traditional marketplaces, becoming increasingly regional and national in scope.

HANNA STEEL CORPORATION

The determination of a 16-year-old boy to share in his nation's World War I military responsibilities, despite the Army's minimum age requirement, is reflected today, sixty-two years later, in a strong and still growing Birmingham steel fabricating company.

Still underage in 1919, after the conclusion of World War I, Walter J. Hanna was accepted as an enlistee in the Alabama National Guard by fabricating his birth date. Within a few weeks, his rise through the ranks began with his promotion to corporal and it was not to stop until he reached the grade of lieutenant general before his retirement in 1963.

In the interim, the name "Crack" Hanna, acquired through his expertise with a rifle, had been indelibly imprinted on the nation's military history, just as the name Hanna has become prominent in the southern steel industry.

World War II marked a critical period in both the military and business careers of Crack Hanna. In 1940 he was a captain in the National Guard. By the termination of the war he held the rank of brigadier general, an assistant division commander, a tribute to his capability as a battlefront leader in the Southwest Pacific. Prior to the war he had created a sales agency, Hanna & Co. On his return to Birmingham, Hanna launched a business manufacturing highway signs and signs cautioning safety in plants and industrial operations. The business flourished and soon it became the largest manufacturer of traffic and safety signs in the South.

Meanwhile, Hanna saw new opportunities in the steel processing field. In 1953 a new business was launched under Hanna's leaderhip, a plant and warehouse specializing in carbon sheet steel and strip products processed to the buyer's requirements.

Never one to let a flourishing business interfere with his military obligations, Hanna returned to active duty in the Korean War as an assistant division commander. A heated disagreement

Lieutentant General Walter J. Hanna has enjoyed great success in both his military and business careers.

with the division commander over what Hanna regarded as inadequate training methods led to the opportunity of his assuming responsibility as Alabama adjutant general under Governor Gordon Persons and his involvement in one of the most dramatic law enforcement episodes in Alabama history—the Phenix City cleanup.

The assassination of Attorney General-elect Albert Patterson, important leader in efforts to erase the designation of "Sin City" from references to his hometown, brought Adjutant General Hanna onto the scene. Within a short time he was able to convince Governor Persons to declare Phenix City under martial law. Due to the efforts of General Hanna and a strong team of special prosecutors, Phenix City became the cleanest it had been since its establishment as an Indian trading post early in the previous century.

Hanna retired as a lieutenant general in 1963. Soon he was creating another

successful facet of his steel business, which from the first had been predicated on the use of domestic steel only. U.S. Steel and Republic Steel have been Hanna's traditional suppliers. With the purchase of three tube mills, Hanna Steel started moving to the front line with welded tubing. The company soon opened another steel service center in Gadsden. Between 1972 and 1979, Hanna sales increased from $12.5 million to over $40 million.

Crack Hanna's son Pete was with him as a private in the National Guard when the general marched into Phenix City. He has kept pace with his father in the business, moving up through the ranks to become president and then board chairman. A longtime associate in the company, John E. Montgomery III is president and those three men form the Hanna Steel executive committee.

Having given up the position of board chairman, what is Crack Hanna's identification today with the company? Some in the company call him "the general," but other term the 80-year-old leader, still involved daily in business decisions, the "supreme advisor." A grin spreads across Crack's face when he hears that appellation.

199

HARDIE-TYNES MANUFACTURING CO.

Hardie-Tynes Manufacturing Company of Birmingham is unique in that it is better known in many other states, and in some far corners of the globe, than it is in its own backyard.

The firm makes air compressors, steam turbines, hydraulic machinery, and special machinery to operate under demanding circumstances—on warships, in deep mines, and inside the vital workings of some of the great dams of America, to cite just a few uses.

The company traces its beginnings back to two Mississippians, William D. Tynes and William Hardie, who came to Birmingham in 1897 and set up a foundry and machine business on First Avenue North in that year. When fire destroyed their first plant in 1901, the firm moved to 800 North Twenty-eighth Street and has been at that location ever since.

After the death of Hardie in 1916, Tynes took over full direction of the company, guiding it until his death in 1932. During that period, the firm became preeminent in its own field and continues to rank among the industry greats to this day.

Hardie-Tynes early on began to demonstrate its ability to turn out new products to meet new conditions and new demands. It began to make mine hoists, air and gas compressors, as well as special machinery in the early 1900s, and during World War I the plant performed vital defense work. Among the products turned out for the war effort were marine engines, shells and other munitions, and special equipment for other key industries.

A historic turn of events for the company came about during World War I, when it was awarded contracts for the construction of marine engines ranging up to 3,800 horsepower. These engines, installed in new ships being launched to meet the demands of the conflict, proved so successful that they reportedly set the standards for the government's dealings with other such companies throughout the United States.

200 Indeed, versatility has been a Hardie-

Tynes trademark down through the years. The company in 1922 agreed to rebuild 100 locomotives, although the firm had done no such work before that time. To do the job Hardie-Tynes had to install trackage, roundtables, and other railroading equipment not normally associated with a foundry-type operation.

In the early years the company devoted most of its efforts to steam engines, both the slide valve and Corliss types,

William D. Tynes cofounded Hardie-Tynes Manufacturing Company in 1897.

and built motor-driven and steam-driven mine hoists. Company president G.L. Flynn notes that "some of those old engines and mine hoists are still in operation in sawmills and sugar refineries in the United States and in Caribbean and South American areas."

Hardie-Tynes' large stationary air compressors were a standard fixture in such noted Birmingham industries as McWane, U.S. Steel, Connors Steel, and ACIPCO as well as in the U.S. naval yard at Portsmouth, New Hampshire, and at the huge naval base at Pearl Harbor. The largest of the massive Hardie-Tynes mine hoists were built during the 1940s. Four are still in operation in France and one in a South African gold mine.

High pressure air compressors designed by Hardie-Tynes in the 1930s coincided with the critical needs that came about when America entered World War II. Hardie-Tynes built all such air compressors installed in submarines and warships during World War II and many are still in active use in the U.S. Navy and in foreign navies.

For more than fifty years the firm has manufactured gate valves, hollow jet valves, needle valves, and butterfly valves, which have been installed in dams and water-flow controls in forty states, including Boulder Dam, the New York City sewer system, the Los Angeles County Flood Control District, and numerous large government and municipal projects.

"In more recent years," says Flynn, "Hardie-Tynes has been involved in the design and manufacture of the auxiliary steam turbines for the U.S. Navy, the most frequent application being steam-driven, forced-draft blowers. These have been installed in more than 100 ships of modern U.S. naval vessels built between 1955 and 1981. Hardie-Tynes is one of only three manufacturers who are on the U.S. Navy Approved Products List for steam-driven forced-draft blowers.

The company at present is developing nonlubricated high-pressure air compressors and, says president Flynn, "we think more will be heard from these in the near future."

JEFFERSON COUNTY COMMISSION

The Creek Indians, fighting to preserve their home and hunting grounds in Alabama, had had their hopes of effectively resisting the encroachment of the white man destroyed by the battle of Horseshoe Bend and Congress had just voted affirmatively to create a new state, Alabama, out of the Mississippi Territory when the settlers in a southwestern area of Blount County united in an effort to create their own government and system of justice.

The newly created Alabama Legislature established by law Jefferson County, Alabama, on December 13, 1819, honoring the third President of the United States in its selection of a name. Major Moses Kelly, chief justice of the Blount County Quorum, whose home was in Jones Valley (which over half a century later would become the site of the newly created city of Birmingham), was selected as chief justice of the new county. The first commissioners of the new county were William Irvin, John Adams, John Cochrane, William Prude, and Reuben Read.

The first circuit court term for Jefferson County was held at a settlement called Carrollsville. In 1820 Elyton was incorporated and the following year it was named the county seat. It so remained until 1871 when the newly

established city of Birmingham, whose limits later absorbed Elyton, was named the county seat. In 1887 a branch of the county administration for justice and law enforcement was established for the south-western section of the county in Bessemer (the Bessemer Cutoff).

With the sudden explosive growth of Birmingham through rapid industrial utilization of the rich deposits of iron ore, coal, and limestone, Jefferson County soon became Alabama's leading metropolitan area, one of the South's most economically dynamic centers.

Today Jefferson County has a population of 632,000, with thirty-three thriving incorporated communities within its borders. Its complex governmental responsibilities are in the hands of a commission of three members, a president, and two associate commissioners, elected concurrently to four-year terms by the qualified voters of the county. The commission holds a public meeting each Tuesday at 10 a.m. at the Jefferson County Courthouse and meets every second Wednesday at the Bessemer Courthouse to conduct business for the Cutoff.

The president of the commission heads the Department of Finance and General

Administration, which is charged with administration of the county's financial affairs; purchase of supplies; collection of taxes, licenses, and other sources of income; county expenditures; management of public buildings; county accounting; and records.

Associate commissioner No. 1 heads the Department of Public Works, having supervision over all public improvements of highways, streets, bridges, ferries, sewage disposal plants, sewage lines, and erection of all public buildings. The department has ten major divisions of operations.

Associate commissioner No. 2 heads the Department of Public Welfare, which has supervision over all eleemosynary, correctional, and welfare institutions of the county (including county hospitals, clinics, institutions for the aged and indigent, prisons and jails, juvenile courts, the health department, county farm and county home demonstration agents, social service agencies, and the medical examiner's office).

It is unlikely that Major Moses Kelly's aspirations in 1819 for a separate county could have anticipated the economic and governmental giant that Jefferson County, Alabama, has become.

JOHN'S RESTAURANT

Alabama's most popular restaurant? Many Alabamians, particularly those in the northern section of the state, would have a rapid answer: John's of Birmingham.

Each weekday (the restaurant is closed on Sunday), John's, an institution in downtown Birmingham, serves 1,300 to 1,600 luncheons and dinners in a facility with accommodations for 240. Standing in line waiting for a table is a tradition for John's enthusiasts and has been since the restaurant opened at 214 Twenty-first Street North in September 1944.

It was in 1914 that a 15-year-old youth from Sparta, Greece, John Proferis, alone and with no knowledge of the English language, landed at New York City. Through a distant relative he obtained employment in a confectionery, easing his trips through the strange city from his boarding house to his place of work by marking the route with chalk on telephone poles.

After a year in New York the lad went to Pennsylvania where a sister lived, working there for two years in confectioneries until 1919 when he came to Alabama, finding employment in Ensley at the U.S. Cafe, owned by acquaintances from Sparta.

In 1920 John Proferis made his first investment in his new country, purchasing 50 percent interest in the Faust Cafe on Twentieth Street in Birmingham. He improved his fluency in the English language by attending night classes at Phillips High School.

Proferis in 1935 opened the Casino restaurant on Twentieth Street and soon afterward found happiness through his marriage to Cleo Kontos, daughter of Alex Kontos. After a period of operating the cafeteria for the Childersburg ordnance plant during World War II, Proferis returned to Birmingham, sold the Casino, and was ready to open a restaurant carrying his own name. Over the next twenty-eight years John (with most of his patrons his surname became surplus) became a leading Birmingham restauranteur, his seafood dinners in particular attracting people in crowds to Twenty-first Street.

Meanwhile, political turmoil following World War II again had made Greece a battlefield with little promise of a bright future for Sparta's young people, so 18-year-old Phil Hontzas decided to follow two uncles to Birmingham. There he found employment with one uncle, John Collas, at Niki's restaurant on Second Avenue North.

With the exception of two years' service in the U.S. military, Hontzas remained at Niki's until 1972, when his uncle John, fatally ill, persuaded him to shift his attention to John's. When John died, Hontzas purchased the restaurant, retaining its original name.

Despite the urging of friends, John had chosen over the years to keep the restaurant in the small location at 214 North Twenty-first Street. In 1978 Hontzas, recognizing the need for more spacious facilities, acquired the location at 112 North Twenty-first, historic as a restaurant location since French restauranteur Galatoire had first opened a cafe there in 1895.

With the seating more than doubled to 240, Phil Hontzas continued the principles that had made his uncle so successful—maintaining the same varied menu and exercising close personal supervision over the preparation of quality food. The long lines of patrons at each mealtime awaiting assignment to seating attests to the success of the formula.

Left: *John Proferis founded the restaurant that bears his name in 1944.*

Right: *Phil Hontzas, John Proferis' nephew, purchased John's Restaurant upon the latter's death in 1972.*

LEEDY MORTGAGE COMPANY

Birmingham was booming in 1887. In the sixteen years since Birmingham had been incorporated, the city had grown to a population of 65,000 with almost 90,000 residents in Jefferson County.

Tennessee Coal & Iron Company had acquired a plant in Birmingham the year before and the firm was launched on a pattern of growth that, under the direction of U.S. Steel, was to make it Alabama's largest employer and the major economic thrust for the Birmingham area well into the middle of the next century. Also that year, the Columbus & Western Railroad brought its tracks into Birmingham and the Alabama Rolling Mills Company was established.

A real estate boom gripped Alabama's newest city and W.B. Leedy saw the opportunity and grasped it. He established a business under the Leedy name in real estate sales and rentals. Ninety-four years later the name "Leedy" remains of signal importance in real estate mortgages and general insurance in Birmingham.

Nourished by the immediate availability of large deposits of iron ore, coal, and limestone, the basic ingredients of iron and steel production, Birmingham developed rapidly into one of the major cities of the Southeast, becoming a national leader in iron and steel production and metal fabrication. It became known as the "Magic City," a name by which it is still identified.

Above: *In 1887, W.B. Leedy established the firm known today as Leedy Mortgage Company, Inc.*

Below: *Today, the Leedy Mortgage Company, an important part of the Birmingham business community for nearly a century, still maintains its mortgage and insurance operations at the historic Leedy address of 2131 Third Avenue North.*

Leedy, utilizing solid business principles in a most heady economic atmosphere, prospered along with the city. The founder of the firm died in 1924 and his son, W.B. Leedy, Jr., took over the reins of the company. Thomas N. Beach and W.D. Caldwell played major roles in the operations of the firm, and the junior Leedy rewarded them with equal stock options in what is now the oldest mortgage banking company in Alabama. During the next eight years Leedy Jr. and W.D. Caldwell both passed away, and Thomas N. Beach, after exercising his options, became the

sole owner of Leedy. During this period the firm also expanded into real estate management and ownership.

After World War II the mortgage banking operations of the company continued to expand and branches were established in Louisiana, Mississippi, Georgia, and Florida. Thomas Beach retired from active management of Leedy and was succeeded by his brother, Henry F. Beach. The company later ceased originating new loans for a period of approximately fifteen years, beginning in the early 1960s. In 1977 Charles Parrish acquired the real estate sales and management operation, while a Beach family member, Mason Dillard, acquired the mortgage banking business. Dillard had served with the firm since 1952 and was its longtime president.

Today, the Leedy Mortgage Company still maintains its mortgage and insurance operations at the historic Leedy address of 2131 Third Avenue North, with offices in Virginia and Pennsylvania and an area of operations encompassing Texas, Louisiana, Mississippi, Florida, Georgia, South Carolina, and Tennessee, as well as Pennsylvania, Virginia, and Alabama.

Under the present leadership of Daniel B. Haralson, Richard J. Micheel, C. Whit Walter, Lawrence Deaton, John Graham, and others, Leedy represents over sixty institutional investors and maintains a loan-servicing portfolio in excess of $150 million. In its 94-year history, Leedy has helped many thousands of Alabamians to acquire home ownership and the company continues to serve the community well. Leedy is now owned by Pennsylvania interests who spend so much of their time in Alabama that they can almost be considered natives.

Leedy is now affiliated with a real estate investment trust, a real estate management company, a title insurance company, a real estate appraisal company, and other entities in related fields. The firm has modernized its historic offices in Birmingham and has now been computerized as they plan their entrance into the twenty-first century.

LIBERTY NATIONAL

When Heralds of Liberty was founded in 1900 as a small fraternal benefit society in Huntsville, Alabama, few people envisioned its later transformation into a major insurance company. However, once Robert P. Davison and Frank P. Samford took control of the society's operations in the 1920s, that is precisely what began. Today, Liberty National Life Insurance Company is the largest life insurance company in Alabama and one of the largest in the United States.

One of Davison and Samford's earliest achievements was to move the society's headquarters back to Alabama from its temporary home in Philadelphia. In 1927, controlling interest in Birmingham's 10-story Pioneer Building at Twentieth Street and Third Avenue South was purchased. The structure, which was renamed the Liberty National Building, has been a city landmark since 1958, when a 31-foot-tall replica of the Statue of Liberty was erected atop the structure. Since then the building has been enlarged twice as the company has grown.

Samford succeeded Davison as president of the business in 1934, and guided the company's destiny for more than 50 years. Starting in the 1940s, Liberty National began an aggressive program of growth —both internally and through acquisitions. Brown-Service Insurance Company, with more than one million policy holders in Alabama, was purchased in 1944; Atlas Life (of Tampa, Florida) in 1949; Family Reserve Life Insurance Company in 1950; and Cherokee Life (of Nashville, Tennessee) in 1964.

The company expanded into the Midwest with the acquisition of Rockford Life Insurance Company in 1974, and by the end of 1979, Liberty National and Rockford were licensed in forty states and the District of Columbia. In 1980, the company purchased Globe Life and Accident Insurance Company for $200 million. The Globe purchase inspired the reorganization of Liberty National Life, Globe Life, and their subsidiaries under Liberty National Insurance Holding Company. This was accomplished on December 30, 1980, and the next day the common stock of the holding company was listed on the New York Stock Exchange under the symbol "LNH."

Liberty National Life and its subsidiaries now market a complete line of life, accident, and health insurance on the "home service" basis—through agents calling on clients and prospects in their homes. Globe Life and its subsidiaries also market a complete line of life, accident, and health insurance through its agency force and by direct mail. In addition, Liberty National Fire Insurance Company offers fire insurance and accepts reinsurance on U.S. risks, while two international subsidiaries in Ireland and Bermuda handle reinsurance on foreign risks.

The company has come a long way since its humble beginnings at the turn of the century, and Liberty National looks forward to another eighty years and more of growth and prosperity from its home base in the city of Birmingham.

Top left: *The Liberty National Building has been a city landmark since 1958, when a 31-foot-tall replica of the Statue of Liberty was erected atop the structure.*

Left: *Frank P. Samford was an early leader of the major insurance company known today as Liberty National.*

Below: *Liberty National's headquarters are located at Twentieth Street and Third Avenue South.*

McGRIFF & SEIBELS

With its roots in the Magic City going back to the turn of the century, the insurance firm of McGriff & Seibels has been a dynamic segment of Birmingham throughout much of its existence.

Today the company, located in a distinctive headquarters building at 2211 Seventh Avenue South, is a recognized leader in its field and a respected corporate name in Birmingham's business and civic community. A service organization, it helps its clients obtain insurance coverage tailored to their specific needs and today has over 125 employees, with branches in Florence, Fairhope, and Huntsville, Alabama, and Orlando, Florida.

The internal structure, which has expanded rapidly over the years to meet the challenges of growth, includes a commercial sales department, employee benefits department, personal lines department, marketing and general services department, financial department, and two subsidiaries, Insurers Services Inc. and Data Processing Systems.

The predecessors of McGriff & Seibels began at the turn of the century as two separate insurance agencies—Ed S. Moore, Inc., and Jemison Real Estate and Insurance Company. In 1912 the former became Ed S. Moore and Lee McGriff; then in 1935 it became Lee McGriff, Inc. The firm merged in 1953 with Fowlkes & Jones, Inc., a local organization dating from 1925 and managed by Henry S. Fowlkes and Raymond M. Jones. The merged firm became Fowlkes, Jones & Lee McGriff, Inc. On the death of Raymond Jones in 1956, the agency became Fowlkes & McGriff, Inc., and over the next six years acquired several small agencies.

Jemison Real Estate and Insurance Company was organized by the well-known developer, Robert Jemison, Jr. H.G. Seibels joined the company in 1903 and in 1909 he separated the insurance agency from the real estate business. The firm became Jemison-Seibels Insurance Agency, with H.G. Seibels as president. As Birmingham grew during the teens and

Above: *Lee McGriff (1880-1945) was a partner with Moore & McGriff from 1912 to 1928, branch manager of U.S. F.&G. from 1928 to 1935, and president of Lee McGriff, Inc., from 1935 to 1945.*

Above right: *H.G. Seibels (1876-1967) entered the insurance business in 1903, was president of Jemison-Seibels, predecessor of today's McGriff & Seibels, from 1909 to 1923, and served as president and chairman of the Birmingham Fire Insurance Company from 1925 to 1960.*

Below: *Executives of McGriff & Seibels are Lee McGriff, Jr., chairman of the board (left); and H.G. Seibels, Jr., vice-chairman of the board.*

the 1920s the agency prospered along with the real estate company. In 1925 the Birmingham Fire Insurance Company was organized by Seibels and the original stock of the company was over-subscribed by local investors. The home office insurance firm prospered and became highly regarded as an Alabama company, doing business throughout the Southeast and as far west as Texas. The Jemison-Seibels Agency was the largest stockholder in the Birmingham Fire Insurance Company until the latter merged with the St. Paul Insurance Company after thirty-five years of operation.

In 1963 Fowlkes and McGriff merged with Jemison-Seibels, Inc., the name changing to Fowlkes, McGriff & Seibels, Inc. In 1967 the agency became McGriff & Seibels, Inc. The top executive team at McGriff & Seibels is composed of Lee McGriff, Jr., chairman and chief executive officer; H.G. Seibels, Jr., vice-chairman; and Richard M. Womack, president and chief operating officer.

The firm's practice of recruiting and employing bright young people, training them, and giving them the support they need to be successful is credited with contributing substantially to the agency's $30-million growth in the past eight years. The firm is currently projecting a sizable increase in new revenues each year, while making certain that service capabilities are able to accommodate the new volume. This is the philosophy that has transformed McGriff & Seibels from a $5-million agency to a $40-million agency in less than a decade.

McWANE, INC.

A tradition in foundry operations originating in the invention of the McCormick grain reaper in 1841 distinguishes the background of McWane Inc., a thriving, multi-division corporation with operations in three states.

An associate of Cyrus McCormick in visualizing and manufacturing the machine that would revolutionize agricultural harvesting was James McWane. His son, Charles Philip McWane, initiated the family's involvement in the foundry business by starting a firm in Wytheville, Virginia, to produce plows and other farm implements. Two of Charles McWane's sons, James Ransom and Henry Edward, entered business for themselves in Lynchburg, Virginia, when they formed the Lynchburg Foundry, which they later expanded to include pipe plants in Radford, Virginia, and Anniston, Alabama.

In 1904, James R. McWane left Lynchburg and moved to the booming young city of Birmingham, Alabama, where he took over the presidency of the Birmingham Steel and Iron Company. A memento of that company still stands high above Birmingham on Red Mountain, the giant statue of Vulcan, the god of the forge, which was originally cast for the St. Louis World's Fair. J.R. McWane personally supervised the casting of this world-renowned symbol of the Birmingham steel industry and was himself the second largest contributor to the Vulcan Fund.

McWane joined the American Cast Iron Pipe Company in 1907, serving as its president from 1915 to 1921. In 1922 he resigned to establish the McWane Cast Iron Pipe Company, and four years later he organized the Pacific States Cast Iron Pipe Company in Provo, Utah.

While serving as president of the two companies, J.R. McWane greatly improved the horizontal method of casting pipe by using his multi-spout pouring ladle and a new process of anchoring the cores so as to produce a more uniform section of metal. He invented and patented the precalked

bell and spigot pipe joint —one of seventy-five patents issued to him for developing and improving the foundry process and its pipe products.

Upon J.R. McWane's death in 1933, his son William became president of the McWane Pipe Company, which served the nation with pipe, fittings, valves, and fire hydrants. He guided the firms through the Great Depression into the

Above: *James R. McWane is chairman of the board of McWane, Inc.*

Below: *McWane Cast Iron Pipe Company of Birmingham began in a frame building in 1922 (inset). Today, the plant is located at 1201 Vanderbilt Road.*

economic boom created by World War II. From 1945 to 1975 he served as chairman of the board.

In 1971 James R. McWane, named for his grandfather, became president of the family business. Under his leadership McWane has expanded to include Empire Coke Company (formerly DeBardeleben Coal Company); SIMSCO (with foundries in Columbiana, Centreville, Demopolis, and Selma, Alabama); Atlantic States Cast Iron Pipe Company of Phillipsburg, New Jersey; Union Foundry Company of Anniston, Alabama; and American Foundation Insurance, which moved from Little Rock, Arkansas, to Birmingham.

Representing the fifth generation of McWanes are James R. McWane, Jr., vice-president and general manager of Empire Coke Company; and Philip McWane, administrative assistant, McWane Inc. With its foundry still on Vanderbilt Road, McWane has established corporate headquarters in Inverness Office Park.

With a proud tradition of serving the nation with cast-iron pipe and fittings, the McWane family looks toward the completion of almost two centuries of leadership as masters of the forge and foundry.

MASON CORPORATION

From a four-man work crew in a leased basement to a corporation with operations extending into forty-four states—and all in three decades. That is the record of Birmingham's Mason Corporation, which originally manufactured just three items and now offers more than 2,600 products to the home improvement and light commercial markets.

The Mason Corporation was formed in April 1948, operating as a tool and die shop producing special tooling and machinery for other companies. Originally known as Southeastern Tool and Die Company, it changed its name in 1969 in honor of the founder, Samuel L. Mason. The Mason leadership continues today in the presence of Frank L. Mason, son of the founder, who became president of the corporation in 1959. Frank Mason, who virtually grew up in the business, has provided the key leadership during the company's years of greatest expansion.

From its beginnings in that leased basement, the firm prospered and then moved to larger facilities in the Birmingham suburb of Powderly. During the next sixteen years the company made nine additions to the Powderly facility and then moved to its present location on West Oxmoor Road in March 1965.

Mason Corporation took its first steps toward expansion in 1959 when it opened a distribution center in a leased building in Dallas, Texas. Mason later moved to its own building and expanded the Dallas operation. In 1976 Mason Corporation acquired a manufacturing facility in a separate operation, a 32,000-square-foot leased building. Then, in 1977, the company completed construction of a 100,000-square-foot building in the Dallas suburb of Carrolton, consolidating its warehouse and manufacturing operations. The warehouse has a complete inventory of Mason materials and the Mason Aluminum Products plant is engaged in roll-forming aluminum and steel storefront facing panels, steel structural roof panels, galvanized steel C channels, screen frame, and glass mold.

Above: *Mason Corporation was headquartered in this 100,000-square-foot facility from 1965 through 1981.*

Right: *In 1948 Samuel L. Mason founded the company known today as Mason Corporation.*

Below right: *The Mason leadership continues today under Frank L. Mason, son of the founder, who has been president since 1959.*

The corporation reached out again in 1969, this time to Raleigh, North Carolina, where it acquired the Southern Roofing and Metals Company from stockholders. The firm made awning sheets and other home improvement products. Southern Roofing and Metals was purchased chiefly because it made 31-inch step-down awning sheets and because the location also served as an excellent distribution point for other products. The warehouse in Raleigh has been enlarged from 15,000 to 49,000 square feet and four acres of land have been acquired for expansion.

In August 1975 Mason Corporation expanded once again, this time into Kansas City, where it acquired a leased building with 24,000 square feet. The Kansas City outlet was established to facilitate service to Mason's customers throughout the Midwest.

It is interesting to note that Mason in its beginnings actually produced only three items—a window screen frame, aluminum spline, and corner insert. The 2,600-plus items offered today include lineals for the manufacture of window screens, screen doors, storm doors and windows, carports, canopies, patio covers, replacement windows, commercial store facing, and of course, Mason Corporation's original line—

tools and dies for the manufacture of its products.

The firm in 1948 boasted four employees. Today Mason employs about 170 persons in twelve states. And, when it started, it had no customers in the home improvement market. Today it has several thousand in forty-four states.

The main plant in Birmingham covers everything from conception and design to cost estimation to ultimate production and a complete operation extending through engineering, manufacturing, and sales.

207

MALONE FREIGHT LINES, INC.

Left: *Joshua R. Oden, Sr. (left), purchased Malone Freight Lines in 1941. Joshua R. Oden, Jr., is president of the company today.*

Opposite: *Great strides have been made in the trucking industry since Joshua Oden, Sr., acquired Malone Freight Lines in 1941. Compare the company's fleet of carriers, circa 1942, to this modern tractor-trailer rig.*

The trucking industry is a powerful factor in the Alabama economy, to a far greater extent than it is in other states of similar size. And in the forefront of the Alabama trucking industry is Malone Freight Lines of Birmingham.

To understand the Malone Freight Lines of today one must retrace its management history back to a lumber mill ancestry and, even beyond that, back to one man's part-time timber leasing activities in the 1890s.

That individual was Joshua Webb Oden, who was employed during the closing years of the nineteenth century as a Southern Railroad stationmaster at Childersburg, Alabama. Oden's intimate knowledge of the people, the landowners, and the terrain in his particular part of the state eventually led to his being retained by area brokers and builders to acquire timber rights for them.

So Oden, the railroad stationmaster, began to work up leases and to handle the installation of new sawmills about the countryside. After some time, the timber activities were consuming more of his time than the railroad was, and the railroad urged the enterprising Oden to give up his sideline and take on new and bigger responsibilities in Selma.

But Oden by now was intrigued with the opportunities that lay in timber. So he rejected his railroad's offer, had a younger brother hired as his own replacement, and launched a full-time career in the timber business with a firm known as the Oden-Elliott Lumber Company.

The Alabama timber business then as now was an extensive operation which took great swatches of the state's forest-lands. Oden, with the knowledge he had acquired, obtained timber rights to thousands of acres and the firm went on to cut millions of board feet of lumber for a growing Alabama. The company at one point had seven sawmills in north-central Alabama, some of them self-reliant, backwoods mills familiar to the state's "piney woods" oldtimers.

In partnership with well-known businessman Erskin Ramsey, Oden in 1919 bought the Alabama Mineral Land Company, a sizable operation which had been started by northern interests in the state's Reconstruction period.

Oden's son, Joshua Rowen Oden, joined the company after graduating from Yale in 1920, and their venture thrived during a decade when business and industry enjoyed unprecedented prosperity. But the affluent '20s gave

way to the Great Depression of the 1930s, and the firm, along with virtually every other business in the country, suffered severe setbacks.

By 1935 it became obvious to J.R. Oden that because of economic conditions he must close down the sawmills. Oden looked to transportation as a new business because he was familiar with the railroads which transported his lumber and because a new field was opening up with the federal regulation of motortrucks.

Oden became director of the Alabama Motor Vehicle Association under Governor Frank Dixon. In this position he was responsible for helping to implement a motor vehicle act for the state of Alabama. Trucking was an infant industry, waiting for advanced technology and improved roads, both of which were developing rapidly. The public demand for motortruck service was increasing because of the flexibility of that service, which railroads could not offer.

Oden saw these developments and another important fact about trucklines—one could buy two trucklines and run them as one as long as they had had one common point or city served by both. Oden realized this presented an opportunity to buy a number of small, inexpensive trucklines and from them create one large line. He

208

interested some of his friends in the idea, a corporation was formed, and in October 1941, it purchased Malone Freight Lines of Decatur, Alabama. The name was retained so that company signs and stationery would not have to be changed.

Other trucklines were purchased according to plan, and by 1950 Malone was operating in nineteen states. Today Malone Freight Lines is one of the largest irregular-route trucklines in the country. It offers truckload service to a large number of industries.

Malone is again expanding, this time by taking advantage of the deregulation law recently enacted by Congress for the trucking industry. Malone operations seem to have come full circle. Oden's son, Joshua Jr., is now president, and while Joshua Sr. built a truckline during a time of government regulation, Joshua Jr. is expanding that line on the basis of government deregulation.

MOORE-HANDLEY, INC.

Sidestepping mud puddles created by spring rains in the unpaved streets of Birmingham, B.F. Moore often paused to talk with local settlers to learn all he could about the decade-old town.

While in Birmingham to sell machinery, which he peddled throughout the state, Moore, observing the town's few businesses, envisioned Birmingham someday becoming a large industrial city with limitless possibilities for growth. Excited about this idea of setting up a business in the small town, he returned home to Roanoke, Alabama, to tell his brother, James Dolphin Moore, about his dream.

The Moore brothers, convinced that their dream could become a reality, persuaded their friend, Colonel W.A. Handley, to join them in establishing a hardware and machinery business in the visionary boom town of Birmingham. After much talk, speculation, and planning, Moore, Moore and Handley, on February 2, 1882, with a capital of $3,000, began business in a one-story building on Second Avenue between Twenty-first and Twenty-second streets.

Within a year the infant company's capital had doubled, prompting a move to more spacious quarters on Crittenden. This site, purchased from the Elyton Land Company for $15,000, was, at that time, the largest property sale for business purposes in the young city. The structure was one of the most imposing in the city, measuring 50 by 100 feet with three stories and a basement.

By the fall of 1886, sales had soared to over $25,000 a month. A year later a decision was made to specialize in wholesale hardware and the company again moved, this time to Powell Avenue between Twentieth and Twenty-first streets. The following year the firm incorporated under the name of Moore and Handley Hardware Company, with annual sales of $300,000.

Catastrophe struck in 1903 when fire destroyed the building on Powell Avenue with an almost total loss of stock. Items salvaged, reportedly mostly pocket knives, were literally sold by the

Top: *Within a year of its founding, Moore, Moore and Handley's capital had doubled, prompting a move in 1883 to more spacious quarters on Crittenden.*

Top right: *Today, Moore-Handley serves the wholesale trade throughout a six-state area of the Southeast, offering full service and merchandise availability through its giant distribution center in Pelham.*

Above: *By the fall of 1886, sales had soared to over $25,000 a month, and the company moved to an even larger facility on Powell Avenue.*

barrel. A new facility was erected, but again in 1905, this building also burned. Surviving these destructive fires and the 1908 depression, Moore and Handley continued to grow and in 1909 the company reincorporated under the name Moore-Handley Hardware Company.

After the deaths of the three founders, W.W. French, Sr., who began his career with Moore-Handley as a stenographer in 1895, was named president. Under his leadership, the company continued to grow and prosper. In 1947, W.W. French, Jr., succeeded his father as president of the firm, his father becoming chairman of the board. In

1972 W.W. French III followed his father as president. In 1968 Moore-Handley, Inc., was purchased by the Union Camp Corporation and continues to operate as a wholly owned subsidiary of this firm. In 1979 Bruce H. Jacobs was named president and chief executive officer.

In the early days, Moore and Handley contributed greatly to the growth of Birmingham by supplying the area's expanding coal mining and steel-making industry needs with various kinds of heavy machinery and equipment, as well as a multitude of hardware items to merchants serving a growing populace. But time has brought changes to the firm established in 1882. Today Moore-Handley operates a chain of fifty home-improvement stores, with more on the drawing board. Within the greater Birmingham area, seven of these stores are strategically located to serve a growing do-it-yourself consumer market as well as to supply the needs of the professional home builder. Further, the company continues to serve the wholesale trade throughout a six-state area of the Southeast, offering full service and merchandise availablility through its giant distribution center in Pelham.

From its modest beginning, the firm has grown to over 1,500 employees, a far cry from those early days when a single peddler sold industrial machinery. Starting from a vision of Birmingham as a major industrial city, Moore-Handley has grown with the times, expanding its operation, broadening its product line, hiring personnel to supplement the talent and vision of its three founders, and keeping pace with the adolescent city that gave the company its first home.

O'NEAL STEEL

Naval Lieutenant Kirkman O'Neal returned home to Alabama from overseas at the end of World War I, looked about for a challenge in industrially booming Birmingham, and found one.

Today O'Neal Steel, Inc., is one of the great success stories in steel supply and service and, with distribution outlets in seven southern states, is one of the largest operations of its kind. It wasn't always so, however. O'Neal Steel began in 1922 as a steel fabrication adventure in a small shack in Birmingham's west end. There was much hope, but few resources and little stock.

Kirkman O'Neal, grandson of Alabama Governor Edward A. O'Neal and son of Alabama Governor Emmet O'Neal, borrowed $2,000 in 1921 and invested in a small steel-fabricating firm, which at the time had no orders. A 1913 graduate of the U.S. Naval Academy with some postwar experience with U.S. Steel, O'Neal made it a point to know his punch presses and rip saws as well as he knew the bridge of a U.S. destroyer. O'Neal Steel began to compete. The firm, as a result, was doing $350,000 in annual sales by the advent of the Great Depression.

Struggling through the depression, the company began to pick up momentum again as war engulfed Europe in 1939 and America began to rearm and retool. In the meantime, the firm had inaugurated its warehouse service, providing an instant supply of bolts, sheets, plates, and other steel products from stock. This supermarket for steel was one of the first in the South and the company today, now out of steel fabricating altogether, operates thirteen such metal-service centers in Alabama, Louisiana, Tennessee, Arkansas, Florida, Georgia, and Mississippi.

Coinciding with America's entry into World War II, O'Neal Steel moved into a huge new plant in Birmingham's east end and went into round-the-clock production for a war whose appetite for metals knew no end. O'Neal Steel turned out steel materials for other war plants, built gun platforms and

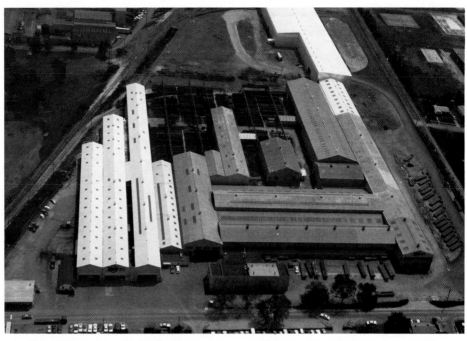

The parent plant of one of the nation's largest steel service centers, O'Neal Steel is located on Forty-first Street North in Birmingham

superstructures for navy destroyers and landing craft, and turned out hundreds of thousands of bomb casings for a variety of aerial bombs. At one time, in July 1945, O'Neal Steel was making twice as many bombs as any other plant in the nation and O'Neal personnel even devised a way to cut in half the time required to machine a bomb — something the war production experts in Washington said could not be done. For this and other valiant work in meeting America's wartime needs, O'Neal Steel was awarded Army and Navy E awards with two citations for excellence.

The company began adding a number of specialty metal products in the 1950s and 1960s and also began its significant switch from fabrication to service centers. In the mid-1970s, O'Neal put special emphasis on products manufactured from hot-rolled coil, adding new heavy-gauge, cut-to-length slitting and edging equipment.

Kirkman O'Neal retired as president in 1959 and became chairman of the board. He was succeeded by his son, Emmet O'Neal II, who holds an

engineering degree from Vanderbilt University and who served as a lieutenant in the navy during World War II.

Departments were established to handle specialty metals, consisting of tool and alloy steels and brass, tubing, pipe and cold-finished bars, aluminum, grating and expanded metals, and stainless steel. Each of the departments has the overall marketing responsibility for its product. The processing of these products is accomplished on the most modern and sophisticated equipment available. The handling equipment associated with the movement of these products is equally up-to-date.

Another reason O'Neal is one of the largest service centers in the country, and possibly the largest privately held service center, is its sophisticated in-house data processing system, which allows sales, purchasing, and credit personnel instant access to information. Real-time order entry assures the absolute minimum delay in converting a customer's desire to a delivered item.

In 1979, Jack H. Blackwell became president and chief operating officer, succeeding Emmet O'Neal. O'Neal then became chairman of the board and his father, Kirkman O'Neal, became chairman of the executive committtee.

PROTECTIVE LIFE INSURANCE COMPANY

The story of Protective Life Insurance Company parallels the story of twentieth-century Birmingham itself. Each has a record of growth and challenge, of change and daring, of problems met and problems solved.

Now a powerful institution in the insurance field both regionally and nationally, Protective Life's beginnings were considerably more modest. The company was founded in 1907 by former Alabama Governor William D. Jelks and operated originally out of a one-room office. But Jelks, known as a "business governor" and an uncommonly successful newspaper publisher before that, set a standard of quality and high aims at the beginning that was to be followed down through the years.

Protective sold its very first policy in September 1907; had $183,500 worth of insurance in force at the end of that first year; moved into a new two-story building in 1915; and in 1916, nine years after it opened its doors, paid its first stockholders' dividend. With the exception of the year 1918, when America was in the throes of a great influenza epidemic, the company hasn't missed a stockholders' dividend.

Protective merged with Alabama National Insurance in 1927 and the strengthened, prospering company erected a 14-story office building in downtown Birmingham at a price tag — paid for entirely out of operating income for that year — of $900,000.

The depression, so devastating to many of the nation's businesses, was less hard on Protective itself. Under the leadership of president Samuel F. Clabaugh, Protective showed an increase in life insurance in force for each of the depression years, with the exception of the rock-bottom years of 1931 and 1932. Indeed, between 1927 and 1937, Protective actually doubled its insurance in force and increased its assets by 67 percent.

It was in 1937, too, that Colonel William J. Rushton — who was to play a powerful role in the company's destiny

for the next several decades — became president of Protective Life. A scholar and champion debater at Washington and Lee University, Rushton was president of a longtime family business, Birmingham Ice & Cold Storage Company, when he was persuaded to change roles from that of a director of Protective to that of the company's president.

And although he took time out to serve with distinction as an army ordnance

Above: *In 1927, Protective merged with Alabama National Insurance and erected a 14-story office building in downtown Birmingham.*

Below: *Protective Life Insurance Company moved in 1976 to a new and magnificently landscaped 28-acre headquarters site in suburban Mountain Brook.*

officer in World War II, Rushton by 1957, after twenty years at the head of Protective, could point with satisfaction to a phenomenal record — insurance in force, assets, and net worth had grown to eight times its 1937 figures.

Growth, however, was sometimes acquired by timely revisions in business strategy. One such major change came in 1963, when Protective elected to concentrate on the upper income, business insurance, and estate planning market and, coincidentally, to expand its geographical horizons and become a national company.

A continued era of Rushton leadership at Protective was assured in 1969 when William J. Rushton III, son of Colonel Rushton, became chief executive officer. Colonel Rushton was then named chairman of the board, retiring from that position in 1976.

William Rushton III graduated magna cum laude in mathematics from Princeton, served as an artillery officer in the Korean war, joined Protective's Actuarial Department and became a fellow of the Society of Actuaries, later switched to sales, and qualified for the Million Dollar Round Table.

Still charting the road ahead, Protective Life in 1976 moved from its 14-story landmark office building in downtown Birmingham to a new and magnificently landscaped 28-acre headquarters site in suburban Mountain Brook, where today it continues to pursue its objectives of quality and growth.

SAINT VINCENT'S HOSPITAL

In 1898 the young, rapidly growing city of Birmingham sorely needed a hospital. The United Charities Hospital had just burned down. The smallpox outbreak in 1897 was to be repeated every year for the next fifteen years. Tuberculosis and typhoid were still very common. Hazardous working conditions resulted in numerous accidents in area mines and steel mills.

Responding to the urgent need, Father Patrick O'Reilly, pastor of St. Paul's Church, journeyed to Provincial House of the Daughters of Charity in Emmitsburg, Maryland, to ask the sisters to establish and staff a hospital in Birmingham. The Daughters consented.

In November 1898, the sisters converted the H.F. DeBardeleben residence on Birmingham's south side into a temporary hospital accommodating thirty patients. Thus, St. Vincent's Hospital was born.

With Father O'Reilly's support, construction was immediately initiated, and on Thanksgiving Day in 1900 a fine hospital, costing $250,000 and located at Twenty-seventh Street and Ninth Court South, was dedicated. The first administrator of the hospital and also the first graduate nurse registered in the state of Alabama was Sister Chrysostom Moynahan. In 1900 St. Vincent's opened the first recognized school of nursing in the state, and in 1912 the State Board of Health approved the hospital for graduate nursing education. St. Vincent's has graduated almost 1,500 registered nurses.

Additional construction has continued since the turn of the century. The dynamic growth of the city put excessive demands on the new 100-bed hospital, and in 1911 a west wing was constructed. An east wing was added at a cost of $1.5 million in 1950.

In the early 1960s, Sister Carlos McDonnell initiated plans for a new St. Vincent's, and in 1972 the $12-million, seven-story facility was dedicated. By 1974 a four-million-dollar professional office building and parking deck had been completed. Historically pressed for space for beds and services, St.

Vincent's in 1978 embarked on a major $31.7-million expansion and renovation program.

Despite the tremendous physical growth and scientific and technological advancement of the institution, St. Vincent's philosophy of care remains constant. The emphasis is on the value of the individual as a creation of God, and the hospital strives to be responsive to the needs of the total person — physical, spiritual, familial, social, and emotional.

From its beginning, the spirit of St. Vincent's has been one of ecumenism. The Daughters of Charity have received constant encouragement from the hospital's outstanding medical staff and from friends throughout the community. This support has enabled the sisters to meet the many challenges with which they have been faced in providing a progressive ministry of healing in the "Magic City" for more than eighty years.

Left: *St. Vincent's first administrator, and the first graduate nurse registered in the state of Alabama, was Sister Chrysostom Moynahan.*

Below: *In this photograph taken in 1909, St. Vincent's nurses check Birmingham's first motorized ambulance, or "invalid carriage."*

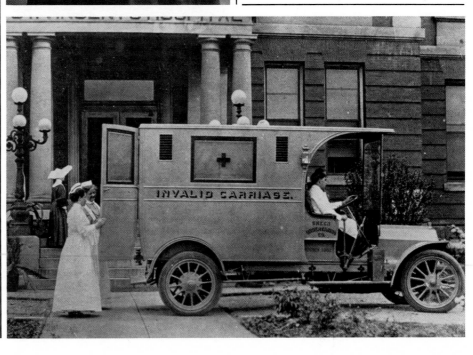

SAMFORD UNIVERSITY

Samford University, Alabama's largest and finest privately supported institution of higher learning, has been an important factor in the development of metropolitan Birmingham since 1887. However, the institution predates that year and, indeed, is older than the city of Birmingham itself.

Samford, third in size among the nation's Baptist senior colleges and universities, was chartered as Howard College in Marion, Alabama, in 1841 and opened its doors to students on January 3, 1842. The college moved to Birmingham in 1887 and became Samford University in 1965. The school is named for prominent Alabamian Frank Park Samford and his family and is an agency of the Alabama Baptist State Convention.

The university moved to its present location—400 acres of picturesque, rolling campus in Shades Valley six miles south of downtown Birmingham—in 1957. The Georgian-Colonial architecture and the beauty of its suburban location make Samford an ideal setting for both serious study and pleasant campus activities for the 4,000-member student body and the community as well. Samford students come from forty-one states and twenty foreign countries.

Samford's enrollment increased by more than 150 percent during the 1960s and 1970s, and through its growth Samford has played an important role in the area by contributing millions of dollars to the local economy. In addition, Samford's academic growth has matched its physical growth. The percentage of the 275 faculty members holding the earned doctoral degree stands far above the national average. Faculty members earned their terminal degrees at more than 100 distinguished universities. The school maintains a highly favorable student-faculty ratio of 20 to 1, and Samford offers programs leading to nineteen degrees, including eight at the postgraduate level.

One of the South's oldest and most respected universities, Samford is noted for its programs offering academic excellence in a distinctly Christian environment. Samford alumni serve in every state and around the world in a wide range of business careers, the professions, and in Christian ministries. Samford ranks in the top 10 percent of the nation's 800 private colleges and universities in the number of graduates listed in the latest edition of *Who's Who in America*. In Alabama, Samford ranks first in this category.

The university is comprised of eight colleges—the Howard College of Arts and Sciences, Cumberland School of Law, Ida V. Moffett School of Nursing, Orlean Bullard Beeson School of Education, School of Graduate Studies, and schools of Business, Music, and Pharmacy. Samford also offers degree programs in the divisions of Anesthesia and Paralegal Studies.

Samford's preprofessional curricula in medicine, dentistry, law, forestry, and engineering have been rated at the top in the southeastern United States. Annually more than 50 percent of Samford's graduating class continue their studies at leading graduate and professional schools throughout the United States and in other countries. Larger numbers of Samford graduates are accepted at medical schools, law schools, and schools of dentistry than from any other privately supported

college or university in Alabama. The percentage of such acceptances from Samford compares most favorably with outstanding colleges and universities throughout the Southeast. A Samford student was Alabama's only Harry S. Truman Scholar in 1980 and 1981.

Ever alert to societal changes and the needs of its students, Samford added six programs in 1980 which are designed to prepare students for useful careers. The programs are communications, computer science, environmental science, international business, public administration, and public affairs. Samford is involved in cooperative education, in which students alternate school and work years. However, regardless of the major field of study, all students take a required curriculum in the liberal arts.

Growth is never achieved at the expense of excellence at Samford. The university's standards, as might be expected of an institution now halfway through its second century, remain high. Results bear this out. After winning the National Four-man Debate title three out of four years in the 1970s, Samford's debate team ranked third in the nation in 1980, trailing only Northwestern and Harvard universities; Cumberland Law School's annual Law

Left: *Memory Leake Robinson Hall is the home of Cumberland School of Law of Samford University. One of the nation's oldest and most respected law schools, Cumberland was founded in 1847 and has produced numerous distinguished members of the judiciary and bar including Cordell Hull, who served as Secretary of State under President Franklin D. Roosevelt.*

Right: *Founded in 1841, Samford University is the nation's third largest Southern Baptist institution of higher learning.*

Below left: *The Samford University campus is situated on 400 picturesque, rolling acres in Shades Valley, six miles south of downtown Birmingham.*

Below: *The Ralph W. Beeson Student Center provides outstanding facilities for various student service programs at Samford University. The student center houses a beautifully appointed main dining room with a seating capacity of more than 1,200, as well as recreational lounges, snack bar, post office, bookstore, health service area, and offices for student publications, student government and campus ministry programs.*

Week program was judged the finest in America three times in a period of five years during the past decade; in the 1981 National Mock Trial Competition, Cumberland Law students won first place; Samford's Chair of Private Enterprise was the first in Alabama and is the most active; Samford's internationally known A Cappella Choir made highly acclaimed concert tours of Great Britain, France, Sweden, and Japan during the past ten years; and the 60-bell Rushton Memorial Carillon, cast in Holland and housed in the library tower, is the only such instrument in the world with an inscription from the Bible or the great poets engraved on every bell.

Offering the only ROTC program at a private academic institution in Alabama, Samford provides opportunities for Air Force careers to Samford students and students from six nearby colleges.

Birmingham area residents have enthusiastically accepted Samford's numerous evening, summer, and non-credit courses, in which students have the options of earning a degree part-time, upgrading their professional skills, or simply pursuing the joys of learning. Samford's Extension Division enrolls an additional 2,500 adults in centers located throughout Alabama.

Construction is nearly complete on the 31-structure master plan of the new campus. Most recently finished were the Leslie Stephen Wright Fine Arts Center, a major addition to the Memory Leake Robinson Law Building, and the Orlean Bullard Beeson School of Education Building. Samford trustees have launched a $12.5-million Preserving Excellence Campaign to complete all nonresidential portions of its campus and to make significant additions to the university's endowment.

Dr. Leslie S. Wright, head of the university for more than two decades, is the dean of college and university presidents in Alabama. An impressive 3,000-seat Fine Arts Center, housing the performing arts, is named in his honor.

215

SHAW WAREHOUSE COMPANY

An enterprise that began as a small warehouse-distribution outlet in the 1920s has evolved into Birmingham's major, multi-building warehouse complex in the 1980s. Today, the Shaw Warehouse Company can boast of over 300,000 square feet in Birmingham and Montgomery. And the Shaw facilities handle a wide range of goods for many Birmingham industries, including hospital and medical supplies, raw materials for local manufacturers, construction materials, electronics, and appliances, as well as grocery products with which the company first began operations over fifty years ago.

The firm was founded in 1927 by Jack Gates (J.G.) Shaw. The former president of a wholesale grocery company, Shaw recognized the need for warehousing and distribution facilities in the growing city of Birmingham. Though the firm primarily warehoused canned food and other household products in its early years, it also handled some industrial products as well.

By the early 1930s, business growth forced the company to move from its old building on Thirteenth Street and First Avenue South to larger quarters at 8 South Eighteenth Street. In those days, Birmingham food stores were small neighborhood groceries, of course, and wholesalers and grocers had to restock their supplies on a weekly and sometimes even daily basis. The new Shaw warehouse served as the local distribution hub for the stores, acting as a storage facility and a delivery system.

Though the times were difficult, the firm managed to survive the depression and continued to grow in the 1940s. J.G.'s son Sam joined the organization after a career in banking, and together they planned the future expansion of both warehouse space and services. J.G. died in 1949 and Sam took over as president, carrying through with his father's plans—new facilities on Thirty-fifth Street, built in 1950 and 1951, provided additional warehouse, distribution, and office space and are still a major aspect of the firm's operations.

216   As chain supermarkets gradually

Above: *By the early 1970s, the Shaw Warehouse Company filled four city blocks—from 2500 to 2800 Second Avenue North. In 1980, the firm constructed another facility at 2900-3000 Second Avenue North.*

Below: *With the proliferation of chain supermarkets in the 1950s and 1960s, Shaw wisely deemphasized food products storage and enhanced its warehouse capabilities for other types of manufactured goods.*

replaced the ''Mom and Pop'' groceries in the 1950s, Shaw wisely deemphasized food products storage and enhanced its warehouse capabilities for other types of manufactured goods. Along with product expansion for industry and retail businesses came more physical expansion—by the early 1970s, the company's warehouses filled four city blocks, from 2500 to 2800 Second Avenue North. In 1980, the firm completed its long-term expansion program with the construction of another building at 2900-3000 Second Avenue North.

Shaw Warehouse Company has always been a family-owned business. After Sam Shaw passed away in 1976, his son and daughter, S. Gates Shaw and Dorothy Shaw, took over the reins— the third generation of the Shaw family to run the company.

With Birmingham's industrial and business future looking bright, Shaw Warehouse Company will continue to serve the city's widely varied wholesale and retail businesses—as it has done so successfully for more than fifty years.

SHEPHERD REALTY COMPANY, INC.

Birmingham was ten years old and already exhibiting the dynamics and economic potential that marked its rapid rise to a major industrial center when Crutcher Duty Shepherd came to the city from Mississippi. There, he had been a farmer and had worked for the railroad, after serving with distinction during the War Between the States with the First Mississippi Light Artillery, rising from private to major.

A widower with two children and little in financial resources, he entered the real estate business. After fifteen years of struggling, he found his niche in this booming, young city. He became a highly successful businessman and a community leader.

Three generations later, his great-grandsons, James W., Everett Jr., and Robert W. Shepherd look proudly from their office window toward one of the area's largest and most prosperous shopping malls, Brookwood Village. It is the latest in a series of successful real estate ventures that the Shepherd family has carried out in Birmingham.

After World War I Everett Shepherd, Sr., and A. Page Sloss formed an organization and in the early 1920s entered the real estate business. The firm, Shepherd-Sloss Realty Company, concentrated at first on residential building. During the strong economic thrust of the period, Shepherd-Sloss turned its attention to commercial construction.

An early project, the stores at Twentieth Street and Highland Avenue, became the first in Birmingham to provide off-street parking. Later, after the completion of the Highland Plaza development at Twenty-third Street, came a truly remarkable achievement in commercial development—Five Points West. One of the first regional shopping centers in the Southeast, Five Points West was for many years the largest shopping center in the South.

In 1966, the Shepherd-Sloss firm was dissolved and Shepherd Realty Company, Inc., was formed, with Everett Shepherd, Sr., as chairman;

Original officers of Shepherd Realty were (seated) Everett Shepherd, Sr., chairman; (left) Robert W. Shepherd, in charge of sales and rentals; James W. Shepherd, manager and comptroller; and (right) Everett Shepherd, Jr., in charge of construction and development.

James W. Shepherd as manager and comptroller; Everett Shepherd, Jr., in charge of construction and development; and Robert W. Shepherd in charge of sales and rentals.

Brookwood Village, a worthy successor to Five Points West, was a recent Shepherd Realty project, completed in association with Charles E. Sharp. It has 100 retail establishments, including 90 stores and specialty shops, a movie theater, and 10 restaurants in the mall and the adjacent convenience center. The mall, visited by 1.2 million shoppers each year, has made a significant impact on Birmingham shopping habits.

The Shepherd name stands tall in Birmingham land development, real estate, and the investment business. With the fourth generation of the family in command, Shepherd Realty can be expected to exert a strong influence in the future in Birmingham land and commercial development.

SHOOK & FLETCHER SUPPLY CO.

Early in 1901 P.G. Shook and John F. Fletcher, Jr., who had recently resigned as executives of the Tennessee Coal, Iron and Railroad Company, formed the firm of Shook & Fletcher. The following statement, an exact facsimile of the original, was mailed to all prospective customers May 14, 1901:

We beg to announce the formation of the firm of Shook & Fletcher, composed of P.G. Shook, formerly Secretary and Treasurer of the Alabama Steel & Ship Building Co., and Assistant General Superintendent of the Steel Works Division of the Tennessee Coal, Iron & R.R. Co., and John F. Fletcher, Jr., formerly Secretary and Assistant Treasurer of the Tennessee Coal, Iron & R.R. Co., both having been connected with the Tennessee Company for the past ten years.

This firm will open a brokerage office in Birmingham, Ala., on May 20th, and will conduct a general commission business, covering the purchase and sale of Pig Iron, Bar Iron, Steel, Coke, Coal, Fire Brick and all manufactured products.

A number of Agency connections with manufacturing concerns, in both the North and South, have been formed.

We are in position to save you money on anything you have to buy, and to make you money on anything you have to sell.

Some of our lines are Pig Iron, Bar Iron and Plates, Steel in all forms, Steel Castings, Coal, Coke, Boilers, Engines, Pumps, Rolling Mill Machinery, Crushers, Steam Shovels, Ore Washers, Electric Overhead Cranes, Pipe Covering, Fire Brick, etc., etc.

Prompted by the belief that the Southern Territory offers at this time flattering inducements for the successful conduct of such a business, we enter the field with a determination to succeed, and, from encouragement already received, consider that we are starting in under most favorable auspices.

If you are in the market, either to buy or sell anything, let us hear from you.

TO THE SOUTHERN FOUNDRYMAN.

A special feature of our business will be pig iron for Southern consumers. We desire to get into direct communication with every Foundryman in the South. Let us correspond with you about your mixture, the grades and brand of iron you are now using. Certainly an exchange of ideas can do no harm, and may result in something mutually advantageous.

In order that we may get in close touch with your practice and requirements, will you kindly answer the following queries:

What grades of iron do you use?
What brand of iron do you use?
What tonnage do you melt monthly?
What coke do you use?

We earnestly solicit your enquiries and promise prompt and satisfactory attention to all business entrusted in our hands.

SHOOK & FLETCHER.

Under the direction of the partners the firm prospered. In 1910 the company name was changed to Shook & Fletcher Supply Co. J.H. Adkins was employed as sales manager and secretary of the corporation at that time. Under his guidance the company became the representative for a large number of manufacturers throughout the United States involved in the iron, steel,

Above: *This is a facsimile of the original statement announcing the formation of Shook & Fletcher, mailed to prospective customers on May 14, 1901.*

Left: *The general office building of Shook & Fletcher Supply Co. was located at 1814 First Avenue North.*

electric utilities, and mining industries.

In 1913 Paschal Shook's brother, James Warner Shook, bought John Fletcher's interest in Shook & Fletcher Supply Co., bringing with him his expertise in the brown iron ore business. In the following years Shook & Fletcher Supply Co. became the largest independent iron ore producer in the Southeast, operating mines in Blount, Franklin, Bibb, Tuscaloosa, Shelby, St. Clair, and Jefferson counties, Alabama; Cedartown, Georgia; and two locations in southeast Missouri. The ore from all of these mines was shipped to Birmingham and sold to iron and steel industries there. Two of Warner Shook's most able assistants in this effort were E.N. Vandegrift of Tate's Gap, Alabama, and E.H. Craddock of Russellville, Alabama. These mines were successfully operated until they were phased out in 1973. ⬦

In the late 1920s and early 1930s the company organized a mechanical contracting division for the installation of heating and cooling equipment. A contract was signed with Carrier Corporation of Syracuse, New York, for its complete line, under the direction of J.H. Adkins. In 1943 C.L. Gaines, Jr., was employed as manager of this division. That part of the company was divided into two operations, one contracting, the other for dealer sales. This was a very successful venture and continued to operate until 1972 when it was sold to Gene Dykes and James Traywick, who were members of this company, and to members of the firm of Banks, Ellett and Ramsay who used their plumbing expertise to make it a complete mechanical contracting unit.

In 1954 T.A. Gearhart was employed to succeed J.H. Adkins, who had died. During his administration he employed two very able assistants, Carl Jones and Michael Lauderdale. Under their direction this division of the company made tremendous strides. Volume of business of Shook & Fletcher increased to the extent that today the company is constructing a new warehouse and field office facility in western Jefferson County, to supply the coal mining industry in Jefferson, Walker, Tuscaloosa, and other counties in Alabama and coal mines in Tennessee.

Products of the following companies will be handled through the new facility: Anaconda-Ericsson, electrical mining cables; Anixter-Cable Service, electrical cable couplers; Bacharach Instrument Company, methane gas detection equipment; D & E Tool Company, drill rods, mining augers; Electro Devices, Inc., annunciators; Industron Corporation, electrical tapes; Kennametal Inc., coal mining tools; Kerite Company, insulated wires and cables; S.P. Kinney Engineers, Inc., automatic water strainers, blast furnace equipment; Mining Machine Parts, Inc., replacement parts for mining machines; Minnesota Mining and Manufacturing Company, portable electrical cable splicing kits; Ohio Brass Company, rectifiers, power centers, mining line materials; Parker-Hannifin Corporation, hydraulic hose and fittings; Pyott-Boone, Inc., electronic communication and monitoring equipment; Sigmaform Corporation, electrical cable splicing kits; TJB, Inc., high- and medium-voltage electrical cable couplers; T & T Machine Company, pumps; and Treadwell Corporation, hot-metal cars, steel mill equipment.

Officers of the company today are A.M. Shook III, president, chief executive officer, treasurer; Paschal G. Shook, Jr., executive vice-president; Charles L. Gaines, Jr., vice-president; H.O. Thomas, Jr., vice-president, controller; and T.A. Gearhart, secretary.

SOUTH CENTRAL BELL

Birmingham sprang to life in 1871 as the result of its fortuitous proximity to all the elements needed to produce steel. Its growth, from the first, was prodigious. Within the first decade of the city's existence, the telephone in Birmingham came to symbolize the same forward-looking spirit and progressiveness that made the "city of steel" possible. And for 100 years, telecommunications have been in the forefront of Birmingham's growth and development.

What some described as Alexander Graham Bell's "toy" first appeared in Birmingham in 1879. That year, North & South Railroad dispatcher F.H. Britton obtained two of the Bell Company's instruments—one for installation in his Birmingham office and one for the railroad's Decatur depot.

The two telephones were connected to telegraph wires, and one Sunday afternoon, by prearrangement, what may well have been the first long-distance call within Alabama took place. The words spoken were clear and distinct. News of the successful conversation spread, and Birmingham businessmen soon became interested.

Others who arranged for private installations included Dr. George Morrow, the Pratt Coal and Coke Company, and the Elyton Land Company. Because they were such a novelty for customers and friends, the first telephones were often busy and could not be used for business much of the time.

In early 1882, a Southern Bell Telephone Company representative ventured to the steel boom town in an effort to sign up twenty-five subscribers and form a telephone exchange. After coming up with only seventeen names, the representative was about to leave Birmingham, his mission a failure. At that point Birmingham grocer James A. Van Hoose (later to become mayor), whose own name topped the list of subscribers, agreed to go scrounging for the last eight signatures. He was warned that the entire city had been canvassed and that there was no hope of additional

signings. Within an hour, however, he was back with the necessary subscriptions.

His explanation? "Why, I got eight men to agree to be the twenty-fifth subscriber." To each of the prospects he had asked the question, "If I can secure twenty-four men to subscribe for a telephone, will you be the twenty-fifth man?" Each of the men agreed, and Birmingham's first telephone exchange was created.

On May 8, 1882, the exchange (with thirty-nine subscribers by then) opened on the third floor of the Hughes Drug Store building on the southeast corner of Second Avenue North and Nineteenth Street. The names of the subscribers represent a roll call of the city's early business and community leaders—including Van Hoose, the Relay House, Alabama Great Southern Railroad, and F.P. O'Brien, who had telephones installed in his home, his opera house, and his lumber company. The march was on. In four years the number of subscribers skyrocketed to between four and five hundred. Long-distance service became available to outlying towns.

During the late 1880s, Birmingham's two operators spent long hours sitting opposite each other helping customers who shouted into their mouthpieces, "Central, connect 248 with 256." The operator took the plugs representing those numbers, touched the battery strip, and rang both bells.

As the century ended, Birmingham's population had swelled to 38,000 citizens and its telephones to over 1,400. New switchboard offices were installed in Ensley, Pratt City, Woodlawn, and Bessemer. As the city continued to grow, another telephone company in the area was organized. The People's Home Telephone Company offered service to Birmingham and Bessemer residents. Because some users chose Bell and others chose People's Home, some business firms were forced to have service with both companies in order to deal with all their customers.

In 1907, Southern Bell erected a new two-story building at 1814 Second Avenue North in Birmingham. A few years later, when that space proved inadequate, four additional floors were added. (The building still stands today between the former Loveman's and Calder's Furniture downtown.)

During the early decades of the twentieth century, the company's operations were centered at the Second Avenue building. Later a small structure was secured at 1715 Sixth Avenue North to serve as a barn-garage for the company's horses and wagons. This

Birmingham's remarkable telephonic progress can be traced through these photographs—from Southern Bell's first telephone operation in Birmingham (below), to South Central Bell's corporate headquarters (right), to the newly constructed Alabama operations headquarters of South Central Bell (page 222).

structure later became part of Birmingham's Main and Toll building.

On August 21, 1912, Southern Bell finalized agreements to purchase People's Home Telephone Company (at a combined price, for the Birmingham and Bessemer properties, of $525,000). This action effectively ended a period of two phone companies in the area and the subsequent duplication of services.

By the time of the 1930s and the onslaught of the Great Depression, the Woodlawn office had been replaced, a manual office installed in Boyles, and a dial office installed in Homewood. By 1930 there were 43,000 telephone subscribers in the Birmingham area. By 1950, subscribers numbered 135,179 and by 1963 that figure had soared to 230,372.

By 1968 Southern Bell was an 89-year wonder, changing and struggling to meet the demand for more and better communications services. While telephones in the nationwide Bell System more than tripled after World War II, they increased more than five times in Southern Bell's nine-state territory. It was this growth and the complexities involved with operating the business that led to a major structural change within the telephone company in the Southeast—one which greatly boosted the economic picture of Birmingham and its surrounding area. The decision was made to divide Southern Bell's territory into two companies.

On July 1, 1968, the South Central Bell Telephone Company was formed, covering a five-state area—Alabama, Kentucky, Louisiana, Mississippi, and Tennessee. Birmingham was selected as the site for the company's corporate headquarters. At that time, South Central Bell became the largest corporation ever newly formed in American business. With $2 billion in assets it became the twenty-third operating company of the Bell System. It immediately began to serve 5.5 million telephones. Of those, 278,042 were in the Birmingham

(continued on next page)

221

calling area.

In 1971, South Central Bell's $20-million, 30-story corporate downtown headquarters complex was completed. It houses over 1,600 employees responsible for the five-state area operation and is Alabama's largest office complex. In addition to these facilities, Birmingham utilizes microwave towers and electronic switching systems to provide the most up-to-date communications service anywhere for the 675,000 telephones in the greater Birmingham calling area. Customers in the 2,636 square miles of this calling area, which encompasses all of Jefferson and Shelby counties and the town of West Blocton, have the third largest toll-free calling area in the United States, behind Atlanta and Denver.

Capital investment during 1980 for new and improved services in Alabama approached $290 million, with over 14,000 South Central Bell employees in Alabama.

The new Alabama Operations Center will be completed by mid-1981. All employees who supervise and perform administrative duties for the company's more than two million telephones in Alabama will be located in this complex. Initially the center will house over 1,500 employees with eventual facilities for over 2,000.

Birmingham and America now confront the "Information Age"—an age the scope and impact of which few are able to define. But one generalization seems inescapable—it will mean an incredible bombardment of information. Another generalization seems likely—the major delivery system will be the Bell System.

Solid-state electronics will make possible pocket-sized portable telephones, wristwatch phones, Picturephone®, home sentinel service, information retrieval over telephone wires, lightwave communications, fiber optics, paying bills by phone, and more. These innovations are not really "the future"; they are available now,

although some of them are not yet economically feasible for general distribution.

Change begets change. Along with the significant technological innovations recently implemented, the Bell System and South Central Bell have changed their organizational structures to accommodate new market and regulatory conditions. The Bell System was born and matured in an era of intense competition. That background—together with an eagerness to take on new opportunities—should stand it in good stead as telecommunications move into an era of increasing competition and deregulation.

"The Bell System will be an organization vastly different from the one we know today," AT&T Chairman Charles Brown has said. One thing that will not change, however, is the Bell System's commitment to serve the many telecommunications needs of its customers.

SOUTHERN NATURAL RESOURCES, INC.

Southern Natural Resources, a Birmingham firm with worldwide interests, began in 1929 as Southern Natural Gas Corporation, a natural gas pipeline company shipping gas from fields in northeast Louisiana, across Mississippi and Alabama into Birmingham. Gas deliveries to Birmingham began in December 1929 and service was extended to Atlanta the following June.

From 1929 until 1959 the company was engaged almost entirely in the interstate shipment of natural gas. In spite of a promising beginning, the young firm was dealt some damaging blows by the depression following the stock market crash of 1929. But Southern Natural Gas Company, the predecessor of Southern Natural Resources, emerged unscathed and began paying dividends in 1936. So successful were the first thirty years, in fact, that by the end of the fifties Southern Natural pipelines extended over 5,000 miles and the company could point to revenues of $122 million for 1959, with earnings of $9.2 million.

However successful the firm many have seemed after its first thirty years, its truly phenomenal years lay ahead, due chiefly to new policies of opportunity through diversification. During the next two decades annual revenues for the emergent parent corporation, Southern Natural Resources, increased to nearly $1.8 billion and earnings increased

every year at a similar pace to over $139 million by 1980.

The days when Southern Natural was merely a shipper of natural gas, however, are long since gone. Today the actual exploration and development of oil and gas fields are two of the company's most important activities. Southern Natural's subsidiary, SONAT Exploration Company, has oil and gas interests in about 100 offshore lease blocks, mostly in the Gulf of Mexico, and in about two million acres onshore in the South and in the Rocky Mountains. Another subsidiary, The Offshore Company, owns and operates one of the world's largest fleets of mobile offshore drilling rigs and ships, as well as a number of land drilling rigs, representing a total investment of more than $500 million. These drilling rigs operate all over the world, from the Shetland Islands in the North Sea to Tierra del Fuego off the southern tip of Argentina and from the Gulf of Mexico to the Gulf of Suez.

During this same 1960-1980 period, Southern Natural moved into the forest products industry in a joint venture with Boise Cascade Corporation. The Boise-Southern venture erected a vast new paper mill complex at DeRidder, Louisiana, in 1969, then the world's largest new forest products operation ever constructed at one time. Today it includes a complex of paper, pulp, plywood, and lumber mills supported by over 800,000 acres of some of America's best timberlands.

Southern Natural acquired the South Georgia Natural Gas Company in 1969 and, in that same year, began a 30-story headquarters building in downtown Birmingham in partnership with the First National Bank of Birmingham.

Another major growth step came in 1980, with the acquisition of Interstate and Ocean Transport Company of Philadelphia, Pennsylvania, which operates one of the nation's largest fleets of coastal tank barges and tugs. A new regional headquarters facility, the Southern Natural Resources Tower in

Houston, Texas, was also occupied in 1980 to accommodate the company's expanding operations in the Southwest.

Obviously, it is a long way from a Louisiana gas field to vast forest tracts to an oil drilling rig in the North Sea. That the company has crossed beyond these business frontiers reflects a spirited sense of growth, an eye for opportunity, and a tradition of careful but aggressive management.

It is significant to note that Southern Natural has had but four chief executives in its 50-plus years. Henry C. Goodrich has recently succeeded John S. Shaw, Jr., as chairman, president, and chief executive officer. Shaw had followed C. Pratt Rather in 1967, and Rather in 1965 had succeeded Christopher T. Chenery, the company's first chief executive.

Above: *Modern energy technology is seen in the world's tallest offshore oil-producing platform, known as "Cognac," which stands in over 1,000 feet of water in the Gulf of Mexico about 100 miles south of New Orleans. A Southern Natural Resources subsidiary, SONAT Exploration Company, has an ownership interest in the oil and gas field on which the giant platform stands.*

Above left: *Muscle and mule power marked the early days of interstate pipeline construction, shown in this 1929 photograph of workers installing one of the first Southern Natural gas lines in the Birmingham area.*

STERNE, AGEE & LEACH, INC.

Sterne, Agee & Leach, Inc., operates the oldest investment securities business in Alabama. The company acts as underwriter, distributor, dealer, and broker in municipal bonds and corporate bonds and stocks and is a market maker in many local securities. It is the only member firm of the New York Stock Exchange with headquarters in Alabama.

The firm of Ward, Sterne & Company was established August 1, 1919, when George B. Ward, twice mayor of Birmingham, and Mervyn H. Sterne, recently retired from military service in France, entered into partnership to conduct an investment securities business. Each had previous business experience in trading securities. On November 1, 1919, Rucker Agee, who was runner at the local branch of the Federal Reserve Bank, was employed by the firm. Edmund C. Leach was employed in 1921 and soon thereafter opened an office for the company in Montgomery. Agee and Leach were admitted to partnership in 1927. After the death of George Ward in 1940, the name of the firm was changed to Sterne, Agee & Leach.

In 1955 Henry S. Lynn, who had joined the organization some years before, acquired a seat on the New York Stock Exchange. That same year Alonzo H. Lee acquired an associate membership on the American Stock Exchange. The business was incorporated in 1964. In 1974 the investment banking business conducted in Mobile by H. Ogden Shropshire was acquired. The firm now operates in the three locations — Birmingham, Montgomery, and Mobile.

Since 1920 the company has been active in public finance in Alabama. Jefferson County had an election which authorized road bonds and the county let contracts for construction to road contractors, but the bond market collapsed and interest on bonds was legally limited to 5 percent. Local headlines announced that the county was bankrupt. The bonds could not be sold. The firm arranged with the county to issue warrants bearing interest at 8 percent to the road contractors, took options from the contractors on the warrants, and proceeded to market them.

Municipal bond laws in Alabama were archaic. There was no attorney in Alabama who specialized in municipal bond law. The firm employed Boston attorneys to draft a modern bond code requiring bonds to be paid in annual serial installments. This law was adopted in 1927 as the Municipal Bond Code.

In 1923 the company purchased $1 million of highway bonds, which were the first ones issued by the state of Alabama for internal improvements since Reconstruction times. Five years later the firm, together with Lehman Brothers, purchased $4 million of Alabama State Bridge Corporation corporate bonds payable from bridge tolls. These were the first revenue bonds issued by the state.

Early in 1927 the company purchased all of the capital stock of the Traders National Bank, invited John C. Persons of Tuscaloosa to be its president, and organized a new board of directors. Before the year was out the bank had merged with American Trust & Savings Bank as American Traders National Bank, with Persons as its president. On July 1, 1930, this bank was merged with First National Bank, with Oscar Wells as chairman and Persons as president.

The three offices of Sterne, Agee & Leach are now conducted under the guidance of a board of directors and in Birmingham by Henry S. Lynn, chairman of the executive committee; Arthur B. Durkee, chairman of the board; and W.K. McHenry, president; in Montgomery by Major General Will Hill Tankersley, senior vice-president; and in Mobile by Frank B. Frazer, senior vice-president.

STOCKHAM VALVES & FITTINGS

William H. Stockham had done well with his own Chicago foundry, but when his business was decimated by the financial panic of 1893 he cast a discerning eye toward the South.

It was obvious that in one locale in particular, history was in the making. Iron, ore, coal, and limestone had come together in the vigorous city of Birmingham to produce an industrial boom. So Stockham, along with his wife and two sons, moved to Alabama in 1903.

With borrowed money, Stockham rented an abandoned car barn for forty dollars a month and opened Stockham Pipe & Fittings Company with a crew of five. The fledgling firm manufactured brake shoes, sash weights, meter boxes, car wheels, manhole covers, and, somewhat later, cast-iron soil pipe

Today—nearly eight decades after Will Stockham moved south and rolled up his sleeves in that rented car barn—Stockham Valves & Fittings produces one of the most extensive lines of valves and fittings in the world and its products are found in some of the greatest plants and institutions in America.

Stockham's original plant was twice swept by fire. But the firm, with 200 employees by 1914, looked adversity in the face and rebuilt four years later on a 30-acre site at 4000 Tenth Avenue North.

The company flourished. A new shipping room and warehouse were added in 1921 and the first Los Angeles warehouse was built in 1923. In that year, too, founder Will Stockham died. His wife, Kate Clark Stockham, became chairman, and his son, Herbert Clark Stockham, became president.

H.C. Stockham began plant mechanization and directed numerous expansions and improvements—electrical cranes, a variety of continuous-molding units, continuous-cleaning mills, and new regional warehouses in several states. The firm was seriously hit by the Great Depression. Despite this, the plant began production of its bronze valves during the 1930s.

Above: *William H. Stockham founded Stockham Pipe & Fittings Company, headquartered in Birmingham, in 1903. The company name was changed in 1948 to Stockham Valves & Fittings.*

Top: *The firm's original facility was an abandoned car barn, rented for forty dollars a month.*

With America's entry into World War II, Stockham built a new shop to forge 75-MM shells and turned out nearly 4.5 million such shells for the armed forces. The company also produced alloy steel castings for tank armor plating, millions of grenades and practice bombs, and cast steel fittings for naval vessels. For its outstanding efforts, Stockham was awarded three Army-Navy E production citations.

Following the war, a program of reconditioning and expansion was launched. Kate C. Stockham died in 1946 and H.C. Stockham became chairman as well as president. The brass foundry switched to electric furnaces. The main Birmingham office building was remodeled. The malleable foundry's third unit went into operation. A push-button malleable cupola charger was installed. An automatic-galvanizing kettle was added. Stockham branched into steel plug valves, steel valve production was begun, and continuous annealing went into operation in 1953. Richard J. Stockham was elected president that same year.

The bronze department moved into a new building in 1958. Upon the death of H.C. Stockham in 1958, his brother Douglass W. Stockham was named chairman, and his son, Herbert Cannon Stockham, became vice-chairman and general manager. Today, Herbert Cannon Stockham is the company's chairman and president.

The Stockham of today is a nationwide organization, much more complex than it was twenty years ago. The valve line includes gate, globe, angle, check, plug, waffer check, ball, and butterfly valves made in bronze, iron, ductile, carbon, and stainless steel. Threaded, flanged, and grooved fittings of all types are manufactured in cast, malleable, and ductile iron.

THOMPSON TRACTOR CO., INC.

Hall Thompson, son of Nashville, Tennessee, Caterpillar dealer DeWitt C. Thompson, Jr., left his native state in 1957 to follow in the footsteps of his father and acquired the J.D. Pittman Tractor Company of Birmingham and the local Caterpillar dealership.

In the ensuing twenty-three years Thompson Tractor Co., Inc., has grown to major status in the North Alabama heavy-equipment field, and Hall Thompson has become one of the area's most effective and most respected civic, cultural, and economic leaders.

Thompson chose a manufacturer with a reputation that was and is at the top in the heavy-equipment field. By 1957 Caterpillar Tractor Company had held a leadership position in heavy-equipment manufacturing for fifty-three years, based on a predecessor firm's innovative conversion of steam tractor machines from wheels to tracks.

At that time the Holt Manufacturing Company, based in Stockton, California, was servicing the agricultural, construction, and industrial markets throughout the world with tractors, but the massive machines were not suitable for much of the farmland in

central California where wheeled machines would quickly bog down during the rainy season. Holt devised a machine replacing the large chain-driven iron wheels with treadmills of wooden slats, opening thousands of acres to cultivation.

Since that time, product improvement has continued to be the keynote of Caterpillar's efforts; the continuing search for more reliable, productive, and serviceable products has stimulated the company's unparalleled growth. With products built around the world Caterpillar offers the most complete earth-moving line in the industry, as well as materials-handling equipment and engines. Today Caterpillar manufactures eighty versions of track-type tractors and loaders, standard wheel scrapers and loaders, dozers, compactors, graders, skidders, track pipe layers, and off-highway trucks. The

Caterpillar name is synonymous with massive earth-moving machinery.

Thompson Tractor has been a dynamic contributor to the Caterpillar company's growth. Thompson's servicing area, comprised of the thirty-nine North Alabama counties, now has three major branch operations in Decatur, Anniston, and Tuscaloosa, and smaller branches in Scottsboro and Opelika. The main office and shop at 2401 Pinson Highway is a leading sales and service installation in the Birmingham area.

Hall Thompson has done much more as a Birmingham resident than promote his tractor firm to a leadership position. As a citizen of Birmingham, Jefferson County, and Alabama he has assumed responsibility in exploiting the area's many resources and strengthening its civic and economic structures. He has been particularly active in encouraging stronger athletic programs for the city's sports fans.

Of particular note is his single-handed effort resulting in a new golf course and country club of national prominence, Shoal Creek in north Shelby County. With Jack Nicklaus as the course architect, Thompson has converted 600 acres in the shadow of Double Oak Mountain into one of the nation's most challenging golf courses. The Professional Golfers' Association selected the course as the site for its 1984 tournament, one of the four top U.S. golf tournaments each year. Nicklaus as course architect calls it, "The best I have ever done."

Thompson Tractor Co., Inc., most definitely has made an affirmative impact on Birmingham in the comparatively few years it has been a part of the community.

Right: *Hall Thompson, one of Birmingham's most respected civic leaders, founded Thompson Tractor Co., Inc., in 1957.*

Below: *Headquarters of Thompson Tractor Co., Inc., are located at 2401 Pinson Highway, Birmingham.*

UNIVERSITY OF ALABAMA IN BIRMINGHAM

The University of Alabama in Birmingham (UAB) is a comprehensive urban university and medical center complex extending over some sixty square blocks on the city's Southside. The current enrollment of nearly 15,000 students is particularly impressive in view of the University's brief existence. Begun in 1936 as an extension center of the University of Alabama in Tuscaloosa, UAB's first enrollment was a mere 116 students.

From the modest beginning, UAB's history has been one of exceptional growth and achievement. Today, UAB embraces the Schools of Business, Community and Allied Health, Dentistry, Education, Engineering, Humanities, Medicine, Natural Sciences and Mathematics, Nursing, Optometry, and Social and Behavioral Sciences, as well as the University of Alabama Hospitals with affiliated clinics. Adding to the educational offerings are the Graduate School—with some thirty-five master's and seventeen doctoral programs—and UAB Special Studies, which offers special-format and nontraditional degree courses and programs.

In addition to the academic and health-care components, UAB also includes numerous specialized centers and programs—many of them internationally recognized—conducting research into mankind's most challenging health and social problems. These centers are an intricate part of the educational programs, making the latest advances readily available to students and professionals.

Outstanding research programs also benefit the patients who come to the University of Alabama Hospitals—the state's leading referral center. Patients come from around the world, due to the Hospitals' reputation for excellence in such important areas as open-heart surgery, cancer, kidney transplantation, burns, nutrition, diabetes, trauma, and the treatment of critically ill newborns. Indeed, such has been the University's contribution that Birmingham—once a city known for its heavy industry—is today known for both industry and health care.

Above: *The Lister Hill Library of the Health Sciences is the major library source for the five health care schools of the University of Alabama in Birmingham.*

Top: *Mortimer Jordan Hall is the central administrative building for the University, housing the office of the president.*

Such growth and success actually got underway in 1945, when the Medical College of Alabama was relocated to Birmingham, expanded to a four-year program, and renamed the University of Alabama School of Medicine. The University of Alabama School of Dentistry was established by the state legislature that same year, and the first class was enrolled in 1948.

The Extension Center was also growing. By 1946, the original single building could no longer accommodate the students. With enrollment approaching 500, extra space was obtained at Philips High School. Plans were begun for undergraduate facilities—and the first building was put into use in 1954. A theater was donated that same year, and an engineering building was completed in 1963. In 1966, the four-year, degree-granting College of General Studies (now University College) was established.

In 1967, the University of Alabama School of Nursing was moved to UAB. The School of Optometry opened in 1969, the same year the legislature established the School of Community and Allied Health Resources (now the School of Community and Allied Health).

Graduate studies at UAB were also growing, keeping pace with interest in various academic areas. The UAB Graduate School was established in 1970, incorporating all previously approved graduate activities. Graduate programs have continued to increase since that time.

When all Birmingham programs were formally designated the University of Alabama in Birmingham in 1966, UAB became one of three campuses of the University of Alabama System. In June 1969, UAB was given autonomy within the system and established its own administrative structure with a president as the chief executive officer.

Today, UAB is truly an outstanding resource—serving the state, nation, and world as it meets its threefold mission of education, research, and service.

TRACTOR & EQUIPMENT CO., INC.

"We'll do whatever it takes to keep you moving."

Adherence to that promise has made Tractor & Equipment Co. of 5336 Airport Highway, Birmingham, a major factor in providing machinery for the construction, mining, forestry, aggregate, manufacturing, and materials-handling industries of Alabama. And it's evident that the application of that promise to the operation of the firm itself has enabled Tractor & Equipment Co. to keep moving. Established in Birmingham in 1943, today the firm has six branches and 325 employees.

It was in January 1943 that the late L.J. Moore, in the machinery business in Georgia, and the late E.J. Anderson, Alabama representative for Northwest Engineering Company, formed Tractor & Equipment Co. of Birmingham.

The newly established company served the thirty-three northern counties of Alabama and represented, among other machinery manufacturers, the International Harvester Company. Demonstrating the successful business practices of the firm in the intervening thirty-seven years, Tractor & Equipment Co. in 1979 was named by International Harvester as the number one distributor in the world for International's construction equipment division.

In 1948 Jack F. Davies joined the firm and achieved the offices of president and chairman of the board before he retired. In 1945 Jim W. Waitzman, who had served as an aviator and flight instructor for the U.S. Navy during World War II, joined Tractor & Equipment Co. as a parts department helper and floor sweeper. Receiving his first sales assignment in 1949, Waitzman advanced to sales manager, to vice-president of sales, and in 1962 was elected as company president; he presently serves as chairman of the board.

Waitzman's business philosphy has made a major impact on the firm's development in the succeeding years. He says, "We want the people who

Above: *Early executives of Birmingham's Tractor & Equipment Co. were Jack Davies (third from left) and Ed Anderson (second from right).*

Left: *Jim W. Waltzman is chairman of the board of Tractor & Equipment Co.*

work for us to reach the potential they would like to reach. We try to lead them and help them reach their goals. Many times our goals for them are higher than the ones they set for themselves. One of the primary reasons for our success is that we give top management, middle management, and lower management as much responsibility as we feel they are willing to accept. And when we give it to them it's with no strings attached." And without doubt Tractor & Equipment Co. employees find comfort in Waitzman's personal axiom: "I never learned anything by doing it right. You've got to make some mistakes in order to learn."

Starting with a Decatur, Alabama, branch in 1952, Tractor & Equipment Co. now has branches in Tuscaloosa, Anniston, Montgomery, Mobile, and Panama City. The new facility in Mobile has almost as many square feet as the company's original headquarters in Birmingham—a sure indication of corporate growth.

In addition to International Harvester, manufacturers represented today include Drott, Barber-Greene, Tel Smith, Dynapac, Galion, Driltech, and Northwest (the company represented by E.J. Anderson when he formed Tractor & Equipment).

The officers, most of whom started with the company at an entry level and most of whom have twenty-five years' service with Tractor & Equipment Co., are W.N. Arnwine, vice-chairman of the board. Bill J. Roberts, president; Jim Waitzman, Jr., executive vice-president W.G. Hazelrig, vice-president and Decatur manager; D.W. Pettis, secretary and treasurer; and T.R. Stuedeman, vice-president sales, Birmingham.

228

WAPI . . . Where radio began in Alabama!

The station started in Birmingham in April 1922, as WSY. In 1925, the enterprise was donated to Alabama Polytechnic Institute (now Auburn University), merged with WMAV, previously relocated from Birmingham to the campus, and the call letters were changed to WAPI.

In 1928, after broadcasting programs of service to the community relating to Alabama agriculture, homemaking, education, and industry, WAPI Radio was moved from the Auburn campus to Birmingham, where the city government acquired joint ownership with the school. WAPI basically maintained its former public service programming format until after 1930, when commercials were introduced.

When the Great Depression hit, the city of Birmingham could no longer afford to contribute to the upkeep of the station. Ownership was then allocated by the state of Alabama to be shared by Auburn University, the University of Alabama, and Alabama College for Women (now the University of Montevallo). Actual operation and management, however, passed into the hands of local businessmen on a lease basis. This arrangement was in effect until 1961, when Newhouse Broadcasting Corporation, the current owner, purchased the rights to WAPI-AM from the three universities.

In the early years, WAPI's innovative leadership astonished the entire radio world with unique live broadcasts utilizing rare technical moves to promote significant changes in power, frequency, and broadcast time. Some of these marvels included . . . A broadcast by Speaker of the U.S. House of Representatives, William B. Bankhead, from the stage of the Alabama Theatre after being introduced from Hollywood by his equally famous daughter, Tallulah Bankhead . . . When it became technically necessary to relocate the radio towers, they were jacked up and rolled to their new site without taking the station off the air, an astonishing feat . . . Discovering that band leader

Glen Miller was stationed at nearby Maxwell Field during World War II, station management persuaded him to conduct his army band in a live concert on WAPI . . . Broadcasting a man's voice as he parachuted to the ground, another technical marvel for that time . . . A live performance by Guy Lombardo and his orchestra, an unusual event in that the concert took place in an airplane flying above Birmingham and was accompanied by a vocalist on the ground.

WAPI-FM, the first FM station in Alabama, began broadcasting on a permanent basis as a separate facility in January 1947. Actual experimental operations started in 1944 during

World War II. Mirroring the growth of other FM stations, WAPI-FM increased its power to 100,000 watts in 1964 and introduced stereo broadcasting in 1969.

In 1930, WAPI-AM Radio moved its headquarters to the top floor of the Protective Life Building, renowned for its cathedral studios and pipe organ. In 1953, WAPI-AM and FM were relocated in Radio Park atop Red Mountain, and on July 1, 1980, the stations moved to spacious new offices on Highland Avenue South.

In its nearly six decades on the air, WAPI has been a pacesetter in Alabama radio. When radio was thought to be a curiosity, WAPI demonstrated to advertisers that radio is a powerful selling medium. When sports coverage was considered the domain of newspapers, WAPI demonstrated that sports events could be brought to the fan, live and exciting. WAPI instigated and helped organize the School of Radio (now the School of Communications) at the University of Alabama in Tuscaloosa. WAPI built its reputation on innovation, enterprise, service, and entertainment. These standards remain current!

Left: *WAPI's former Birmingham facility was situated downtown.*

Below: *WAPI-AM and FM have been located at 2146 Highland Avenue South since July 1, 1980.*

VULCAN MATERIALS COMPANY

The history of Birmingham's Vulcan Materials Company is an American success story—a modest, family-owned business prosperous in its field rapidly expands through a series of mergers to become one of the largest and most profitable operations of its kind in the United States.

Vulcan Materials, under that name, dates only to its incorporation in 1956. But its forerunners were many and varied. Chief among those was the Birmingham Slag Company, founded in 1910 by Birmingham businessmen Solon Jacobs and Henry L. Badham. With the advent of the automobile, the demand for highways in Alabama provided a use for slag, the waste product of Birmingham's blast furnaces. It was an excellent material for the construction of roads.

Controlling interest in Birmingham Slag was purchased in 1916 by Charles L.

Ireland of Ohio, along with his three sons, Glenn, Eugene, and Barney. By the early 1920s, the firm had opened modernized slag plants at Ensley, Fairfield, Thomas, and Alabama City.

Despite the advent of the Great Depression, the company continued to grow, installing ready-mixed concrete, asphalt, and concrete block plants in several towns in Alabama and Georgia. In 1939, Birmingham Slag began a series of projects with the TVA, and during World War II provided slag and concrete for the Oak Ridge atomic project, the Redstone Arsenal, and a major munitions depot near Anniston. By 1956, 600 people were employed by Birmingham Slag, annual sales had increased to $22 million, and net profits amounted to nearly $2 million a year.

Then president Charles Ireland could look about and see that things were

good, but not good enough. There was a dilemma—whether to face the crunch of inheritance taxes that would force the sale of shares of the small, family-dominated company, probably at a disadvantageous price; or via a merger, to become a publicly held company whose share were listed on the New York Stock Exchange. The decision was made to go public.

A means of expansion presented itself in 1956 in the form of the Vulcan Detinning Company of Sewaren, New Jersey. Oddly, Vulcan Materials Company acquired its name not from Birmingham's big iron man atop Red Mountain, but from this New Jersey metals recycling business. The merger with Vulcan Detinning, orchestrated by Barney Monaghan, then chief legal counsel and destined to become president and later chief executive officer, gave Birmingham Slag its new name, a public listing on the New York

230

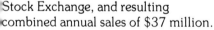

Stock Exchange, and resulting combined annual sales of $37 million.

Overnight the slag company was in the secondary metals business. Vulcan's Metals Division, which today produces secondary aluminum alloys, detinned steel, and tin chemicals, operates plants in Pennsylvania, Ohio, Maryland, Indiana, Arkansas, California, Wisconsin, England, and Wales. Sales and pretax earnings in 1980 reached record levels of $181.65 million and $8.2 million.

In 1957, Vulcan acquired Union Chemical and Materials Company. The main attraction to Union was its subsidiary, the Consumers Company, a Chicago-based building materials business. But the only way to obtain it was to acquire the parent chemical company. In this way Vulcan also acquired the company that is now its Chemicals Division.

The merger strategically placed Vulcan in the midwestern aggregates market, provided a foothold in the basic chemicals industry, and afforded an excellent opportunity for further capital investment. In 1980, the Chemicals Division, which produces a wide range of industrial chemicals, enjoyed record sales of $251 million and pretax earnings of $51.7 million. Vulcan's Chemicals Division plants operate in Louisiana, Texas, Kansas, and Wisconsin, with shipping terminals and sales offices located from San Francisco to New Jersey and throughout the South and Midwest.

A series of mergers through the late 1950s with family-owned stone and gravel companies in the South greatly expanded and fortified the company's position in construction materials. Within four years the firm had become the nation's largest producer of

construction materials, a position it retains today. Today, Vulcan's Construction Materials Group operates plants in twelve states throughout the South and Midwest and in Saudi Arabia. In 1980, the Construction Materials Group enjoyed record sales of $314 million and pretax earnings of $69.7 million.

In 1980, after twenty years of outstanding leadership, with company sales and pretax earnings at record levels of $754 million and $112.5 million, B.A. Monaghan stepped aside as chief executive officer in order to provide for an orderly transfer and was elected principal officer of the board. He was succeeded as chief executive officer by W. Houston Blount. Charles Ireland has remained as chairman of the board since 1959.

THE GEORGE F. WHEELOCK COMPANY

It was just sixteen years after Birmingham became a city that 30-year-old George F. Wheelock settled there and subsequently set up shop on south Twenty-first Street. Today the George F. Wheelock Company is one of the oldest and most respected members of the Birmingham business community.

Wheelock was convinced that the city provided an opportunity for a business centered on skylights, window caps, galvanized cornices, and other types of elaborate sheet metal work incorporated into the ornate construction designs of the Victorian Age.

His company had established an excellent reputation by the time of Wheelock's death in 1904. His widow, Addie Wheelock, took over as president. But she was well ahead of her time and since the rest of the world wasn't yet ready for a successful female business executive, she worked largely behind the scenes. She died in 1924.

Wheelock Company outgrew its original location and in 1914 moved to 2309 Fifth Avenue South. The firm at that time took on a distributing branch known as Phoenix Supply Company in addition to its sheet metal and roofing contract work, and this ultimately proved to be the most far-reaching decision made by the organization. Distribution is now the entire basis of operation for the company.

George Frederick Wheelock, son of the founder, succeeded his mother as president in 1916; he had begun as an apprentice with the company at a young age.

It was after World War I that the Wheelock Company left lasting imprints through participation in some of the city's great projects—lush residential developments; large apartment projects; west end industrial plants; the Liberty National, Alabama Power Company, and Jackson buildings; the Molton, Redmont, Bankhead, and Thomas Jefferson hotels; and the Birmingham Country Club. Increased business created corresponding demands on the physical facilities of the

The George F. Wheelock Company was originally located on South Twenty-first Street, Birmingham. An early work crew takes a moment to pose for this photograph taken around the turn of the century.

firm, so in 1928 larger quarters were secured at 3013 Second Avenue South.

It was about this time, too, that the company underwent an extensive restructure, changing chiefly from retailer to wholesaler. Wheelock changed product brands, eliminated its roofing contract business, and merged the Phoenix Supply Company into the parent firm. The sheet metal division continued intact.

Wheelock was hit hard by the Great Depression—a familiar story to most American businesses. But the company survived mainly because of the acumen of its president, who was described enthusiastically by one longtime employee as "the greatest businessman the world ever produced."

World War II threw a major obstacle in the path of Wheelock. Sheet steel for the manufacture of domestic items was siphoned off for the war effort, and the firm had to cast about for ways to survive. So Wheelock went into a temporary partnership with E.M. Quintana to manufacture metal ammunition boxes, shell casings, bomb crates, and other items designed for military use.

After the war Wheelock expanded its facilities, adding another warehouse east of the present building. The move signaled the beginning of a new era, with Wheelock diversifying into the air-conditioning field.

George F. Wheelock, Sr., who had worked for the company for sixty years, died in 1965. He was succeeded as president by his son, George F. Wheelock, Jr. The younger Wheelock had joined the family business in 1949, after serving in the Philippines during World War II. After graduating from LaGrange College, George F. Wheelock III joined the company. In 1977, he was named branch manager of the newly organized warehouse in Decatur, Alabama. Wheelock remains the major wholesale building supplier in its line in Alabama.

Birmingham's pioneers are usually thought of as a group of industrial movers and doers. And while this is largely true, there was one non-industrial, non-business pioneer almost from the beginning—the Birmingham Young Men's Christian Association. The local YMCA dates from 1884—thirteen years after the city was incorporated—and it has been a keenly felt part of the city's physical and spiritual life ever since.

From its main downtown location, which itself dates back to the early part of this century, the YMCA has since expanded into five other branches plus its popular Camp Cosby on nearby Logan Martin Lake. And on the way to its present role in the growing community of Birmingham, the YMCA has traveled an adventuresome and fulfilling road.

The local YMCA was incorporated on March 7, 1887, and was originally located at 1906 Second Avenue North. In 1893, the YMCA merged with the Birmingham Athletic Club and utilized the facilities of the old First Methodist Church at Nineteenth Street and Fourth Avenue North.

The downtown branch location at 526 North Twentieth Street was acquired from Birmingham businessman R.S. Munger in 1903 for $19,500. A campaign for a building fund of some $200,000 was launched in 1909 and a new structure was completed the following year. Renovated, expanded, and modernized since that time, the venerable building remains the local YMCA flagship, and its replacement value at this time is estimated at nearly $4.25 million.

Generally speaking, the Birmingham YMCA, in common with YMCAs everywhere, offers programs aimed at meeting individual needs and problems; developing recreational, vocational, cultural, intellectual, and social interests; deepening religious faith and sharpening moral convictions; maintaining health and physical fitness; and helping individuals become responsible members of society. This

This photograph taken in 1910 shows the ground-breaking ceremonies of the downtown branch location of the Birmingham YMCA. The venerable building, at 526 North Twentieth Street, remains the local YMCA flagship.

work is carried out under the direction of volunteers who serve as members of boards and committees, activity leaders, or group officers, and under the leadership of professionally trained directors and associates.

The Birmingham YMCA has come a long way since it offered little more than exercise, showers, and night classes for young men in the city. Its fitness programs for adults and youths cover individual exercise, slimnastics for women, special senior citizens' exercise classes, raquetball and handball, jogging and walking tracks, swimming and lifesaving lessons, organized basketball and volleyball games, weight room and exercise equipment, and tennis lessons and tournaments.

In the field of community service, the Y conducts exercise, sports, and swimming lessons for senior citizens; Back-A-Boy and other activities for underprivileged youths; and a community outreach program involving fitness, games, and sports programs in nursing homes, schools, and juvenile care facilities.

Special youth programs include camp leadership and counseling training; basketball, soccer, football, and swim teams; preschool programs; After-School Fun Club; cheerleading; and the activities at Camp Cosby. Camp Cosby, of course, is one of the outstanding success stories in the history of the local Y effort. The camp site at Lake Logan Martin, just an hour's drive from Birmingham, covers 135 acres of woods and rolling hills. The camp is fully equipped with a lodge-dining hall seating 250, comfortable cabins for campers and their counselors, swimming pool, open-air gym, three tennis courts, softball field, paved track, stables, riding ring, archery range, and boat dock. Activities at the camp continue year-round.

233

BIBLIOGRAPHY

For specific citations and extensive bibliographical information, please consult the typed footnoted manuscript of this book on deposit at the Department of Archives and Manuscripts, Birmingham Public Library, and at the Special Collections Department of the Samford University Library.

Akin, Eugenia Thompson. *Bull Frog Bend: Echoes from Turkey Creek in Jefferson County.* Birmingham: Jefferson County Historical Commission, 1978.

Anderson, Fletcher. "Foundations of a Musical Culture in Birmingham, Alabama, 1871-1900," *Journal of the Birmingham Historical Society,* 4 (January 1980), pp. 2-17.

Armbrester, Margaret England. "John Temple Graves and the New Deal, 1933-1940." Unpublished M.A. thesis, Vanderbilt University, 1967.

Armes, Ethel. *The Story of Coal and Iron in Alabama.* Birmingham: Chamber of Commerce, 1910.

Avery, Mary Johnston. *She Heard With Her Heart: Life of Mrs. R.D. Johnston.* Birmingham: Birmingham Publishing Company, 1944.

Badham, H.L., Jr. "History of the Bessemer Coal, Iron, and Land Company." Unpublished typed manuscript in possession of Bessemer Coal, Iron and Land Company.

Bailey, Barbara Connell. "Ten Trying Years: A History of Bessemer, Alabama, 1929-1939." Unpublished M.A. thesis, Samford University, 1977.

Beavers, Theresa Aguglia. "The Italians of the Birmingham District." Unpublished M.A. thesis, Samford University, 1969.

Bee, Fanna K., and Allen, Lee N. *Sesquicentennial History of Ruhama Baptist Church, 1919-1969.* Birmingham: Ruhama Baptist Church, 1969.

Beiman, Irving. "Birmingham: Steel Giant with a Glass Jaw." In *Our Fair City,* edited by Robert S. Allen. New York: Vanguard Press, 1947.

Benfield, Steve. "The 1963 Bombing of the Sixteenth Street Baptist Church, Paradigm for Social Change." Historical essays, vol. 21, Colonial Dames, Samford University.

Bigelow, Martha Mitchell. "Birmingham: Biography of a City of the New South." Unpublished Ph.D. dissertation, University of Chicago, 1946.

Birmingham Area Chamber of Commerce.

Century Plus, A Bicentennial Portrait of Birmingham, Alabama, 1976. Birmingham: Oxmoor Press, 1976.

Birmingham Centennial Corporation. *Portrait of Birmingham, Alabama.* Birmingham: Oxmoor Press, 1971.

Blake, Thomas Harry. *Birmingham Since 1885.* Birmingham: Birmingham Publishing Company, 1973.

Boles, W.J. "Jonesboro, Rich in History." In *A Journal of History,* 5 (Winter, 1977), pp. 358-363.

Bowron, James. Autobiography. 3 vols. Typed manuscript, William S. Hoole Special Collections Department, University of Alabama Library.

Bowron, James. Diary and papers. William S. Hoole Special Collections Department, University of Alabama Library.

Brown, Charles Allen. *The Origin and Development of Secondary Education for Negroes in Metropolitan Area of Birmingham, Alabama.* Birmingham: Birmingham Commercial Printing, 1959.

Brown, Virginia P., and Nabers, Jane Porter. "The Origin of Certain Place Names in Jefferson County, Alabama," In *The Alabama Review,* 5 (July, 1952), pp. 177-202.

Brown, Virginia P., and Turner, Mabel Thuston. "The Birmingham Public Library, From Its Beginning Until 1927." In *The Journal of the Birmingham Historical Society,* 5 (July, 1978), pp. 26-32; 6 (January, 1979), pp. 24-30.

Brownell, Blaine A. "Birmingham, Alabama: New South City in the 1920's." In *Journal of Southern History,* 38 (February, 1972), pp. 21-48.

Brownell, Blaine A. "The Notorious Jitney and the Urban Transportation Crisis in Birmingham in the 1920's." In *The Alabama Review,* 25 (April, 1972), pp. 105-118.

Brownell, Blaine A., and Goldfield, David R., eds. *The City in Southern History.* Port Washington, New York: Kennikat Press, 1977.

Caldwell, Henry M. *History of the Elyton Land Company and Birmingham, Alabama.* Birmingham: 1892. Reprint. Southern University Press, 1926.

Centennial Committee. *Century of Worship: 1872-1972: The Story of a Century of Service to God and Man, First Methodist Church, Birmingham, Alabama.* Birmingham: Oxmoor Press, 1972.

Chiles, Ruth. "The Birmingham Theatres,

1886-1900." Unpublished M.A. thesis, Birmingham Southern College, 1936.

Corley, Robert Gaines. "The Quest for Racial Harmony: Race Relations in Birmingham, Alabama, 1947-1963." Unpublished Ph.D. dissertation, University of Virginia, 1979.

Cruikshank, George M. *A History of Birmingham and Its Environs.* 2 vols. Chicago: Lewis Publishing Company, 1920.

Davis, Elias, Letters. Southern Historical Collection, University of North Carolina, Chapel Hill.

DuBose, John Witherspoon. "Birmingham." In *Northern Alabama Historical and Biographical,* pp. 744-758. Birmingham: Smith and DeLand, 1888.

DuBose, John Witherspoon. *Jefferson County and Birmingham, Alabama: Historical and Biographical.* Birmingham: Teeple and Smith, 1887.

DuBose, John Witherspoon. *The Mineral Wealth of Alabama and Birmingham Illustrated.* Birmingham: N.T. Green and Company, 1886.

Duffee, Mary Gordon. "Sketches of Alabama, Jones Valley, Birmingham." Typed manuscript, Works Progress Administration, 1937, Tutwiler Collection of Southern History, Birmingham Public Library.

Durham, Tramel W. "History of the City of Bessemer, 1887-1917." Unpublished M.A. thesis, Birmingham Southern College, 1962.

Elovitz, Mark H. *A Century of Jewish Life in Dixie: The Birmingham Experience.* Tuscaloosa: University of Alabama Press, 1974.

Elyton Land Company. Papers. Department of Archives and Manuscripts, Birmingham Public Library.

Ely, William. Letters. William S. Hoole Special Collections Department, University of Alabama Library.

Fell, Charles A. "The Crash and the Moratorium." In *Journal of the Birmingham Historical Society,* 1 (January, 1960), pp. 7-10.

Ferguson, Hill. *Historical Collections of Birmingham, Jefferson County and Alabama.* Scrapbooks. Department of Archives and Manuscripts, Birmingham Public Library.

Flynt, J. Wayne. "Religion in the Urban South: The Divided Mind of Birmingham, 1900-1930." In *The Alabama Review,* 30 (April, 1977), pp. 108-134.

Franke, Will. "Jefferson County in 1850." Typed manuscript. Hill Ferguson Papers,

BIBLIOGRAPHY

Department of Archives and Manuscripts, Carbon copy in the William S. Hoole Special Collections Department, University of Alabama Library.

Fuller, Justin. "History of the Tennessee Coal, Iron and Railroad Company, 1852-1907." Unpublished Ph.D. dissertation, University of North Carolina at Chapel Hill, 1966.

Fussell, Richard, *Demographic Atlas of Birmingham: 1960-1970.* Tuscaloosa: University of Alabama Press, 1975.

Goodrich, Gillian. "Romance and Reality: The Birmingham Suffragists, 1892-1920." In *The Journal of the Birmingham Historical Society,* 5 (January, 1978), pp. 5-21.

Gorman, Ethel Miller. *Red Acres.* Birmingham: Vulcan Press, 1956.

Grambs, Fred L. Scrapbooks. Department of Archives and Manuscripts, Birmingham Public Library.

Grace, Francis Mitchell. "Autobiography." Typed manuscript compiled by Janie Grace Robinson. Tutwiler Collection of Southern History, Birmingham Public Library. Also appears in *A Journal of History,* 5 (Fall, 1976), pp. 331-348.

Grace, Francis Mitchell. "Early History of the Development of the Iron and Coal Resources of the Birmingham District." In *A Journal of History,* 5 (Fall, 1976), pp. 349-353.

Greene, Julius C. "Reminiscence of Julius C. Greene." Typed manuscript, Tutwiler Collection of Southern History, Birmingham Public Library.

Hamilton, Virginia Van der Veer. *Alabama: A Bicentennial History.* New York: W.W. Norton and Company, 1977.

Harris, Carl V. *Political Power in Birmingham, 1871-1921.* Knoxville: University of Tennessee Press, 1977.

Harrison, Mary Phyllis. "A Change in the Government of the City of Birmingham." Unpublished M.A. thesis, Montevallo University, 1974.

Hassinger, Bernice Shield. *Henderson Steel: Birmingham's First Steel.* Birmingham: Jefferson County Historical Commission, 1978.

Heldman, Max. *Max Heldman's Birmingham.* Birmingham: Commercial Printing Company, 1971.

Henckell, Robert Barnwell, comp. "Information About Birmingham, Jefferson County, and Alabama." 3 vols. Typed manuscript, Tutwiler Collection of Southern History, Birmingham Public Library.

Hendricks, Charles F. Diary. Western Historical Manuscripts Collection, University of Missouri, Columbia, Missouri.

Henley, John C., Jr. *This is Birmingham: The Story of the Founding and Growth of an American City.* Birmingham: Southern University Press, 1960.

Holmes, Jack D.L. *A History of the University of Alabama Hospitals.* Birmingham: University Hospital Auxiliary, 1974.

Hoole, William Stanley. *The Birmingham Horrors.* Huntsville: Strode Publishers, 1980.

Hornaday, John R. *The Book of Birmingham.* New York: Dodd, Mead and Company, 1921.

Hudson, Alvin W., and Cox, Harold E. *Street Railways of Birmingham.* Privately published, 1976.

Huntley, Horace. "Iron Ore Miners and Mine Mill in Alabama: 1933-1952." Unpublished Ph.D. dissertation, University of Pittsburgh, 1977.

Johnson, Daniel Milo. "Black Return Migration to a Southern Metropolitan Community: Birmingham, Alabama." Unpublished Ph.D. dissertation, University of Missouri, 1973.

Johnson, Evans C. *Oscar W. Underwood: A Political Biography.* Baton Rouge: Louisiana State University Press, 1980.

Kilian, Clarence, M., ed. *"The Old First": A History of the First Presbyterian Church of Birmingham, Alabama.* Birmingham: Birmingham Publishing Company, 1952.

King, Jere C., Jr. "The Formation of Greater Birmingham." Unpublished M.A. thesis, University of Alabama, 1935.

LaMonte, Edward S. *George B. Ward: Birmingham's Urban Statesmen.* Birmingham: Birmingham Public Library, 1974.

LaMonte, Edward S. "Politics and Welfare in Birmingham: 1900-1975." Unpublished Ph.D. dissertation, University of Chicago, 1976.

LaMonte, Edward S. *The Faces of Birmingham: Past, Present, and Future.* Birmingham: University of Alabama in Birmingham, 1977.

LaMonte, Edward S. "The Mercy Home and Private Charity in Early Birmingham." In *Journal of the Birmingham Historical Society,* 5 (July, 1978), pp. 5-15.

Leighton, George R. "Birmingham, Alabama: The City of Perpetual Promise," *Harper's,* 175 (August, 1937), pp. 225-242.

Lovett, Rose Gibbons, "Centennial History of Saint Paul's Parish, Birmingham, Alabama,

1872-1972." Typed manuscript, Department of Archives and Manuscripts, Birmingham Public Library.

McDavid, Mittie Owen. *Church of the Advent, Its History and Traditions.* Birmingham: Birmingham Publishing Company, 1943.

McDavid, Mittie Owen. *John Smith, Esquire.* Privately printed, 1948.

McKenzie, Robert H. "The Great Birmingham Iron Boom, 1880-1892." Typed manuscript, Alabama Department of Archives and History, Montgomery.

McMillan, Malcolm C. *Yesterday's Birmingham.* Miami, Florida: Seemann Publishing, 1975.

Mellown, Bennie Catherine. *Memoirs of a Pre-Civil War Community* (Crumly's Chapel). Birmingham: 1950.

Milner, Willis Julian. "Autobiography." In *Journal of the Birmingham Historical Society,* 5 (January, 1977), pp. 5-27.

Mims, William Jemison. Letters. In possession of Dr. Glover Moore, Starkville, Mississippi.

Mitch, William. "Labor's Depression Recovery." In *Journal of the Birmingham Historical Society,* 1 (January, 1960), pp. 18-19.

Moore, Glover. *William Jemison Mims: Soldier and Squire.* Birmingham: Birmingham Publishing Company, 1966.

Morgan, Charles. *A Time to Speak.* New York: Harper and Row, 1964.

Morgan, Roberta. "Social Implications and the Human Side." In *Journal of the Birmingham Historical Society,* 1 (January, 1960), pp. 11-17.

Munger, Rose McDavid. *Mortimer Jordan, Pioneer.* Privately published, 1974.

Munger, Rose McDavid, comp. *Pioneer Scrapbook Compiled Largely from the Papers of Mittie Owen McDavid Dealing with the Early History of Jones Valley in Jefferson County, Alabama.* Birmingham: Birmingham Publishing Company, 1967.

Newton, Wesley P. "Lindbergh Comes to Birmingham." In *The Alabama Review,* 26 (April, 1973), pp. 105-121.

Norton, Bertha Bendall. *Birmingham's First Magic Century.* Birmingham: Lakeshore Press, 1970.

Owen, Thomas McAdory. *History of Alabama: Dictionary of Alabama Biography.* 4 vols. 1921. Reprint. Spartanburg, South Carolina: Reprint Company, 1978.

Painter, Nell Irvin. *The Narrative of Hosea Hudson.* Cambridge, Massachusetts: Harvard University Press, 1979.

BIBLIOGRAPHY

Parke, Thomas Duke. Papers. Department of Archives and Manuscripts, Birmingham Public Library.

Parker, Arthur H. *A Dream that Came True.* Birmingham: Industrial High School, 1932-1933.

Parks, Joseph Howard. *Birmingham-Southern College, 1856-1956.* Nashville, Tennessee: Parthenon Press, 1957.

Perkins, Crawford A., comp. *An Industrial History of Ensley, Alabama.* Birmingham: Advance Publishing Company, 1907.

Pioneer Club. *Early Days in Birmingham.* Birmingham: Birmingham Publishing Company, 1937.

Purcell, Douglas Clare. *The Making of a City, Trussville, Alabama, 1820-1970.* Privately published, 1970.

Raines, Howell. *My Soul is Rested.* New York: G.P. Putnam's Sons, 1977.

Register of County Officials of Jefferson County, 1819-1900. Typed manuscript. Bledsoe-Kelly Collection, Samford University Library.

Rikard, Marlene Hunt. "George Gordon Crawford: Man of the New South." Unpublished M.A. thesis, Samford University, 1971.

Roebuck, Cora Elizabeth. "The History of Birmingham from 1871 to 1890." Unpublished M.A. thesis, University of Alabama, 1931.

Rogers, Rebecca Pegues. *The Strength of Her Towers: Episcopal Church of the Advent, Birmingham, Alabama.* Birmingham: 1973.

Rutledge, William Summer. "An Economic and Social History of Ante-bellum Jefferson County, Alabama." Unpublished M.A. thesis, University of Alabama, 1939.

Satterfield, Carolyn Green. *Historical Sites of Jefferson County, Alabama.* Birmingham: Jefferson County Historical Commission, 1976.

Scroggins, Raymond. "A Cultural and Religious History of Birmingham, Alabama, 1871-1931." Unpublished A.B. thesis, Howard College, 1939.

Shipman, S.V. Diary. State Historical Society of Wisconsin, Madison, Wisconsin.

Snell, William R. "Masked Men in the Magic City: Activities of the Revised Klan in Birmingham, 1916-1940." In *Alabama Historical Quarterly,* 34 (Fall-Winter, 1972), pp. 206-227.

Snell, William Robert. "The Ku Klux Klan in Jefferson County, Alabama, 1916-1930."

Unpublished M.A. thesis, Samford University, 1967.

Spence, Ruth S., comp. *Bibliography of Birmingham, Alabama, 1872-1972.* Birmingham: Oxmoor Press, 1973.

Starr, J. Barton. "Birmingham and the 'Dixiecrat' Convention of 1948." In *Alabama Historical Quarterly,* 32 (Spring-Summer, 1970), pp. 23-50.

Sterne, Ellin. "Prostitution in Birmingham, Alabama, 1890-1925." Unpublished M.A. thesis, Samford University, 1977.

Stewart, George R. "Birmingham's Reaction to the 1954 Desegregation Decision." Unpublished M.A. thesis, Samford University, 1967.

Straw Richard A. "The United Mine Workers of America and the 1920 Coal Strike in Alabama." In *The Alabama Review,* 28 (April, 1975), pp. 104-128.

Sulzby, James F., Jr. *Annals of the Southside Baptist Church.* Birmingham: Birmingham Printing Company, 1947.

Sulzby, James F., Jr. *Birmingham Sketches From 1871 Through 1921.* Birmingham: Birmingham Printing Company, 1945.

Sulzby, James F., Jr. *Historic Alabama Hotels and Resorts.* Tuscaloosa: University of Alabama Press, 1960.

Sulzby, James F., Jr. Scrapbook: Sesquicentennial Celebration, 1946-1947.

Tennessee Coal and Iron Division, United States Steel Corporation. *Biography of a Business.* Privately published, 1960.

The Hill Country of Alabama, U.S.A., or The Land of Rest. London: n.p., 1878.

Tower, J. Allen. "The Changing Economy of Birmingham and Jefferson County." In *Journal of the Birmingham Historical Society,* 1 (January, 1960), pp. 11-17.

The Survey. 27 (January 6, 1912).

Underwood, Anthony Paul. "A Progressive History of the Young Men's Business Club of Birmingham, Alabama, 1946-1970." Unpublished M.A. thesis, Samford University, 1980.

Vann, Samuel King. Letters. Alabama Department of Archives and History, Montgomery.

Vines, R.U. "Pleasant Hill, near McCalla, Jefferson County, Alabama." Typed manuscript in possession of Betty McAdory, Opelika, Alabama.

Ward, George. Scrapbooks. Department of Archives and Manuscripts, Birmingham Public

Library.

Ward, Robert David, and Rogers, William Warren. *Labor Revolt in Alabama: The Great Strike of 1894.* Tuscaloosa: University of Alabama Press, 1965.

White, Marjorie Longenecker. *Downtown Birmingham: Architectural and Historical Walking Tour Guide.* Birmingham: Birmingham Historical Society and First National Bank of Birmingham, 1977.

Wilson, James Harrison. Diary. Historical Society of Delaware, Wilmington, Delaware.

Windham, Kathryn Tucker. *The Ghost in the Sloss Furnaces.* Birmingham: Birmingham Historical Society and First National Bank of Birmingham, 1978.

Woodward, Joseph H., II. "Alabama Iron Manufacturing, 1860-1865." In *The Alabama Review,* 7 (July, 1954), pp. 199-215.

Woodward, Joseph H. Diary. Typed manuscript, William S. Hoole Special Collections Department, University of Alabama.

Works Progress Administration. "Historical Collections of Jefferson County." Typed manuscript, 1937, Tutwiler Collection of Southern History, Birmingham Public Library.

Worthman, Paul. "Black Workers and Labor Unions in Birmingham, Alabama, 1897-1904." *Labor History,* 10 (Summer, 1969), pp. 375-407.

ACKNOWLEDGMENTS

The researching and writing of this history of Birmingham and Jefferson County has been a labor of love. It would be impossible for me to acknowledge all the people who lent me a helping hand along the way, but there are some whose support was so great, I must express to them my deep appreciation for their efforts.

The Birmingham-Jefferson Historical Society enthusiastically approved the project and I am indebted to the publications committee, composed of Dr. Margaret D. Sizemore, Rucker Agee, Richard J. Stockham, Elmer Thuston, and James F. Sulzby, Jr., for asking me to write this history. Rucker Agee was the Birmingham-Jefferson Historical Society's official reader and he spent many hours reading my manuscript, making suggestions, and sharing with me his vast knowledge of Birmingham and Jefferson County history. James F. Sulzby, Jr., also read the manuscript draft, discussed with me the inconsistencies and errors of past histories, answered many of my questions, and allowed me to use his excellent personal library and his extensive collection of Birmingham and Jefferson County materials. To both men I owe my deepest gratitude. I also wish to thank Dr. Margaret Sizemore for reading the manuscript and writing the introduction.

Dr. Marvin Y. Whiting, archivist and curator of manuscripts for the Birmingham Public Library, generously assisted me in locating materials in his department, took time from his busy schedule to talk to me about certain phases of Birmingham history, and also critiqued the manuscript. My colleagues, Dr. Lee N. Allen, Dr. J. Wayne Flynt, Dr. Malcolm C. McMillan, and Professor Marlene Rikard, read portions of the manuscript and made valuable suggestions. I am indebted to Dr. Charles A. Brown and Dr. Horace Huntley for reading the manuscript and sharing their knowledge of Birmingham's black history and culture. Every effort was made to be correct in spelling proper names and in facts, dates, and interpretations. Errors that remain are my responsibility.

Most of the research was done in private libraries and at the Birmingham Public Library, particularly the Department of Archives and Manuscripts where the staff, Robert Corley, Mary Miller, Teresa Ceravalo, and Tom Haslett, were more than courteous, and the Tutwiler Collection of Southern History where Mary Bess Kirksey and her staff willingly found volumes of materials for me. Milo B. Howard, Jr., director of the Alabama Department of Archives and History, and his staff, particularly Joe Caver and Mimi Jones, gathered materials for me and assisted in getting photographic duplications. The staff and directors, particularly Betty Martin and Louise Tommie, of the West Jefferson Historical Society and the Bessemer Hall of History, lent me much assistance. Elizabeth C. Wells, director of the Special Collections Department of the Samford University Library and her staff, particularly Shirley Hutchens and Johnny Dollar, cheerfully searched for materials. The Auburn University Archives staff, Dr. Allen Jones and Bill Summers, assisted me in going through the J.F. Knox Photographic Collection. Joyce H. Lamont, librarian of the William S. Hoole Special Collections Department of the University of Alabama Library at Tuscaloosa and her staff, especially Gunetta R. Rich and Deborah Nygren, were so helpful that researching there was a pleasure. The staffs of the Southern Historical Collection at the University of North Carolina at Chapel Hill and the Special Collections Department of the Perkins Library at Duke University were most generous with their time.

Dicki Arn is responsible for most of the color photography. Spider Martin allowed me to use his famous picture of Birmingham at night and John

Scott reproduced the color portraits in the Archives and Capitol in Montgomery. Lew Arnold, Mickie Hood Blackwell, and Jo Roy, head of the Photographic Services Department of the Birmingham Public Library, did most of the black and white photographic duplications, and all were a pleasure to work with. Jackie and Gary Dobbs allowed me to use the negatives of Fred Arthur Powell, who operated Birmingham View Company and was a Birmingham photographer for almost 50 years. Jackie made all the prints from Powell's negatives and was helpful in many ways.

Eddie Smith tried to answer all my questions about the northwestern area of the county, and Wallace Montgomery was kind enough to show me Turkey Falls, the Blue Hole, and the Pinson area. Eugenia Akin allowed me to read her father's diary, and Mrs. Hugh Nabers shared Bevelle Comer Nabers's remembrance of early Birmingham. Dr. Glover Moore and his sister, Kathleen Peacock, generously lent me their grandfather's Civil War letters which gave me such an appreciation for life in Jefferson County during the war. William Y. Elliott, Sr., shared with me copies of Samuel King Vann's love letters to his sweetheart at Cedar Grove, which illustrate so well the effect this war had on the young people of Jefferson County. Frank Jones located many bits of obscure information and willingly shared them.

Betty Huff and Laurie Orr of the *Birmingham News* Research Library were so pleasant and helpful, and Tom Self and Voncille Williams of the Photographic Department were prompt with photographic duplications. Others who opened their homes, shared their memorabilia with me or assisted me in locating certain information or photographs were Jeff Norrell and Karen Rolen of Birmingfind, Dr. Carolyn Green Satterfield, Professor Frances Hamilton, Dr. Jim Brown, Mr. and Mrs. Mortimer H. Jordan, Dr. and

Mrs. Henley Smith, Virginia Murray, James and Max Price, Betsy Barber Bancroft, Ruby Munger Montgomery, Sam Rumore, Jr., Betty and Henry McAdory, Elmer Thuston, Edward T. Douglass, Jr., Richard and Paul Bowron, Jean Bynum, Paul Earle, Mary Alice Carmichael, Donna Peters of the Alabama Museum of Natural History, Becky and Billy Strickland, Clare Gillam, Debbie Metcalf, Mildred Barber, Pat Brandon, and Elizabeth Agee. Jan Peoples and Nena Beth Moon typed the manuscript. Janie Dowdell Evans relieved me of many responsibilities which left more time for writing. The editorial staff of Windsor Publications, most particularly Lissa Sanders, Teri Greenberg, and Randy Smoot, were a joy to work with and they deserve much credit for their patience and editorial suggestions. Karen Story and Judy Mowinckel did an outstanding job of editing and coordinating the corporate histories that John Bloomer researched and wrote so carefully.

I could never have undertaken the writing of this book without the support and cooperation of Dr. David M. Vess, Dr. Lee N. Allen, Dr. Ruric Wheeler, and Dr. Leslie S. Wright, president of Samford University, who approved a sabbatical semester which allowed me to work full-time on the manuscript and to travel to do research. Finally without the loving cooperation of my husband George, and children Tim, Brian, Laura Leigh, and Jack, and my mother Margaret Rawls, it could never had been completed. I would like to dedicate this book to the memory of my father, Jack Rawls, who all his life loved the valley and the hills.

Leah Rawls Atkins
Birmingham
December 1, 1980

INDEX

242

243

THIS BOOK WAS SET IN
SOVRAN AND PALADIUM TYPES,
PRINTED ON
70 POUND ENAMEL WARRENFLO
AND BOUND BY
WALSWORTH PUBLISHING COMPANY.
COVER AND TEXT DESIGNED BY
JOHN FISH
LAYOUT BY
RANDY HIPKE, DAURI PALLAS, AND
MELINDA WADE